HANDBOOK OF
RESEARCH DESIGN
AND
SOCIAL MEASUREMENT

HANDBOOK OF
RESEARCH DESIGN
AND
SOCIAL MEASUREMENT

DELBERT C. MILLER

PROFESSOR OF SOCIOLOGY AND BUSINESS ADMINISTRATION
INDIANA UNIVERSITY

DAVID McKAY COMPANY, INC.

NEW YORK

HANDBOOK OF RESEARCH DESIGN AND SOCIAL MEASUREMENT

COPYRIGHT © 1964 BY DAVID MC KAY COMPANY, INC.

LIBRARY OF CONGRESS CATALOG CARD NUMBER: 64-10332

MANUFACTURED IN THE UNITED STATES OF AMERICA

VAN REES PRESS • NEW YORK

To

F. STUART CHAPIN

Pioneer in Sociometric Scaling

Preface

THE PURPOSE OF this handbook is to assist the social science researcher in finding information he needs quickly and in brief form when he is designing and conducting research. There are four major areas where aids are commonly required. These are in research functions associated with *research design and sampling, statistical analysis, selection of sociometric scales or indexes,* and, lastly, *research costing and reporting.* Accordingly, the handbook is organized around these functions.

No handbook can replace the training required for qualified research. This handbook is not a text nor a substitute for one. It is a compilation of resources organized to provide reference to the essential materials needed in the design of research. Designed research refers to the planned sequence of the entire process involved in conducting a research study. The steps of this sequence are shown in Guide I.1 as:

1. Selection and definition of a sociological problem.
2. Description of the relationship of the problem to a theoretical framework.
3. Formulation of working hypotheses.
4. Design of the experiment or inquiry.
5. Sampling procedures.
6. Establishment of methods of gathering data.
7. Preparation of a working guide.
8. Analysis of results.
9. Interpretation of results.
10. Publication or reporting of results.

The handbook provides guides to accompany most of these steps. No attempt has been made to include guides to methods of gathering data since it is believed that these could not be put into brief form and that it would be better for a researcher to consult books on research methods when he needs guidance. However, he will find a relatively large number of scales in the handbook from which to choose if these prove useful to his problem.

The selection of guides has been made to insure the widest possible use regardless of the problem selected. Aids have been sought that set forth step-by-step procedures. It is hoped that both the professional worker and the graduate student shall find this handbook useful and timesaving.

Another purpose has motivated the development of this guide book. The author seeks to advance a major goal of all research progress, i.e., to improve research and to expedite the design and other operational phases of research. Investigations into leading sociological journals show that replication of research is infrequent. Measures of sociological variables except for such demographic variables as age, sex, religion, race, etc., are not used uniformly. Researchers often tend to ignore the scales available and to construct new ones. Thus, it is impossible to make careful comparisons with previous research and it is also difficult to build an accumulation of empirically verified relationships. Some exceptions show what might be accomplished. Social researchers have made wide use of the *Bogardus Social Distance Scale, Moreno's Sociometry Measures, Chapin's Social Participation Scale,* and other instruments included in this handbook. The psychologists have some relatively standard instruments in the *Minnesota Multiphasic Personality Inventory* and in the *F-Scale* to measure *Authoritarian Personality.* These scales have led to replication, which has produced accumulative research findings.

This handbook seeks to bring together social scales that have, or promise to have, wide utility and validity. It is expected that new scales will continue to be constructed by the hundreds. Certainly, many new and better scales are needed. Meanwhile, we need an inventory and storage house for selected measures that ought to be used unless there are compelling reasons to the contrary. If the scales included herein are not the most useful and valid, then the author invites communication. The handbook should constantly improve as consensus among experts is achieved. Meanwhile, if the selection helps increase replication and speeds research operations, a major goal of this book will have been achieved.

Another possible outcome of this handbook may be its capacity to suggest new research. The graduate student who is looking for a research problem should begin by examining the section containing the sociometric scales and indexes. These are generally measures of the dependent variables of greatest interest to social researchers. Any one of these scales can suggest to a researcher a new hypothesis requiring a test of a relationship not yet carefully demonstrated in a given population. In many ways, the sociometric scales in the storehouse of knowledge constitute the best seedbed for new research ideas and endeavors. The graduate student can play an important role in replicating good research designs of professional researchers. Graduate students now exceed professional researchers in numbers. They represent manpower of such scope that their combined efforts could make a substantial contribution to verified social science knowledge.

Empirical social research is now being actively encouraged not only in all of the traditional social sciences but also in the applied schools of business, education, social work, and law. Newcomers also include recruits from police administration, hospital administration, medical sociology, recreational administration, schools of communication, library administration, and many others.

I am especially indebted to both the College of Arts and Sciences and the Graduate School of Business at Indiana University for opportunities to serve as a research consultant to the faculty and graduate students. I wish to express my appreciation especially to Deans Arthur M. Weimer and W. George Pinnell for an opportunity to serve in the School of Business. Working with candidates for the masters' and doctors' degrees in business administration has more clearly shown me the needs that exist among graduate students in the basic and applied social sciences. I wish to express my appreciation to those devoted graduate students, Charles E. Starnes, Frank Castro, James Barrett, and Charles E. Leinenweber, for their efforts in assembling and classifying much of the material. I am also grateful to Jane Wellman, Jane Sunderland, and Rita Hosler for their enthusiastic help in preparing the manuscript.

DELBERT C. MILLER

Bloomington, Indiana
May 15, 1964

Contents

Part I. General Description of the Guides to Research Design and Sampling   1

 1. An Outline Guide for the Design of a Social Research Problem   3
 2. A General Statement to Guide the Basic Researcher in the Formulation of Research Problems   6
 3. The Bearing of Sociological Theory on Empirical Research   7
 4. Criteria for Judging Usable Hypotheses   14
 5. Some Observations on Study Design   20
 6. On the Decisions in Verificational Studies   26
 7. General Considerations of Research Design   31
 8. The Shaping of Research Design in Large-Scale Group Research   32
 9. The Sampling Chart   46
 10. A Selected Bibliography on Research Design   51

Part II. Guides to Statistical Analysis   53

 1. The Impertinent Questioner: The Scientist's Guide to the Statistician's Mind   55
 2. A Note on Statistical Analysis in the *American Sociological Review*   61
 3. The Idea of Property-Space in Social Research   65
 4. Summary of Common Measures of Association   72
 5. Four Levels of Measurement and the Statistics Appropriate to Each Level   74
 6. Nonparametric Statistical Tests Appropriate to Various Types of Scales   76

7. Computation Guides 78
   a. *t* Test of Significance between Two Means of Independent Samples 79
   b. Pearsonian *r* to Measure Linear Correlation between Two Variables 81
   c. X^2 Test of Association 85
   d. Spearman's Rank Correlation 86
8. A Bibliography of Statistical Guides 88
9. A Specialized Bibliographic Section for the Advanced Student 89

Part III. Selected Sociometric Scales and Indexes 91

Introduction 93

SECTION A. SOCIAL STATUS 97
1. Alba M. Edwards' Social-Economic Grouping of Occupations 98
2. Revised Occupational Rating Scale from W. L. Warner, M. Meeker, and K. Eells's Index of Status Characteristics 100
3. Hatt-North Occupational Prestige Ratings 106
4. Warner's Evaluated Participation Method of Social Class Measurement 110
5. Chapin's Social Status (Living Room) Scale, Revised 1952 114
6. Sewell's Short Form of the Farm Socioeconomic Status Scale 120

SECTION B. GROUP STRUCTURE AND DYNAMICS 123
1. Hemphill's Index of Group Dimensions 123
2. Bales's Interaction Process Analysis 135
3. Seashore's Group Cohesiveness Index 138
4. Sociometry Scales of Sociometric Choice and Sociometric Preference 140
5. Bogardus Social Distance Scale 143

SECTION C. MORALE AND JOB SATISFACTION 151
1. Short Form of the Minnesota Survey of Opinions (General Adjustment and Morale Scales) 152

Hollingshead 2-factor Index of Social Position (♂, ♀) [handwritten annotation]

2. The Science Research Associates Employee Inventory   173
3. Morse Indexes of Employee Satisfaction   181
4. Guttman Scales of Military Base Morale   185
5. Brayfield and Rothe's Index of Job Satisfaction   188

SECTION D. COMMUNITY   192

1. Community Attitude Scale   194
2. Community Solidarity Index   198
3. Community Rating Schedule   203
4. Scorecard for Community Services Activity   206

SECTION E. SOCIAL PARTICIPATION   208

1. Chapin's Social Participation Scale, 1952 Edition   208
2. Leisure Participation and Enjoyment   213
3. Bernard's Neighboring Practices Schedule   217
4. A Guttman Scale for Measuring Women's
   Neighborliness   220
5. Citizen Political Action Schedule   222

SECTION F. LEADERSHIP IN THE WORK ORGANIZATION   224

1. Leadership Opinion Questionnaire   226
2. Supervisory Behavior Description   230
3. Work Patterns Profile   234

SECTION G. IMPORTANT ATTITUDE SCALES   238

1. Wants and Satisfaction Scale   239
2. Social Insight Scale   246
3. Guttman-Type Scales for Union and Management
   Attitudes toward Each Other   256
4. Perception of Internal Communist Danger   260
5. Willingness to Tolerate Nonconformists   264
6. Semantic Differential   268

SECTION H. FAMILY AND MARRIAGE   273

1. Marriage-Prediction Schedule and Marriage-
   Adjustment Schedule   273

SECTION I. PERSONALITY MEASUREMENTS   294

1. Minnesota Multiphasic Personality Inventory
   (*MMPI*)   295
2. Authoritarian Personality (*F*) Scale, Forms 45 and 40   301

SECTION J. AN INVENTORY OF MEASURES UTILIZED IN THE
AMERICAN SOCIOLOGICAL REVIEW DURING 1951-60   308
  1. Scale Inventory of the *American Sociological
     Review,* 1951-60   308

Part IV. Research Costing and Reporting   **328**

  1. Guide to Research Costing   329
  2. Specifications for Sociological Report Rating   330
  3. Form for Sociological Report Rating   332

HANDBOOK OF
RESEARCH DESIGN
AND
SOCIAL MEASUREMENT

General Description of the Guides to Research Design and Sampling

PART I CONTAINS guides to accompany the first five steps in the sequence of a planned research proposal. These are (1) selection and definition of a sociological problem, (2) description of the relationship of the problem to a theoretical framework, (3) formulation of working hypotheses, (4) design of the experiment or inquiry, and (5) sampling procedures. The brief treatments of these subjects may be enriched by use of the bibliography placed at the end of Part I.

PART I

General Description of the Guides to Research Design and Sampling

I.1. AN OUTLINE GUIDE FOR THE DESIGN OF
A SOCIAL RESEARCH PROBLEM *

Instructions for Use of Guide I.1.

This outline for the design of social research lists all of the essential considerations in designing a research project. It is recommended that all steps be planned before field or laboratory work is undertaken. Each of the guides in Part I has been selected to aid in planning the first five steps shown in the outline. Other guides in Parts II, III, and IV are available to assist the researcher in most of the steps shown.

   I. The Sociological Problem
      1. Present clear, brief statement of the problem with concepts defined where necessary.
      2. Show that the problem is limited to bounds amenable to treatment or test.
      3. Describe the significance of the problem with reference to one or more of the following criteria:
         a. is timely.
         b. relates to a practical problem.
         c. relates to a wide population.
         d. relates to an influential or critical population.
         e. fills a research gap.
         f. permits generalization to broader principles of social interaction or general theory.
         g. sharpens the definition of an important concept or relationship.
         h. has many implications for a wide range of practical problems.
         i. may create or improve an instrument for observing and analyzing data.
         j. provides opportunity for gathering data that is restricted by the limited time available for gathering particular data.
         k. provides possibility for a fruitful exploration with known techniques.

---

* Based on Russell L. Ackoff, *The Design of Social Research*, Chicago: University of Chicago Press, 1953. Adapted by Delbert C. Miller.

II. The Theoretical Framework

1. Describe the relationship of the problem to a theoretical framework.
2. Demonstrate the relationship of the problem to previous research.
3. Present alternate hypotheses considered feasible within the framework of the theory.

III. The Hypotheses

1. Clearly state the hypotheses selected for test. (Null and alternate hypothesis should be stated.)
2. Indicate the significance of test hypotheses to the advancement of research and theory.
3. Define concepts or variables (preferably in operational terms).
   a. Independent and dependent variables should be distinguished from each other.
   b. The scale upon which variables are to be measured (quantitative, semiquantitative, or qualitative) should be specified.
4. Describe possible mistakes and their consequences.
5. Note seriousness of possible mistakes.

IV. Design of the Experiment or Inquiry

1. Describe ideal design or designs with especial attention to the control of interfering variables.
2. Describe selected operational design.
   a. Describe stimuli, subjects, environment, and responses with the objects, events, and properties necessary for their specification.
   b. Describe how control of interfering variables is achieved.
3. Specify statistical tests including dummy tables for each test.
   a. Specify level of confidence desired.

V. Sampling Procedures

1. Describe experimental and control samples.
   a. Specify the population to which the hypotheses are relevant.
   b. Explain determination of size and type of sample.
2. Specify method of drawing or selecting sample.
   a. Specify relative importance of Type I Error and Type II Error.
   b. Estimate relative costs of the various sizes and types of samples allowed by the theory.

VI. Methods of Gathering Data

1. Describe measures of quantitative variables showing reliability and validity when these are known. Describe means of identifying qualitative variables.
2. Include the following in description of questionnaires or schedules, if these are used.
   a. Approximate number of questions to be asked of each respondent.
   b. Approximate time needed for interview.
   c. The schedule as it has been constructed to this time.
   d. Preliminary testing of interview and results.
3. Include the following in description of interview procedure, if this is used.
   a. Means of obtaining information, i.e., by direct interview, all or part by mail, telephone, or other means.
   b. Particular characteristics interviewers must have or special training that must be given them.
4. Describe use to be made of pilot study, pretest, or trial run.
   a. Importance of and means for coping with unavailables, refusals, and response error.

VII. Working Guide

1. Prepare working guide with time and budget estimates.
   a. Planning.
   b. Pilot Study and Pretests.
   c. Drawing sample.
   d. Preparing observational materials.
   e. Selection and training.
   f. Trial plan.
   g. Revising plans.
   h. Collecting data.
   i. Processing data.
   j. Preparing final report.
2. Estimate total man hours and cost.

VIII. Analysis of Results

1. Specify method of analysis.
   a. Use of tables, calculator, sorter, computer, etc.
   b. Use of graphic techniques.
   c. Specify type of tables to be constructed.

IX. Interpretation of Results

1. Discuss how conclusions will be fed back into theory.

X. Publication or Reporting Plans

1. Write these according to department and graduate school requirements.
2. Select for journal publication the most significant aspects of the problem in succinct form (probably not in excess of fifteen typewritten pages double spaced). Follow style and format specified by the journal to which the article will be submitted.

I.2. A GENERAL STATEMENT TO GUIDE THE BASIC RESEARCHER IN THE FORMULATION OF RESEARCH PROBLEMS

Instructions for Use of Guide 1.2.

The first step in the design of research is the selection of a fruitful problem. The range of potential topics for social research is as broad as the range of social behavior itself. The significance of a problem rests on its probable contribution to knowledge. The formulation of the problem becomes of great importance in providing this potential.

Guide I.2 was formulated by a group of researchers to indicate those criteria that should be considered in insuring that a research proposal will be significant. This guide may be most valuable to the professional researcher, but the graduate student should use it as a standard by which to gauge his work. At the same time, the criteria of significance shown in Guide I.1 should be carefully considered.

Suggested Criteria for Research Problems *

A. A concern with basic concepts and relationships of concepts, as distinguished from local, particularized, or exclusively applied research, to the end that the knowledge produced may be cumulative with that from other studies.

B. The development, refinement, and testing of theoretical formulations. At present the theories appropriate as research guides will be more limited in scope than the comprehensive, speculative systems prominent in the early history of social science.

C. Superior research design, including careful specification of the variables involved and use of the most precise and appropriate methods available.

D. A probable contribution to methodology by the discovery, development, or refinement of practicable tools, techniques, or methods.

* From *Report of the Study for the Ford Foundation on Policy and Program,* Detroit, Michigan: Ford Foundation, November, 1949.

E. Full utilization of relevant concepts, theories, evidence, and techniques from related disciplines.

F. The integration of any single study in a planned program of related research to the end that the results become meaningful in a broad context.

G. Adequate provision to train additional research scientists.

H. Provision, wherever feasible, to repeat or check related research of other persons in order to provide a check on the generality of conclusions. A special aspect of this characteristic would be the repetition of studies in more than one culture group.

I.3. THE BEARING OF SOCIOLOGICAL THEORY ON EMPIRICAL RESEARCH

Instructions for Guide I.3.

To advance knowledge, both theory and substantive bodies of fact must be progressively interrelated. Robert K. Merton describes the bearing of theory on empirical research. He says that the ". . . notion of directed research implies that, in part, empirical inquiry is so organized that if and when empirical discoveries are made, they have direct consequences for a theoretic system." Note the functions of theory that are set forth. The researcher must often formulate "middle range" or miniature theories that will link his hypotheses to a more inclusive theory. Zetterberg has written that miniature theories delineate convenient research problems. "Granted that our ultimate purpose is a general theory and that this general theory will in part be made up by means of miniature theories, experimental evidence supporting a miniature theory will support also the inclusive theory of which the miniature theory is a special case." [1]

Milton Friedman has listed the following criteria for significant theory: "A theory is 'simpler' the less initial knowledge is needed to make a prediction within a given field of phenomena; it is the more 'fruitful' the more precise the resulting prediction, the wider the area within which the theory yields predictions, and the more additional lines for further research it suggests. . . . The only relevant test of the validity of a hypothesis is comparison of prediction with experience." [2]

FOOTNOTES

1. Hans L. Zetterberg, *On Theory and Verification in Sociology,* New York: The Tressler Press, 1954, p. 15.
2. Milton Friedman, "The Methodology of Positive Economics," in *Essays in Positive Economics,* Chicago: University of Chicago Press, 1953, p. 10.

Empirical Generalizations in Sociology *

ROBERT K. MERTON

Not infrequently it is said that the object of sociological theory is to arrive at statements of social uniformities. This is an elliptical assertion and hence requires clarification. For there are two types of statements of sociological uniformities that differ significantly in their bearing on theory. The first of these is the empirical generalization: an isolated proposition summarizing observed uniformities of relationships between two or more variables.[1] The sociological literature abounds with such generalizations that have not been assimilated to sociological theory. Thus, Engel's "laws" of consumption may be cited as examples. So, too, the Halbwachs' finding that laborers spend more per adult unit for food than white-collar employees of the same income class.[2] Such generalizations may be of greater or less precision, but this does not affect their logical place in the structure of inquiry. The Groves-Ogburn finding, for a sample of American cities, that "cities with a larger percentage engaged in manufacturing also have, on the average, slightly larger percentages of young persons married" has been expressed in an equation indicating the degree of this relationship. Although propositions of this order are essential in empirical research, a miscellany of such propositions only provides the raw materials for sociology as a discipline. The theoretic task, and the orientation of empirical research toward theory, first begins when the bearing of such uniformities on a set of interrelated propositions is tentatively established. The notion of directed research implies that, in part,[3] empirical inquiry is so organized that if and when empirical uniformities are discovered, they have direct consequences for a theoretic system. Insofar as the re-

* Excerpt from Robert K. Merton, "The Bearing of Sociological Theory on Empirical Research," *Social Theory and Social Structure,* rev. ed., Glencoe, Ill.: The Free Press, 1957, pp. 95-99.

search is directed, the rationale of findings is set forth before the findings are obtained.

Sociological Theory

The second type of sociological generalization, the so-called scientific law, differs from the foregoing inasmuch as it is a statement of invariance derivable from a theory. The paucity of such laws in the sociological field perhaps reflects the prevailing bifurcation of theory and empirical research. Despite the many volumes dealing with the history of sociological theory and despite the plethora of empirical investigations, sociologists (including the writer) may discuss the logical criteria of sociological laws without citing a single instance that fully satisfies these criteria.[4]

Approximations to these criteria are not entirely wanting. To exhibit the relations of empirical generalizations to theory and to set forth the functions of theory, it may be useful to examine a familiar case in which such generalizations were incorporated into a body of substantive theory. Thus, it has long been established as a statistical uniformity that, in a variety of populations, Catholics have a lower suicide rate than Protestants.[5] In this form the uniformity posed a theoretical problem. It merely constituted an empirical regularity that would become significant for theory only if it could be derived from a set of other propositions, a task that Durkheim set himself. If we restate his theoretic assumptions in formal fashion, the paradigm of his theoretic analysis becomes clear:

1. Social cohesion provides psychic support to group members subjected to acute stresses and anxieties.
2. Suicide rates are functions of *unrelieved* anxieties and stresses to which persons are subjected.
3. Catholics have greater social cohesion than Protestants.
4. Therefore, lower suicide rates should be anticipated among Catholics than among Protestants.[6]

This case serves to locate the place of empirical generalizations in relation to theory and to illustrate the several functions of theory.

1. It indicates that theoretic pertinence is not inherently present or absent in empirical generalizations but appears when the generalization is conceptualized in abstractions of higher order (Catholicism–social cohesion–relieved anxieties–suicide rate) that are

embodied in more general statements of relationships.[7] What was initially taken as an isolated uniformity is restated as a relation, not between religious affiliation and behavior, but between groups with certain conceptualized attributes (social cohesion) and the behavior. The *scope* of the original empirical finding is considerably extended, and several seemingly disparate uniformities are seen to be interrelated (thus differentials in suicide rates between married and single persons can be derived from the same theory).

2. Once having established the theoretic pertinence of a uniformity by deriving it from a set of interrelated propositions, we provide for the *cumulation* both of theory and of research findings. The differentials-in-suicide-rate uniformities add confirmation to the set of propositions from which they—and other uniformities—have been derived. This is a major function of *systematic theory*.

3. Whereas the empirical uniformity did not lend itself to the drawing of diverse consequences, the reformulation gives rise to various consequences in fields of conduct quite remote from that of suicidal behavior. For example, inquiries into obsessive behavior, morbid preoccupations, and other maladaptive behavior have found these also to be related to inadequacies of group cohesion.[8] The conversion of empirical uniformities into theoretic statements thus increases the *fruitfulness* of research through the successive exploration of implications.

4. By providing a rationale, the theory introduces a *ground for prediction* that is more secure than mere empirical extrapolation from previously observed trends. Thus, should independent measures indicate a decrease of social cohesion among Catholics, the theorist would predict a tendency toward increased rates of suicide in this group. The atheoretic empiricist would have no alternative, however, but to predict on the basis of extrapolation.

5. The foregoing list of functions presupposes one further attribute of theory that is not altogether true of the Durkheim formulation and which gives rise to a general problem that has peculiarly beset sociological theory, at least, up to the present. If theory is to be productive, it must be sufficiently *precise* to be *determinate*. Precision is an integral element of the criterion of *testability*. The prevailing pressure toward the utilization of statistical data in sociology, whenever possible, to control and test theoretic inferences has a justifiable basis, when we consider the logical place of precision in disciplined inquiry.

The more precise the inferences (predictions) that can be drawn from a theory, the less the likelihood of *alternative* hypotheses that will be adequate to these predictions. In other words, precise predictions and data serve to reduce the *empirical* bearing upon research of the *logical* fallacy of affirming the consequent.[9] It is well known that verified predictions derived from a theory do not prove or demonstrate that theory; they merely supply a measure of confirmation, for it is always possible that alternative hypotheses drawn from different theoretic systems can also account for the predicted phenomena.[10] But those theories that admit of precise predictions confirmed by observation take on strategic importance since they provide an initial basis for choice between competing hypotheses. In other words, precision enhances the likelihood of approximating a "crucial" observation or experiment.

The internal coherence of a theory has much the same function, for if a variety of empirically confirmed consequences are drawn from one theoretic system, this reduces the likelihood that competing theories can adequately account for the same data. The integrated theory sustains a larger measure of confirmation than is the case with distinct and unrelated hypotheses, thus accumulating a greater weight of evidence.

Both pressures—toward precision and logical coherence—can lead to unproductive activity, particularly in the social sciences. Any procedure can be abused as well as used. A premature insistence on precision at all costs may sterilize imaginative hypotheses. It may lead to a reformulation of the scientific problem in order to permit measurement with, at times, the result that the subsequent materials do not bear on the initial problem in hand.[11] In the search for precision, care must be taken to see that significant problems are not thus inadvertently blotted from view. Similarly, the pressure for logical consistency has at times invited logomachy and sterile theorizing, inasmuch as the assumptions contained in the system of analysis are so far removed from empirical referents or involve such high abstractions as not to permit of empirical inquiry.[12] But the warrant for these criteria of inquiry is not vitiated by such abuses.

FOOTNOTES

1. This usage of the term "empirical" is common, as Dewey notes. In this context, *"empirical* means that the subject-matter of a given proposition which has existential inference, represents merely a set of uniform conjunctions of traits repeatedly observed to exist, without any understanding of *why* the conjunction occurs; without a theory which states its rationale." John Dewey, *Logic: The Theory of Inquiry* (New York: Henry Holt & Co., 1938), p. 305.

2. See a considerable collection of such uniformities summarized by C. C. Zimmerman, *Consumption and Standards of Living* (New York: D. Van Nostrand Co., 1936), p. 55 ff.

3. "In part," if only because it stultifies the possibilities of obtaining fertile new findings to confine researches *wholly* to the test of predetermined hypotheses. Hunches originating in the course of the inquiry that may not have immediately obvious implications for a broader theoretic system may eventuate in the discovery of empirical uniformities that can later be incorporated into a theory. For example, in the sociology of political behavior, it has been recently established that the larger the number of social cross-pressures to which voters are subjected, the less interest they exhibit in a presidential election (P. F. Lazarsfeld, Bernard Berelson, and Hazel Gaudet, *The People's Choice,* New York: Duell, Sloan & Pearce, 1944, pp. 56-64). This finding, which was wholly unanticipated when the research was first formulated, may well initiate new lines of systematic inquiry into political behavior, even though it is not yet integrated into a generalized theory. Fruitful empirical research not only tests theoretically derived hypotheses; it also originates new hypotheses. This might be termed the "serendipity" component of research, i.e., the discovery, by chance or sagacity, of valid results that were not sought for.

4. E.g., see the discussion by George A. Lundberg, "The concept of law in the social sciences," *Philosophy of Science,* 1938, 5, 189-203, which affirms the possibility of such laws without including any case in point. The book by K. D. Har, *Social Laws* (Chapel Hill: University of North Carolina Press, 1930), does not fulfill the promise implicit in the title. A panel of social scientists discussing the possibility of obtaining social laws finds it difficult to instance cases. Herbert Blumer, *An Appraisal of Thomas and Znaiecki's The Polish Peasant in Europe and America* (New York: Social Science Research Council, 1939), pp. 142-50.

5. It need hardly be said that this statement assumes that education, income, nationality, rural-urban residence, and other factors that might render this finding spurious have been held constant.

6. We need not examine further aspects of this illustration, e.g. (1) the extent to which we have adequately stated the premises implicit in Durkheim's interpretation; (2) the supplementary theoretic analysis that would take these premises not as given but as problematic; (3) the grounds on which the potentially infinite regression of theoretic interpretations is halted at one rather than another point; (4) the problems involved in the introduction of such intervening variables as social cohesion that are not directly measured; (5) the extent to which the premises have been empirically confirmed; (6) the comparatively low order of abstraction represented by this illustration; and (7) the fact that Durkheim derived several empirical generalizations from this same set of hypotheses.

7. Thorstein Veblen has put this with typical cogency: "All this may seem like taking pains about trivialities. But the data with which any scientific inquiry has to do are trivialities in some other bearing than that one in which they are of account." *The Place of Science in Modern Civilization* (New York: Russell & Russell, 1961), p. 42.

8. See, e.g., Elton Mayo, *Human Problems of an Industrial Civilization* (New York: Macmillan Co., 1933), p. 113 *et passim*. The theoretical framework utilized in the studies of industrial morale by Whitehead, Roethlisberger, and Dickson stemmed appreciably from the Durkheim formulations, as the authors testify.

9. The paradigm of "proof through prediction" is, of course, logically fallacious: If A (hypothesis), then B (prediction).
B is observed.
Therefore, A is true.
This is not overdisturbing for scientific research, inasmuch as other than formal criteria are involved.

10. As a case in point, consider that different theorists had predicted war and internecine conflict on a large scale at midcentury. Sorokin and some Marxists, for example, set forth this prediction on the basis of quite distinct theoretic systems. The actual outbreak of large-scale conflicts does not in itself enable us to choose between these schemes of analysis, if only because the observed fact is consistent with both. Only if the predictions had been so *specified,* had been so precise, that the actual occurrences coincided with the one prediction and not with the other, would a determinate test have been instituted.

11. Stuart A. Rice comments on this tendency in public opinion research; see *Eleven Twenty-six: A Decade of Social Science Research,* ed. Louis Wirth (Chicago: University of Chicago Press, 1940), p. 167.

12. It is this practice to which E. Ronald Walker refers, in the field of economics, as "theoretic blight." *From Economic Theory to Policy* (Chicago: University of Chicago Press, 1943), chap. IV.

ADDITIONAL READINGS

N. R. HANSON, *Patterns of Discovery: An Inquiry into the Conceptual Foundations of Science,* Cambridge, Eng.: Cambridge University Press, 1958. See chap. IV "Theories."

CARL G. HEMPEL AND P. OPPENHEIM, "Studies in the Logic of Explanation," *Philosophy of Science,* 1948, 15: 135-75.

ABRAHAM KAPLAN, *The Conduct of Inquiry, Methodology for Behavioral Science,* San Francisco: Chandler Publishing Co., 1964. See chap. VIII "Theories."

FRANK R. WESTIE, "Toward Closer Relations between Theory and Research: A Procedure and an Example," *American Sociological Review,* April, 1957, 22: 149-54.

HANS L. ZETTERBERG, *On Theory and Verification in Sociology,* 2nd rev. ed., Totowa, N.J.: The Bedminster Press, 1963.

I.4. CRITERIA FOR JUDGING USABLE HYPOTHESES *

Instructions for Guide I.4.

The formulation of usable hypotheses is of central importance. The entire study rests upon the potential significance of the hypotheses. In this guide, William J. Goode and Paul K. Hatt prescribe step-by-step methods for evaluating hypotheses against criteria. Note again the emphasis given to the criterion that a hypothesis should be related to a body of theory. It is also important to anticipate the verification problem. Zetterberg has stated three criteria for the acceptance of a working hypothesis: (1) that the empirical data were found to be arranged in the manner predicted by the working hypothesis; (2) that we have disproved the null hypothesis with a certain probability; and (3) that we have disproved alternate hypotheses to the one tested.

WILLIAM J. GOODE and PAUL K. HATT

1. *The hypotheses must be conceptually clear.* The concepts should be clearly defined, operationally if possible. Moreover, they should be definitions that are commonly accepted and communicable rather than the products of a "private world."

What to do: One simple device for clarifying concepts is to write out a list of the concepts used in the research outline. Then try to define them (*a*) in words, (*b*) in terms of particular operations (index calculations, types of observations, etc.), and (*c*) with reference to other concepts to be found in previous research. Talk over each concept with fellow students and other researchers in the field. It will often be found that supposedly simple concepts contain many meanings. Then it is possible to decide which is the desired referent.

2. *Hypotheses should have empirical referents.* It has also been previously pointed out that scientific concepts must have an ultimate empirical referent. No usable hypothesis can embody moral judgments. Such statements as "criminals are no worse than businessmen," "women should pursue a career," or "capitalists exploit their workers," are no more usable hypotheses than is the familiar proposition that "pigs are well named because they are so dirty" or the

---

* By permission from *Methods in Social Research* by William J. Goode and Paul K. Hatt. Copyright 1952 by McGraw-Hill Book Company, Inc., pp. 68-73.

classical question, "How many yards of buttermilk are required to make a pair of breeches for a black bull?" In other words, while a hypothesis may involve the study of value judgments, such a goal must be separated from a moral preachment or a plea for acceptance of one's values.

What to do: First, analyze the concepts that express attitudes rather than describe or refer to empirical phenomena. Watch for key words such as "ought," "should," "bad," etc. Then transform the notions into more useful concepts. "Bad parents" is a value term but the researcher may have a definite description in mind: parents who follow such practices as whimsical and arbitrary authoritarianism, inducing psychic insecurity in the child, failure to give love, etc. "Should" is also a value term, but the student may simply mean, "If women do not pursue a career, we can predict emotional difficulties when the children leave home, or we can predict that the society will not be able to produce as much goods," etc. When, instead, we find that our referent is simply a vague feeling and we cannot define the operations needed to observe it, we should study the problem further and discover what it is that we really wish to investigate.

3. *The hypotheses must be specific.* That is, all the operations and predictions indicated by it should be spelled out. The possibility of actually testing the hypothesis can thus be appraised. Often hypotheses are expressed in such general terms, and with so grandiose a scope, that they are simply not testable. Because of their magnitude, such grand ideas are tempting because they seem impressive and important. It is better for the student to avoid such problems and instead develop his skills upon more tangible notions.

By making all the concepts and operations explicit is meant not only conceptual clarity but a description of any indexes to be used. Thus, to hypothesize that the degree of vertical social mobility is decreasing in the United States requires the use of indexes. (At present there are many operational definitions of the status levels that define mobility. Therefore, the hypothesis must include a statement of the index that is to be used; see Part III for available indexes.)

Such specific formulations have the advantage of assuring that research is practicable and significant, in advance of the expenditure of effort. It furthermore increases the validity of the results, since the broader the terms the easier it is to fall into the trap of using selective evidence. The fame of most prophets and fortune-tellers lies in their ability to state predictions so that almost any occurrence can be interpreted as a fulfillment. We can express this in almost statistical terms: the more specific the prediction, the smaller the chance that the prediction will actually be borne out as a result of mere accident. Scientific predictions or hypotheses must, then, avoid the trap of selective evidence by being as definite and specific as possible.

What to do: Never be satisfied with a general prediction, if it can be broken into more precise subhypotheses. The general prediction of war is not enough, for example: we must specify time, place, and participants. Predicting the general decline of a civilization is not a hypothesis for testing a theory. Again, we must be able to specify and measure the forces, specify the meaning and time of decline, the population segments involved, etc. Often this can be done by conceptual analysis and the formulation of related hypotheses: e.g., we may predict that urbanization is accompanied by a decline in fertility. However, we gain in precision if we attempt to define our indexes of urbanization; specify which segments will be affected, and how much (since in the United States the various ethnic and religious segments are affected differently); specify the amount of fertility decline, and the type (percentage childless, net reproduction rate, etc.). Forming subhypotheses (1) clarifies the relationship between the data sought and the conclusions; and (2) makes the specific research task more manageable.

4. *Hypotheses should be related to available techniques.* Earlier, the point was repeatedly made that theory and method are not opposites. The theorist who does not know what techniques are available to test his hypotheses is in a poor way to formulate usable questions.

This is not to be taken as an absolute injunction against the formulation of hypotheses that at present are too complex to be handled by contemporary technique. It is merely a sensible requirement to apply to any problem in its early stages in order to judge its researchability.

There are some aspects of the impossible hypothesis that may make its formulation worth while. If the problem is significant enough as a possible frame of reference, it may be useful whether or not it can be tested at the time. The socioeconomic hypotheses of Marx, for example, were not proved by his data. The necessary techniques were not available either then or now. Nevertheless, Marxian frameworks are an important source of more precise, smaller, verifiable propositions. This is true for much of Emile Durkheim's work on suicide. His related formulations concerning social cohesion have also been useful. The work of both men has been of paramount importance to sociology, even though at the time their larger ideas were not capable of being handled by available techniques.

Furthermore, posing the impossible question may stimulate the growth of technique. Certainly some of the impetus toward modern developments in technique has come from criticisms against significant studies that were considered inadequate because of technical limitations. In any serious sociological discussion, research frontiers are continuously challenged by the assertion that various problems "ought" to be investigated even though the investigations are presently impossible.

What to do: Look for research articles on the subject being investigated. Make a list of the various techniques that have been used to measure the factors of importance in the study. If you are unable to locate any discussions of technique, you may find it wiser to do a research on the necessary research techniques. You may, instead, decide that this lack of techniques means your problem is too large and general for your present resources.

Some items, such as stratification or race attitudes, have been studied by many techniques. Try to discover why one technique is used in one case and not in another. Note how refinements in technique have been made, and see whether one of these may be more useful for your purposes. Look for criticisms of previous research, so as to understand the weaknesses in the procedures followed.

Again, other problems may have been studied with few attempts at precise measurement. Study the literature to see why this is the case. Ascertain whether some subareas (for example, of religious behavior) may be attacked with techniques used in other areas (for example, attitude measurement, stratification measures, research on choice making, etc.).

5. *The hypothesis should be related to a body of theory.* This criterion is one which is often overlooked by the beginning student. He is more likely to select subject matter that is "interesting," without finding out whether the research will really help to refute, qualify, or support any existing theories of social relations. A science, however, can be cumulative only by building on an existing

body of fact and theory. It cannot develop if each study is an isolated survey.

Although it is true that the clearest examples of crescive theoretical development are to be found in the physical and biological sciences, the process can also be seen in the social sciences. One such case is the development of a set of generalizations concerning the social character of intelligence. The anthropological investigations at the end of the nineteenth century uncovered the amazing variety of social customs in various societies, while demonstrating conclusively that there were a number of common elements in social life: family systems, religious patterns, an organization of the socialization process, etc.

The French school of sociology, including Lucien Lévy-Bruhl, Emile Durkheim, Marcel Mauss, Henri Hubert, and others, formulated a series of propositions, at the turn of the century, which suggested that the intellectual structure of the human mind is determined by the structure of the society. That is, perception and thought are determined by society, not alone by the anatomical structure of our eyes, ears, and other senses. Modes of thought vary from society to society. Some of these formulations were phrased in an extreme form that need not concern us now, and they were often vague. Nevertheless, the idea was growing that the intelligence of a Polynesian native could not be judged by European standards; his thinking was qualitatively, not merely quantitatively, different.

At the same time, however, better techniques were being evolved for measuring "intelligence," which came to be standardized in the form of scores on various IQ tests. When these were applied to different groups it became clear that the variation in IQ was great; children of Italian immigrants made lower grades on such tests, as did Negroes. Northern Negroes made higher grades than whites from many Southern states. American children of Chinese and Japanese parents made rather high scores. Since it was generally assumed that these tests measured "innate intelligence," these data were sometimes generalized to suggest that certain "racial" groups were by nature inferior and others superior.

However, such conclusions were opposed on rational grounds, and liberal sentiments suggested that they be put to the test. There were, then, two major sets of conclusions, one suggesting that intelligence is in the main determined by social experience, the other suggesting that the IQ is innately determined. To test such opposing generalizations, a research design was needed for testing logical expectations in more specific situations. If, for example, it is true that the intelligence of individuals who are members of "inferior" groups is really determined biologically, then changes in their environments should not change their IQ. If, on the other hand, the social experience is crucial, we should expect that such changes in social experience would result in definite patterns of IQ change.

Further deductions are possible. If identical twins are separated and are placed in radically different social experiences at an early age, we might expect significant differences in IQ. Or, if a group of rural Negro children moves from the poor school and social experience of the South, to the somewhat more stimulating environment of the North, the group averages would be expected to change somwhat. Otto Klineberg, in a classic study, carried out the latter research. He traced Negro children of various ages after they had moved to the North and found that, in general, the earlier the move to the North occurred, the greater the average rise in the IQ. The later the move, the smaller the increase. Even if one assumes that the "better," more able, and more daring adult Negroes made this move, this does not explain the differences by time of movement. Besides, of course, the subjects were children at the time of the migration.[1]

In this research design a particular result was predicted by a series of deductions from a larger set of generalizations. Further, the prediction was actually validated. In justice to the great number of scholars who have been engaged in refining and developing IQ tests, it should be mentioned that other tests and investigations of a similar order have been carried out by many anthropologists, sociologists, and social psychologists. They do not invalidate the notion that IQ is based in part on "innate" abilities, but they do indicate that to a great extent these abilities must be stimulated by certain types of experience in order to achieve high scores on such tests.

From even so sketchy an outline of a theoretical development as the foregoing is, it can be seen that when research is systematically based upon a body of existing theory, a genuine contribution in knowledge is more likely to result. In other words, to be worth doing, a hypothesis must not only be carefully stated, but it should possess theoretical relevance.

What to do: First, of course, cover the literature relating to your subject. If it is impossible to do so, then your hypothesis probably covers too much ground. Second, try to abstract from the literature the way in which various propositions and sets of propositions relate to one another (for example, the literature relating to Sutherland's theory of differential association in criminology, the conditions for maximum morale in factories, or the studies of prediction of marital adjustment). Third, ascertain whether you can deduce any of the propositions, including your own hypothesis, from one another or from a small set of major statements. Fourth, test it by some theoretical model, such as Merton's "Paradigm for Functional Analysis in Sociology" (*Social Theory and Social Structure*, pp. 50-54), to see whether you have left out major propositions and determinants. Fifth, especially compare your own set of related propositions with those of some classic author, such as Weber on bureaucracy or Durkheim on suicide. If you find this task of abstraction difficult, compare instead with the propositions of these men as explained by a systematic interpreter such as Talcott Parsons in his *Structure of Social Action*. What is important is that, whatever the source of your hypothesis, it must be logically derivable from and based upon a set of related sociological propositions.

FOOTNOTE

1. Otto Klineberg, *Negro Intelligence and Selective Migration* (New York: Columbia University Press, 1935).

1.5.   SOME OBSERVATIONS ON STUDY DESIGN *

Instructions for Guides to Study Design. Guides I.5, I.6, I.7, and I.8.

The study design involves such decisions as that of whether a statistical sampling survey, qualitative structured observation, or controlled experimentation is needed. At this point one must decide the nature of proof desired, taking into consideration the level of one's hypotheses, the size of one's budget, the amount of personnel and their skills, the time required, etc. It is now generally accepted that the model of the controlled experiment is always a valuable guide even if, in practice, deviation is necessary. *Some Observations on Study Design* (1.5) by Samuel A. Stouffer is re-

---

* Reprinted from Samuel A. Stouffer, "Some Observations on Study Design," *The American Journal of Sociology*, 55 (January 1950), 356-59. Copyright 1950 by the University of Chicago.

garded as the single most useful statement of design requirements for social investigation.

Hans Zetterberg explains the problems facing the researcher who wishes to use controlled observation and explains how alternative hypotheses can be tested with pseudo-experimental designs. See I.6, an excerpt from *On the Evaluation of Designs for the Confirmation of a Working Hypothesis.*

Edward Suchman in I.7 has listed some *General Considerations of Research Design.* These are realistic appraisals often needed when ideal plans must be compromised. The professional researcher keeps these guides before him.

Large scale group research has grown in volume and in scope. Delbert C. Miller has written *"The Shaping of Research Design in Large Scale Group Research"* (I.8) to provide a case study for the team research proposal. The breaking down of the problem into manageable parts is illustrated. The importance of individual differences among researchers is highlighted. Note also the progression of research stages. This guide is for the guidance of design in large-scale research only.

SAMUEL A. STOUFFER

We must be clear in our own minds what proof consists of, and we must, if possible, provide dramatic examples of the advantages of relying on something more than plausibility. And the heart of our problem lies in study design *in advance,* such that the evidence is not capable of a dozen alternative interpretations.

Basically, I think it is essential that we always keep in mind the model of a controlled experiment, even if in practice we may have to deviate from an ideal model. Take the simple accompanying diagram.

	Before	After	After—Before
Experimental group	x_1	x_2	$d = x_2 - x_1$
Control group	x'_1	x'_2	$d' = x'_2 - x'_1$

The test of whether a difference d is attributable to what we think it is attributable to is whether d is significantly larger than d'.

We used this model over and over again during the war to measure the effectiveness of orientation films in changing soldiers' attitudes. These experiences are described in Volume III of our *Studies in Social Psychology in World War II*.[1]

One of the troubles with using this careful design was that the effectiveness of a single film when thus measured turned out to be so slight. If, instead of using the complete experimental design, we simply took an unselected sample of men and compared the attitudes of those who said they had seen a film with those who said they had not, we got much more impressive differences. This was more rewarding to us, too, for the management wanted to believe the films were powerful medicine. The gimmick was the selective fallibility of memory. Men who correctly remembered seeing the films were likely to be those most sensitized to their message. Men who were bored or indifferent may have actually seen them but slept through them or just forgot.

Most of the time we are not able or not patient enough to design studies containing all four cells as in the diagram above. Sometimes we have only the top two cells, as in the accompanying diagram. In this situation we have two observations of the same individuals or

$$
\boxed{x_1 \;|\; x_2} \qquad d = x_1 - x_2
$$

groups taken at different times. This is often a very useful design. In the army, for example, we would take a group of recruits, ascertain their attitudes, and restudy the same men later. From this we could tell whose attitudes changed and in what direction. (It was almost always for the worse, which did not endear us to the army!) But exactly what factors in the early training period were most responsible for deterioration of attitudes could only be inferred indirectly.

The panel study is usually more informative than a more frequent design, which might be pictured thus:

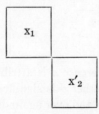

Here at one point in time we have one sample, and at a later point in time we have another sample. We observe that our measure, say, the mean, is greater for the recent sample than for the earlier one. But we are precluded from observing which men or what type of men shifted. Moreover, there is always the disturbing possibility that the populations in our two samples were initially different; hence the differences might not be attributable to conditions taking place in the time interval between the two observations. Thus we would study a group of soldiers in the United States and later ask the same questions of a group of soldiers overseas. Having matched the two groups of men carefully by branch of service, length of time in the army, rank, etc., we hoped that the results of the study would approximate what would be found if the same men could have been studied twice. But this could be no more than a hope. Some important factors could not be adequately controlled, for example, physical conditions. Men who went overseas were initially in better shape on the average than men who had been kept behind; but, if the follow-up study was in the tropics, there was a chance that unfavorable climate already had begun to take its toll. And so it went. How much men overseas changed called for a panel study as a minimum if we were to have much confidence in the findings.

A very common attempt to get the result of a controlled experiment without paying the price is with the design that might be as shown in the accompanying diagram. This is usually what we get

with correlation analysis. We have two or more groups of men whom we study at the same point in time. Thus we have men in the infantry and men in the air corps and compare their attitudes. How much of the difference between x'_2 and x_2 we can attribute to experience in a given branch of service and how much is a function of attributes of the men selected for each branch we cannot know assuredly. True, we can try to rule out various possibilities by matching; we can compare men from the two branches with the same age and education, for example. But there is all too often a wide-open gate through which other uncontrolled variables can march.

Sometimes, believe it nor not, we have only one cell:

$$\boxed{x_2}$$

When this happens, we do not know much of anything. But we can still fill pages of social science journals with "brilliant analysis" if we use plausible conjecture in supplying missing cells from our imagination. Thus we may find that the adolescent today has wild ideas and conclude that society is going to the dogs. We fill in the dotted cell representing our own yesterdays with hypothetical data, where x_1 represents us and x_2 our offspring. The tragicomic part is that most of the public, including, I fear, many social scientists, are so acculturated that they ask for no better data.

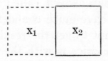

I do not intend to disparage all research not conforming to the canons of the controlled experiment. I think that we will see more of full experimental design in sociology and social psychology in the future than in the past. But I am well aware of the practical difficulties of its execution, and I know that there are numberless important situations in which it is not feasible at all. What I am arguing for is awareness of the limitations of a design in which crucial cells are missing.

Sometimes by forethought and patchwork we can get approximations that are useful if we are careful to avoid overinterpretation. Let me cite an example:

In Europe during the war the army tested the idea of putting an entire platoon of Negro soldiers into a white infantry outfit. This was done in several companies. The Negroes fought beside white soldiers. After several months we were asked to find out what the white troops thought about the innovation. We found that only 7 per cent of the white soldiers in companies with Negro platoons said that they disliked the idea very much, whereas 62 per cent of the white soldiers in divisions without Negro troops said they would dislike the idea very much if it were tried in their outfits. We have:

	Before	After
Experimental		7%
Control		62%

Now, were these white soldiers who fought beside Negroes men who were naturally more favorable to Negroes than the cross-section of white infantrymen? We did not think so, since, for example, they contained about the same proportion of southerners. The point was of some importance, however, if we were to make the inference that actual experience with Negroes reduced hostility from 62 to 7 per cent. As a second-best substitute, we asked the white soldiers in companies with Negro platoons if they could recall how they felt when the innovation was first proposed. It happens that 67 per cent said they were initially opposed to the idea. Thus we could tentatively fill in a missing cell and conclude that, under the conditions obtaining, there probably had been a marked change in attitude.

Even if this had been a perfectly controlled experiment, there was still plenty of chance to draw erroneous inferences. The conclusions apply only to situations closely approximating those of the study. It happens, for example, that the Negroes involved were men who volunteered to leave rear-area jobs for combat duty. If other Negroes had been involved, the situation might have been different. Moreover, they had white officers. One army colonel who saw this study and whom I expected to ridicule it because he usually opposed innovations, surprised me by offering congratulations. "This proves," he said, "what I have been arguing in all my thirty years in the army—that niggers will do all right if you give 'em white officers!" Moreover, the study applied only to combat experience. Other studies would be needed to justify extending the findings to noncombat or garrison duty. In other words, one lone study, however well designed, can be a very dangerous thing if it is exploited beyond its immediate implications.

Now experiments take time and money, and there is no use denying that we in social science cannot be as prodigal with the replications as the biologist who can run a hundred experiments simultaneously by growing plants in all kinds of soils and conditions. The relative ease of experimentation in much—not all—of natural science goes far to account for the difference in quality of proof demanded by physical and biological sciences, on the one hand, and social scientists, on the other.

Though we cannot always design neat experiments when we want to, we can at least keep the experimental model in front of our eyes and behave cautiously when we fill in missing cells with dotted lines. But there is a further and even more important operation we can perform in the interest of economy. That lies in our choice of the initial problem.

FOOTNOTE

1. Carl I. Hovland, Arthur A. Lumsdaine, and Fred D. Sheffield, *Experiments on Mass Communication* (Princeton: Princeton University Press, 1949).

1.6. ON THE DECISIONS IN VERIFICATIONAL STUDIES *

HANS L. ZETTERBERG

The advantages of the experimental design, however, rest with the possibility of a random assignment of cases to the experimental and control groups and on the possibility of producing what the working hypothesis terms the cause. Unfortunately, in sociology we rarely have these possibilities.

Certainly many factors are intentionally introduced into society by politicians, educators, welfare agencies, etc. But these phenomena are seldom or never produced, because they are termed causes in a scientific social theory. Furthermore, when compulsory education,

* From H. L. Zetterberg, *On Theory and Verification in Sociology,* 2nd rev. ed. (Totowa, N.J.: The Bedminister Press, 1963), pp. 61-66.

socialized medicine, public housing projects, etc., are introduced into a society, the very complexity of the new phenomena does not make them suitable as indicators of concepts of a theory.

In the second place, we can rarely introduce randomization of the persons supposed to enjoy these intentionally produced phenomena without violating strong moral sentiments. As to the social programs of the welfare state Chapin makes the comment:

> The conventional method of equalizing factors that are known and also unknown (by R. A. Fisher's design of experiment) is to select at random both the experimental group that receives treatment and the control group that serves as a reference group for comparison. In social research the program of social treatment cannot be directed toward a randomly selected group because the prevailing mores require that this treatment be directed to a group of individuals who are eligible because of greater *need*. Thus precise control of unknown is impossible and the only factors that can be controlled are factors that are known to be in the particular social situation because of previous studies.[1]

It seems that this inability to satisfy the conditions for a profitable use of the experimental design would definitely curtail the sociologist's prospect to verify his theories. However, the situation is by no means disastrous: sciences like meteorology and astronomy have verified theories without the employment of the experimental method.

For control of alternative hypotheses, the sociologist is to a large extent dependent on what might be called *pseudoexperimental* designs. These designs control propositions known as alternative ones, but, unlike the experimental designs, these designs cannot control unknown alternatives.

The most commonly used method in sociology for control of known alternative propositions is multivariate analysis, which has been formalized by Paul Lazarsfeld.[2] Skill in its use has become essential for most sociological research; those who know how to use it deserve to be called "modern sociologists." The technique controls alternative propositions by testing the hypothesis in subsamples that are homogeneous with respect to the determinants specified by the alternative propositions. It can be used to control all known alternative determinants, provided the sample used is large enough.

The simplest relation between two variates x and y is a fourfold table:

	X	non-X
Y		
non-Y		

To discover whether a third variable, z, accounts for any of the relations found in such a table, we break it into two parts:

	X	non-X			Z	X	non-X			non-Z	X	non-X
Y				=	Y				+	Y		
non-Y					non-Y					non-Y		

If the relation between x and y still holds in all subclasses of z, we may retain, for the time being, our trust in the proposition that x affects y. To this kind of design many new alternative determinants can be added, and it works equally well for qualitative and quantitative varieties.

However, the advantages do not end here. We can tabulate:

	X	non-X			Y	X	non-X			non-Y	X	non-X
Z				=	Z				+	Z		
non-Z					non-Z					non-Z		

and also:

	X				X				non-X		
	Y	non-Y			Y	non-Y			Y	non-Y	
Z				Z				Z			
			=				+				
non-Z				non-Z				non-Z			

The purpose of these tabulations is to discover the actual linkage between the three variables. It would carry us far to review all the rules of interpretation involved here. However, if certain assumptions about the time lag between the variates can be made, it is impossible to use such tabulations to disentangle a wide variety of causal chains, as shown in the adjoining diagram adapted from Dahlström.[3]

(1)   X —→ Y —→ Z   (2)   X —→ Z —→ Y

(3)   Z —→ X —→ Y   (4)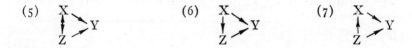

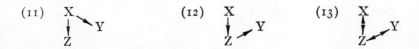

Another method of pseudoexperimental control is that of *matching,* advocated by F. S. Chapin.[4] An experimental group and a control group are made equal on some criteria by discarding cases in one group for which no "twin" can be found in the other group. One disadvantage of this procedure is that the matched groups so obtained are not representative of the original groups. When this way of matching is employed, we do not quite know to what population the results can be generalized.

Control in pseudoexperimental design can be obtained through the use of other statistical adjustments. Various applications of the *multiple regression* approach can be made, provided variables fitting the rather rigid assumptions are used. The most common methods are those of partial correlation and analysis of covariance. These methods become rather laborious if the number of factors to be controlled is more than three or four.

Experimental designs and pseudoexperimental designs may be cross-sectional or longitudinal. We have already pointed out that longitudinal designs are more effective than cross-sectional designs and that experimental designs are more effective than pseudoexperimental designs. We can now reach a typology of designs:

		The test of the null-hypothesis	
		Cross-sectional	Longitudinal
The control of alternative hypotheses	No control		
	Pseudoexperimental		
	Experimental		

The closer a design comes to the longitudinal experimental the better it is. However, we know little or nothing about how to evaluate crosswise combinations of the two criteria. We have no way in which to tell whether a pseudoexperimental longitudinal design (such as a panel with multivariable analysis) is as effective as the cross-sectional experimental design (the conventional laboratory experiment).

FOOTNOTES

1. F. Stuart Chapin, "Experimental Designs in Social Research," *American Journal of Sociology,* LV (1950), p. 402.

2. Paul F. Lazarsfeld, "Interpretation of Statistical Relations as a Research Operation" in Paul F. Lazarsfeld and Morris Rosenberg (eds.), *The Language of Social Research* (Glencoe, Ill.: The Free Press, 1955), pp. 115-25.

3. Edmund Dahlström, "Analys av surveymaterial" in Georg Karlsson, *et al.* (eds.), *Sociologiska metoder* (Stockholm: Svenska Bokförlaget, 1961), p. 193.

4. F. Stuart Chapin, *Experimental Designs in Sociological Research* (New York: Harper & Bros., 1947).

For further reading the advanced student should see F. Stuart Chapin, *Experimental Designs in Sociological Research,* rev. ed., New York: Harper & Bros., 1955; Ernest Greenwood, *Experimental Sociology: A Study in Method,* New York: King's Crown Press, 1945; Claire Selltiz, Marie Jahoda, Morton Deutsch, and Stuart W. Cook, *Research Methods in Social Relations,* rev., 1 vol., chap. 4, New York: Henry Holt, 1959; Russell L. Ackoff, *The Design of Social Research,* chap. 3, Chicago: University of Chicago Press, 1953; Abraham Kaplan, *The Conduct of Inquiry,* San Francisco: Chandler Publishing Co., 1964.

I.7. GENERAL CONSIDERATIONS OF RESEARCH DESIGN *

EDWARD A. SUCHMAN

1. It seems to us futile to argue whether or not a certain design is "scientific." The design is *the plan of study* and, as such, is present in all studies, uncontrolled as well as controlled and subjective as well as objective. It is not a case of scientific or not scientific, but rather one of good or less good design. The degree of accuracy desired, the level of "proof" aimed at, the state of existing knowledge, etc., all combine to determine the amount of concern one can have with the degree of "science" in one's design.

2. The proof of hypotheses is never definitive. The best one can hope to do is to make more or less plausible a series of alternative hypotheses. In most cases multiple explanations will be operative. Demonstrating one's own hypotheses does not rule out alternative hypotheses and vice versa.

3. There is no such thing as a single, "correct" design. Different workers will come up with different designs favoring their own

* From *An Introduction to Social Research,* by John T. Doby (ed.), with the assistance of Edward A. Suchman, John C. McKinney, Roy G. Francis, and John P. Dean, pp. 254-55. By permission of Edward A. Suchman and the Stackpole Company, 1954. The statements above are from chap. 10, "The Principles of Research Design."

methodological and theoretical predispositions. Hypotheses can be studied by different methods using different designs.

4. All research design represents a compromise dictated by the many practical considerations that go into social research. None of us operates except on limited time, money, and personnel budgets. Further limitations concern the availability of data and the extent to which one can impose upon one's subjects. A research design must be *practical*.

5. A research design is not a highly specific plan to be followed without deviation, but rather a series of guideposts to keep one headed in the right direction. One must be prepared to discard (although not too quickly) hypotheses that do not work out and to develop new hypotheses on the basis of increased knowledge. Furthermore, any research design developed in the office will inevitably have to be changed in the face of field considerations.

I.8. THE SHAPING OF RESEARCH DESIGN IN LARGE-SCALE GROUP RESEARCH *

DELBERT C. MILLER

This paper examines some of the problems and opportunities in the shaping of research design posed by a large-scale group research project undertaken by the University of Washington for the United States Air Force.

The project began in June 1951 under a contract with the Human Resources Research Institute calling for an exploration of human relations problems of Air Force personnel manning isolated Air Defense radar stations "with reference to job requirements, morale factors, and leadership under stressful noncombat conditions and to develop methods for improving effectiveness." The contract was concluded in December, 1953. During the 32 months of active research, the project moved from exploration to descriptive and diagnostic study. Some cross-sectional experimental studies were undertaken in the final phase. The full research program included a national survey of the United States Air Defense Command Aircraft Control and Warning Stations, a study of the Japan Air Defense Command (A. C. and W.), and numerous investigations in the

* Reprinted by permission of *Social Forces,* XXXIII (May, 1955), 383-90.

25th Division of the Pacific Northwest. All of these undertakings centered about personnel problems and squadron efficiency.

It is the theme of this paper that research design in a group project is a product of a social process. That process is influenced by a number of organizational demands as well as by the dynamic interplay of personalities and experiences that are encountered by the group as research penetration continues. It is believed that it is entirely fallacious to consider group research as individual research simply grown big.

Research design for group research must be sensitive to needs of individual researchers, to organizational demands, and to research growth through contact with the problem. Indeed, it should be clearly recognized that individual researchers do not become group researchers merely by joining group research. The problem of research design becomes one of wedding the logic of scientific method to the social pressures of many internal and external considerations. Four major factors affected research design on the Air Site Project. These were: (I) the characteristic imperatives of group research; (II) the personal wants of researchers; (III) the demands of education; and (IV) the accumulation of empirical and theoretical knowledge.

I. The Characteristic Imperatives of Group Research

A. *The Restrictions of Interdependent Research Relationships.* The individual researcher confronting group research is asked to change many research habits that he may value highly. The change in habits may be experienced as a set of onerous restrictions. He may find that he cannot choose his problem, and the problem assigned to him may require collaboration with others that reduces still further his area of free movement. He discovers that he has come to live in a web of interrelationships in which his work is intertwined. His own methods of work undergo close scrutiny of the group. He is subordinate to the final approval of a research director. Status and craft comparisons may clearly become causes of interpersonal conflict.[1] If the researcher does not or cannot adjust to this new social environment, conflict processes are intensified and spread to the group. In this atmosphere, even interpretation of words can become a serious source of wrangling.[2] Learning to live together in close interdependence does not come easy. And in group research for a client, many additional pressures are added.

B. *The Demands of a Time Schedule*. Group research for a client usually has a number of deadlines. Our military client required quarterly, interim, and final reports on given dates. No longer could researchers regard as indefinite the date for concluding a study. The demand for a report often meant intensified work, and this brought to some workers a sense of frustration that quality had been sacrificed for lack of time to do one's best.

C. *Conciliation of Other Pressures*. The client—or, as in our project, the monitoring agent—may offer suggestions and instructions as the research proceeds. These are usually accepted as persuasions to modify or intensify work in a given direction. These come to the project director and are transmitted through his actions or instructions to the group researchers. Sometimes the reason is not understood, or it may be understood but resented as an outside idea, foreign to the group process, and emotionally rejected.

Scientific canons of rigor may be opposed by demands for exploratory or applied research on problems for which hypotheses and measurement tools cannot be readied. A researcher whose pride system has incorporated strict and rigid standards of craftsmanship may quail before problems whose solution requires simple exploration or vulgar practicality (especially if he does not see how he can get a published paper from it).

The requirements of expense accounts, security clearances, permission for entry to the research field, "logistic support," and numerous matters of red tape are often further irritations—a headache to researchers and director alike.

The airmen and officers in the research field also exert subtle pressure on the researchers. The questions, "What's this all about? What are you trying to find out?" are continuous and require some kind of answer. The challenge, "You won't be able to do any good" is even more difficult to meet. It can undermine the feeling of acceptance and make fieldwork a resented rather than a welcome experience.

All of these new elements call for personal adjustments. It is apparent that a number of strains must be borne by group researchers who have not confronted these factors before. Who are these researchers that come into the group and what do they want?

II. The Personal Wants of Researchers

A. *Motivations of Researchers*. Young researchers are attracted to group research. If they are graduate students, the prospect of funds and a thesis presents an opportunity both to do research and to eat. Young Ph.D.'s see opportunity for publication, promotion, and freedom from teaching. Both of these groups are seeking to build research reputations through publication. This motive serves to make the burdens of fieldwork sufficiently acceptable to get the necessary data collecting done, but marriage, parenthood, and sedentary proclivities all contrive to make absence from the home an increasing burden. The influence of wives on the shaping of research design is an unknown but promising area of investigation.

B. *Security Needs of Researchers*. Research staffs are often recruited from among those persons who are seeking permanent employment. When contracts are on a year to year basis with no fixed guarantee as to their duration, a job insecurity is added to the social influences that bear upon the researchers' morale and productivity. As individual contracts begin to approach termination, personal insecurities mount and are intensified by group interaction. The feelings of insecurity are expressed in many different ways, which may include demands for more say in both policy and administrative decisions, safeguards for individual publication rights, and almost single-minded preoccupation with the acquisition of the *next* research contract.

A research design is under the stress of individual wants, for group thinking is colored every step of the way by these personal concerns. Each person wants to know what part of the design he can claim for his research publications. Each person wants to have an opportunity to guide his fieldwork in such a way as to minimize its burdens. Each wants the maximum opportunity to determine his working conditions.

C. *Role of the Research Director*. The research director takes his place in the center of all the forces that have been described. His role is to direct group processes, ascertain group sentiment, and make decisions so that research can be designed and executed with harmony and efficiency. He must see that role definitions for each member are clearly outlined. He must interpret the external demands on the project and relate them to his research personnel so that appropriate action is taken. He must come to recognize that he will get little opportunity to do field research himself. And he must accept the fact that some interpersonal friction will accompany his most valiant efforts to make group research palatable, especially during the early period when a number of individual researchers are learning to live together as group researchers. He will come to understand that each member of the group is concerned with his reputation as the result of his membership. He wants to have his say as to what others do when he feels his own standards are being violated. This is at once a source of group power and of group conflict. The director will often be challenged as to how these group motivations can be channeled.

A research director who wishes to manage by the use of democratic methods must know the dilemmas of leadership in the democratic process and find his own way to cope with them.[3] Softhearted, inexperienced democratic leadership rivals autocratic blindness in creating poor conditions for efficiency and morale.

III. The Demands of Education

The major problem facing organization of group research within a university is to secure opportunity for each researcher to have maximum freedom to apply his talents to a project whose major problems have been outlined in a contract for him. This is no little task. A professional researcher, we have said, wants to choose his problem, be given the proprietary right of publication for his work, and have control over his working conditions. The university is concerned that graduate students receive broad research training and not be employed at mere clerical tasks. The research design must be constructed in recognition of these concerns and the staff organized in optimum-size working groups so that the best combination of professional staff and graduate students may be obtained.

The basic research unit of the Air Site Project was made up of a professional sociologist and two graduate students; in 1952-53, there were four such units in the Project. Graduate students alternated fieldwork and classwork so that both types of training were secured. In the close association of professional sociologist and graduate student, both educational and research functions were served.

IV. The Accumulation of Empirical and Theoretical Knowledge

Research progress on a central problem usually proceeds through stages—first, exploration of the social setting of the problem, the factors involved, and the criteria that may be used to measure or appraise the problem; then descriptive and diagnostic study may be possible. Hypotheses are set up, factors are isolated, measured, and relationships ascertained. Still later, experimental studies may be undertaken. Research design keeps changing as hypotheses are modified, eliminated, and substituted. Each stage of research requires the use of new skills, the recasting of theory, the introduction of new revised factors, and perhaps reinterpretation of results.[4]

A. *Exploratory Study.* The Air Site Project began as a military requirement to investigate the morale and personnel problems of Air Force personnel in radar squadrons. We agreed to go to the research field and discover the personnel problems and personnel needs. At the same time we were to find the most significant problems for basic research into morale and motivation. Three professional sociologists developed a plan of sampling and interviewing and devoted three months between July and October 1951 to field visits and analysis of seven squadrons in one Air Defense Division.[5] Detailed interviews were held with a representative sample of Air Force personnel in each squadron. We lived with and observed the operations and leisure activities of each squadron for a number of days. From our interviews and notes a common record was prepared by the research team for each squadron. This record ranked the major personnel problems as reported to us in each squadron, the needs as expressed by Air Force personnel, and research clues that we determined through our experiences in the field. Table 1 gives a record of major personnel needs and research clues for one Air Force squadron.

TABLE 1. Major Personnel Needs and Research Clues for One Air Force Squadron

Problems Encountered

1. Recreational outlets on the base.
2. Access to city or large town.
3. Degree of supervision.
4. Housing for the married man and his family.
5. Living on Indian Reservation and adjustment to Indian people.
6. Restrictions imposed on minors.
7. Career misassignment.
8. Pressures from division and group commands.

Continued on page 38.

9. Irritations from G.I. regulations.
10. Inequities in promotions and advancements.
11. Supply problems.
12. Access to weapon and monotony of tracking.
13. Organizational change to larger unit.
14. Relative deprivation.
15. Organizational cleavages.

Basic Research Clues for Possible Future Study

1. Study relationship between humor and tension. Compare a tense and relaxed site, watching for differences.
2. Study of emotional outbursts as manifested in attitude and in behavior such as A.W.O.L., chewing out, or fighting.
3. Time sampling study of a group of highly motivated and poorly motivated personnel.
4. A study of newcomers over an extended time period to watch acculturation.
5. A study of the effect of increasing size on organizational and morale changes.
6. Relations of age, marital status, military experience, and residence and education to adjustment of highly and poorly adjusted persons.
7. A validation of relative deprivation.
8. A study of language functions, especially jargon and argot.
9. Socialization of the civilian to military culture.
10. Description of military culture.
11. The relation of job satisfaction to civilian training, experience, and goals.
12. Extent to which realization alone of choice of job is related to job satisfaction.

Observation Clues for Possible Future Measurement

1. Evaluate condition of uniform and military bearing at spot point.
2. Number of persons found in various places—barracks, dayroom, mess hall (goldbricking).
3. Count number who leave camp every day—check those who leave on 2-day-off periods.
4. Turnover as a generalized aspect of military organizations.
   —among officers (upward mobility involves spatial mobility).
   —among airmen (stay only 18 months in a site).
5. What is relation of high turnover to problem of morale, organization, and leadership, to identification with the site, fellows, C.O.?

Interviews were coded and an analysis of major personnel problems was made to determine possible associations with age, marital status, education, length of service, and isolation of site. Various tables were constructed to show analyses of interview data—Analysis of Management Problems, Impact of Isolation on Operating Problems, and Personnel Needs as Defined by Site Personnel. All of these tables were prepared especially for top military leaders and were presented in briefing sessions to them for their guidance. On the basis of these facts and others, new facilities were subsequently made available to the squadrons.

Meanwhile, research clues were combed to find the most significant research problems. General clusters of factors that we called research sectors were set forth as the ones we believed to be most directly related to the adjustment of Air Force personnel.[6] We selected (1) The Job and the Career, (2) Organization and Communication, (3) Leadership, and (4) Morale and Motivation. We pressed forward without an overall theory;[7] rather, research teams were formed and these teams selected a research sector, set up hypotheses, and began field research in the fall of 1951.

B. *Descriptive and Diagnostic Study*. In January 1952, six months after the initiation of the project, the research design was composed of the parts shown on page 40. The central problem had become the adjustment of the person to a military organization. Morale, motivation, and management or personnel problems had been chosen as the principal objects of study. Guttman scaling techniques were being applied to the study of various attitude areas. Nonverbal indices, such as rate of promotion, were being developed. Later, as a squadron efficiency rating system was developed by the officers of one Air Division (assisted by the Air Site Project), this criterion was introduced. Against these criteria we sought to determine the relationship of many social and social-psychological variables.

The illustration on page 40, Basic Generalities of Social Organization, became our overall design. It was based essentially on the importance of studying certain difficult sociological problems *intensively* while ascertaining the full scope of other problems *extensively*. The six research sectors that received intensive study were those of Personal History, Job Adjustment, Group Integration, Leadership, Organization, and Family and Community. In these sectors researchers attempted to find relationships in areas where it was

BASIC GENERALITIES of SOCIAL ORGANIZATION

Relationships Validated in the Air Defense Command

Management
Information
Manuals

Basic
Science
Contributions

↑   ↑

EXTENSIVE INTERSITE RESEARCH DESIGNS
Relationships Validated in the 25th Air Division A.D.C.

Site 1	Site 2	Site 3	Site 4	Site 5	Site 6	Site 7	Site 8	Site 9	Site 10
A.C.&W.	E.W.	A.C.&W	A.C.&W	A.C.&W.	E.W.	E.W.	A.C.&W.	A.C.&W.	E.W.

VARIABLES AND RELATIONSHIPS READY FOR INTER-SITE TESTS

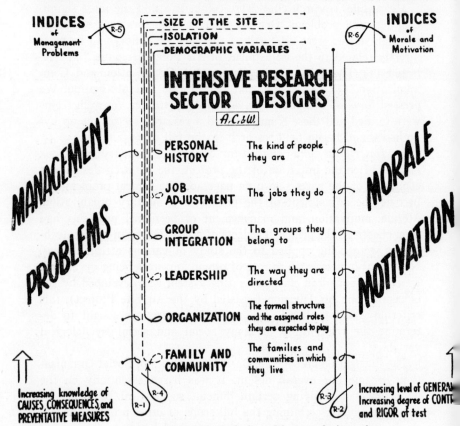

The general research design of large-scale investigation into the human factors affecting morale, motivation, and efficiency of radar sites.

difficult to secure the relevant data and in which understanding could come only through patient, skillful, and persistent study. Such study was usually confined to one or two sites.[8] As crucial variables were identified and quantitative measures were developed, these variables were considered ready for extensive intersite test. The intersite design called for a testing of variables on a selected sample of Air Force men in all (or representative sample of all) sites in the population studied. Here, the criteria of morale, personnel problems, and efficiency were measured by the most refined measures that could be constructed or utilized. Selected social, demographic, and ecological variables were employed as independent variables to determine significant relationships to criteria measures. Intersite questionnaires were administered in 12 sites of one division [9] (May 1952), and in the Japan Air Defense Command [10] (August-September 1952); and a national survey of the Air Defense Command was executed in April and May 1953.

The design reflects the twofold objectives: (1) to carry on basic research in morale (or personal adjustment) at the descriptive level, and (2) to work on personnel problems at the diagnostic level. The design thus reflects both the canons of basic research and the requirements of the client for operational results. The balance between these two foci was often beset by subtle pressures deriving from professional standards, on the one hand, and the practical concerns of the military officials, on the other. The research director who seeks to advance knowledge must see that the research work is so designed that the long-run concerns of basic science are carried along while, at the same time, good diagnostic studies of operational problems are produced that convince his client that research can be of service to him on the problems he faces *now*. He must persuade his staff of the importance of these twin demands, and he must protect them so that there is ample opportunity to achieve both basic and operational research. The basic research design of the Air Site Project grew out of these pressures, and it sought to satisfy them.

But more than this, the design must be understood as an expression of the researcher's desire for freedom to attack his problem in his own way. Some researchers took to the field at once to explore their problem. Others began to devise measuring instruments and to work out sampling plans. Some planned much observational work in the field; others planned fieldwork only to make pretests of questionnaires and scales. These differences seemed to be explained sometimes by differences in research approach (interactionists versus statistical testers) and sometimes by different adjustments to fieldwork. The deprivations of fieldwork and the new role relationships of a fieldworker (in contrast to those of the classroom teacher and library researcher) presented adjustment problems to all staff members. Some found field contact exciting and satisfying; others found absence from home and from customary routines of office a deprivation and sought to center their research in the university. It has already been suggested that the home plays an influential role in shaping the attitudes of the field researcher and thus indirectly the research work itself.

C. *Experimental Study*. Samuel Stouffer has written that "the necessary condition for dealing with a collection of variables is to isolate and identify them and, in addition, it is useful if they can also be measured. Until the relevant variables can be identified, empirical tests of a conceptual scheme involving these variables hardly can be expected." [11]

In the Air Site Project we identified the objects of study and were able to measure some of them. We ascertained many relationships between our criteria and social, demographic, and ecological factors. Many hypotheses were tested by field teams. Experimental work of a cross-sectional type was carried out.[12] Perhaps one of the most important relationships tested was that between morale in a squadron and the efficiency of the squadron. It is widely believed that good human relations are related positively to high efficiency. However, only a few tests have been made under experimental conditions involving a control group.[13]

The assignment of Air Force men is made according to the training specialty of available personnel and according to organizational needs. The assignment of men who are drawn out to fill quotas results in near stratified-random selection. As a result it is possible to find squadrons that have almost identical characteristics as to mean age, length of service, marital status, education, rank structure, degree of isolation, work conditions, and living conditions. In one division we studied 12 squadrons. Efficiency ratings of these squadrons were made each quarter by the responsible division officials. We constructed Guttman type scales or items measuring such areas of morale as satisfaction with air site, satisfaction with Air Force, job satisfaction, and acceptance of mission goals. The relationship of morale to efficiency under controlled conditions was ascertained in our population. Because of the randomization in the squadron populations, control by frequency distribution could be employed. Squadrons were selected from the total universe (one division) and matched on variables believed to affect efficiency. The significance of differences between means was determined. Replication of this design was made on our larger universe of squadrons from all divisions.[14]

D. *Projected Experimentation.* Plans had been made for moving to the stage of true experimental study by taking before and after measures of experimental and control groups under controlled conditions. This would have consummated the direction of research movement. Unfortunately, the sharp curtailment of funds for human relations research in 1953 made it impossible to proceed into this type of experimentation. Projected experiments were not undertaken earlier because needed measures of morale, leadership, and efficiency had to be constructed first. Moreover, a high degree of confidence and cooperation from line military officers had to be earned before such work would have been possible. This is a hard social fact that cannot be ignored.

Conclusion

Four major factors influenced the shaping of research design on one large-scale group research project. These were: the characteristic imperative of group research; the personal wants of researchers; the demands of education; and the accumulation of empirical and theoretical knowledge.

These factors created both problems and opportunities. Problems have been considered in much of this paper, but opportunities were also abundant. Adequate financing of research brings professional, clerical, and technical assistance, permitting a rapid increase in the quantity and quality of research. Access to the research field and cooperation within it opens a new wealth of social data. A long-standing weakness of social science research has been the inability to get enough individual cases or organizational units so that relationships could be validated through replication. This is possible in large-scale group research. These opportunities can be capitalized, but only as the social processes of group research are marshaled. Social processes ever blend with scientific thinking to mold research design. As an end product of group research, it is a precipitate of personal feelings, thoughts, habits, and hopes.

FOOTNOTES

* This paper is based on the conclusions of the writer as director of the Air Site Project. Other members of the project have contributed in many different ways to the experiences described. Appreciation is acknowledged to: Orvis F. Collins, Michigan State University, Edward Gross (University of Minnesota), James F. Davis (Hamline College), Glenn C. McCann (North Carolina State College), Nahum Z. Medalia (National Institute of Mental Health), Charles D. McGlamery (University of Alabama), professional sociologists; David S. Bushnell, Donald L. Garrity, Robert Hagedorn, John Hudson, Harold Kant, Alvin S. Lackey, Robert Larson, Herman Loether, Duane Strinden, Wes Wager, Shirley Willis, and David Yaukey, research fellows.

The research was supported in part by the United States Air Force under contract number AF-33-038-26823, monitored by the Human Resources Research Institute, Air Research and Development Command, Maxwell Air Force Base, Alabama. Permission is granted for reproduction, translation, publication, and disposal in whole and in part by or for the U.S. Government.

I am especially indebted to the continuous encouragement of Dr. Raymond V. Bowers, Director of the Institute from 1949-52, and to Dr. Abbott L. Ferriss, Chief of the Human Relations Division, whose administrative efforts made possible our access to many research fields.

1. Joseph W. Eaton, "Social Processes of Professional Teamwork," *American Sociological Review,* 16 (October, 1951), pp. 707-13; Alfred M. Lee, "Individual and Organizational Research in Sociology," *American Sociological Review,* 16 (October, 1951) pp. 701-7.

2. Urie Bronfenbrenner and Edward C. Devereux, "Interdisciplinary Planning for Team Research on Constructive Community Behavior," *Human Relations,* V (1952), 187-203; William Caudill and Bertram H. Roberts, "Pitfalls in the Organization of Interdisciplinary Research," *Human Organization,* 10 (Winter, 1951), pp. 12-15.

3. Chester I. Barnard, "Dilemmas of Leadership in the Democratic Process," *Organization and Management* (Cambridge: Harvard University Press, 1949), pp. 24-50.

4. Robert K. Merton, "The Bearing of Empirical Research Upon the Development of Social Theory," *American Sociological Review,* 13 (October 1948), pp. 505-15.

5. Squadrons varied in size from approximately 100 to 300 men, depending on type and function of the station.

6. For a full report of this exploratory survey see F. James Davis, Edward Gross, and Delbert C. Miller, *Survey Report on Military Management Problems in Aircraft Control and Warning Stations in the Air Defense Command* (Human Resources Research Institute, Air University, Maxwell Air Force Base, Alabama, 1951).

7. This was a source of much concern to some of our researchers, and we held many staff meetings groping for such a theory. Some members of the staff believed we should not set out at all until a fully-developed theory was in hand. Others believed theory should wait until the research and field experience were more advanced.

8. For published reports of this work see: F. James Davis, "Conceptions of Official Leader Roles in the Air Force," *Social Forces,* 32 (March 1954), pp. 253-58; F. James Davis and Robert Hagedorn, "Testing the Reliability of Systematic Field Observations," *American Sociological Review,* 19 (June 1954), pp. 345-48; Edward Gross, "Some Functional Consequences of Primary Controls in Formal Work Or-

ganizations," *American Sociological Review*, 18 (August 1953), pp. 368-73; Edward Gross, "Primary Functions of the Small Group," *American Journal of Sociology*, 60 (July 1954), pp. 24-29; C. D. McGlamery, "Developing an Index of Work Group Communications," *Research Studies, State College of Washington*, 21 (1953), pp. 225-30; Nahum Z. Medalia, "Unit Size and Leadership Perception," *Sociometry*, 17 (February 1945), pp. 64-67; Nahum Z. Medalia, "Authoritarianism, Leader Acceptance, and Group Cohesion," *Journal of Abnormal and Social Psychology*, 51 (Sept., 1955), 207-13.

9. The Human Resources Research Institute published the following interim reports in 1952: HR-9, "Personnel Problems," Delbert C. Miller and staff; HR-11, "The Development of Efficiency Criteria of Air Surveillance Crews," Charles D. McGlamery; HR-12, "A Study of Small Group Integration," Edward Gross, Herman J. Loether, L. Wes Wager; HR-13, "Organization and Communication," Orvis Collins, Alvin S. Lackey, David S. Bushnell; HR-16, "Leadership," F. James Davis; HR-17, "Family Adjustment to Military Life," Shirley Willis.

10. A final report has been prepared for Human Resources Research Institute by Edward Gross and Orvis Collins, *American Air Sites in Japan: An Analysis of Human Relations in A. C. & W. Detachment Within the Japan Air Defense Force* (January 12, 1953).

11. Samuel A. Stouffer *et. al., The American Soldier* (Princeton: Princeton University Press, 1949), I, 34.

12. Stouffer writes, "I would trade a half dozen army-wide surveys on attitudes toward officers for one good controlled experiment. Keeping the model of the controlled experiment as an ideal, it is sometimes possible for one to approximate it.... Ingenuity in locating ready-made situations is much needed. In any program of future research, I would put far more emphasis on this than ever has been done in the past." Robert K. Merton and Paul F. Lazarsfeld (eds.), *Studies in the Scope and Method of "The American Soldier,"* (Glencoe, Ill.: The Free Press, 1950), p. 211.

13. See Daniel Katz, Nathan Maccoby, and Nancy C. Morse, *Productivity, Supervision and Morale in an Office Situation*, Part I (Ann Arbor: Institute for Social Research, University of Michigan, 1950); Daniel Katz, Nathan Maccoby, Gerald Gurin, and Lucretia G. Floor, *Productivity, Supervision, and Morale Among Railroad Workers* (Ann Arbor: Survey Research Center, University of Michigan, 1951); Irving R. Weschler, Murray Kahane, and Robert Tannenbaum, "Job Satisfaction, Productivity and Morale: A Case Study," *Occupational Psychology*, January, 1952, 1: 1-14; Gunner Westerlund, *Group Leadership, A Field Experiment* (Stockholm: Nordisk Rotogravyr, 1952).

14. This research is described by Nahum Z. Medalia and Delbert C. Miller in "Human Relations Leadership and the Association of Morale and Efficiency in Workgroups: A Controlled Study with Small Military Units," *Social Forces*, May, 1955, 33: 348-52. See also D. C. Miller and N. Z. Medalia, "Efficiency, Leadership, and Morale in Small Military Organizations," *The Sociological Review*, July, 1955, 3: 93-107; Edward Gross and D. C. Miller, "The Impact of Isolation on Worker Adjustment in Military Installations of the United States and Japan," *Estudios de Sociologia*, Buenos Aires, Fall, 1961, 1: 70-86; Glenn C. McCann, Nahum Z. Medalia, and Delbert C. Miller, "Morale and Human Relations Leadership as Factors in Organizational Effectiveness" in *Studies of Organizational Effectiveness*, ed. R. V. Bowers (Washington, D.C.: Air Force Office of Scientific Research, 1962), pp. 85-114.

I.9. THE SAMPLING CHART

Instructions for Use of Guide I.9.

A sample is a smaller representation of a larger whole. The use of sampling allows for more adequate scientific work by making the time of the scientific worker count. Instead of spending much of his time analyzing a large mass of material from one point of view, he can use that time to make a more intensive analysis from many points of view. The researcher can also save much time and money by sampling, thus making possible investigations that could not otherwise be carried out.

The sampling problems may be divided into those that affect (1) the definition of the population, (2) the size of the sample, and (3) the representativeness of the sample. In regard to the definition of the population, the important problem is to decide the group about which the researcher wishes to generalize his findings. In regard to size of sample, consideration must be given to the persistent disappearance of cases in a breakdown analysis. This disappearance should be foreseen as clearly as possible. Dummy tables help provide for such planning. The third and perhaps most intricate sampling problem arises in connection with the method of securing a representative sample. The essential requirement of any sample is that it is as representative as possible of the population or universe from which it is taken.

Three methods of sampling are commonly used. These are *random sampling, stratified sampling,* and *judgmental* or *"purposive" sampling.*

1. *Random sampling.* A random sample is one that is drawn in such a way that every member of the population has an equal chance of being included. The most rigorous method of random sampling employs a table of random numbers. In this method, a number is assigned to each member of the population. Those members are included in the sample whose numbers are taken from the table of random numbers in succession until a sample of predetermined size is drawn. A more common method is to write the names or numbers of the members of a population on cards or discs, shuffling these, and then drawing. A convenient method, known as systematic

sampling, which is not exactly equivalent to random sampling, but is often close enough for practical purposes, is to take every n^{th} item in the population, beginning at some random member in the population.

2. *Stratified sampling.* The aforementioned methods assume that the composition of the total group is not known, and that a representative sample will be best approximated by a strictly random selection or a selection by regular intervals. In some cases the more or less exact composition of the total group with respect to some significant characteristics is known before we select our sample. For example, we may know the exact ratio of men to women in the population and that sex differences are related to the variables we wish to test. In such cases we can increase the chances of selecting a representative sample by selecting subsamples proportionate in size to the significant characteristics of the total population. Thus, we can select a sample that is mathematically absolutely representative with regard to some significant characteristics. There are numerous forms of stratified random sampling techniques as shown in the Ackoff Sampling Chart, which follows on pages 48-49.

3. *Judgmental or "purposive" sampling.* When practical considerations preclude the use of probability sampling, the researcher may seek a representative sample by other means. He looks for a subgroup that is typical of the population as a whole. Observations are then restricted to this subgroup, and conclusions from the data obtained are generalized to the total population. An example would be the choice of a particular state or county as a barometer of an election outcome, relying upon the results of past elections as evidence of the representativeness of the sample for the nation or state. Sampling errors and biases cannot be computed for such samples. For this reason judgmental sampling should be restricted to the following situations: (1) when the possible errors are not serious and (2) when probability sampling is practically impossible. Data from judgmental samples at best suggest or indicate conclusions, but in general they cannot be used as the basis of statistical testing procedures.

These three forms of sampling do not exhaust the range of sampling procedures. The Ackoff Sampling Chart lists such types as multistage random sampling, cluster, stratified cluster, and repetitive sampling. A description of these forms may be found in Russell

Sampling Chart *

Type of Sampling	Brief Description	Advantages	Disadvantages
A. Simple random	Assign to each population member a unique number; select sample items by use of random numbers	1. Requires minimum knowledge of population in advance 2. Free of possible classification errors 3. Easy to analyze data and compute errors	1. Does not make use of knowledge of population which researcher may have 2. Larger errors for same sample size than in stratified sampling
B. Systematic	Use natural ordering or order population; select random starting point between 1 and the nearest integer to the sampling ratio (N/n); select items at interval of nearest integer to sampling ratio	1. If population is ordered with respect to pertinent property, gives stratification effect, and hence reduces variability compared to A 2. Simplicity of drawing sample; easy to check	1. If sampling interval is related to a periodic ordering of the population, increased variability may be introduced 2. Estimates of error likely to be high where there is stratification effect
C. Multistage random	Use a form of random sampling in each of the sampling stages where there are at least two stages	1. Sampling lists, identification, and numbering required only for members of sampling units selected in sample 2. If sampling units are geographically defined, cuts down field costs (i.e., travel)	1. Errors likely to be larger than in A or B for same sample size 2. Errors increase as number of sampling units selected decreases
1. With probability proportionate to size	Select sampling units with probability proportionate to their size	1. Reduces variability	1. Lack of knowledge of size of each sampling unit before selection increases variability
D. Stratified 1. Proportionate	Select from every sampling unit at other than last stage a random sample proportionate to size of sampling unit	1. Assures representativeness with respect to property which forms basis of classifying units; therefore yields less variability than A or C 2. Decreases chance of failing to include members of population because of classification process 3. Characteristics of each stratum can be estimated, and hence comparisons can be made	1. Requires accurate information on proportion of population in each stratum, otherwise increases error 2. If stratified lists are not available, may be costly to prepare them; possibility of faulty classification and hence increase in variability
2. Optimum allocation	Same as 1 except sample is proportionate to variability within strata as well as their size	1. Less variability for same sample size than 1	1. Requires knowledge of variability of pertinent characteristic within strata
3. Disproportionate	Same as 1 except that size of sample is not proportionate to size of sampling unit but is dedicated by analytical considerations or convenience	1. More efficient than 1 for comparison of strata or where different errors are optimum for different strata	1. Less efficient than 1 for determining population characteristics; i.e., more variability for same sample size

* From Russell L. Ackoff, *The Design of Social Research* (Chicago: University of Chicago Press, 1953), p. 124.

Type of Sampling	Brief Description	Advantages	Disadvantages
E. Cluster	Select sampling units by some form of random sampling; ultimate units are groups; select these at random and take a complete count of each	1. If clusters are geographically defined, yields lowest field costs 2. Requires listing only individuals in selected clusters 3. Characteristics of clusters as well as those of population can be estimated 4. Can be used for subsequent samples, since clusters, not individuals, are selected, and substitution of individuals may be permissible	1. Larger errors for comparable size than other probability samples 2. Requires ability to assign each member of population uniquely to a cluster; inability to do so may result in duplication or omission of individuals
F. Stratified cluster	Select clusters at random from every sampling unit	1. Reduces variability of plain cluster sampling	1. Disadvantages of stratified sampling added to those of cluster sampling 2. Since cluster properties may change, advantage of stratification may be reduced and make sample unusable for later research
G. Repetitive: multiple or sequential	Two or more samples of any of the above types are taken, using results from earlier samples to design later ones, or determine if they are necessary	1. Provides estimates of population characteristics which facilitate efficient planning of succeeding sample, therefore reduces error of final estimate 2. In the long run reduces number of observations required	1. Complicates administration of fieldwork 2. More computation and analysis required than in nonrepetitive sampling 3. Sequential sampling can only be used where a very small sample can approximate representativeness and where the number of observations can be increased conveniently at any stage of the research
H. Judgment	Select a subgroup of the population which, on the basis of available information, can be judged to be representative of the total population; take a complete count or subsample of this group	1. Reduces cost of preparing sample and field work, since ultimate units can be selected so that they are close together	1. Variability and bias of estimates cannot be measured or controlled 2. Requires strong assumptions or considerable knowledge of population and subgroup selected
1. Quota	Classify population by pertinent properties; determine desired proportion of sample from each class; fix quotas for each observer	1. Same as above 2. Introduces some stratification effect	1. Introduces bias of observers' classification of subjects and nonrandom selection within classes

* From Russell L. Ackoff, *The Design of Social Research* (Chicago: University of Chicago Press, 1953), p. 125.

Ackoff, *The Design of Experiments* (copyright 1953 by the University of Chicago Press), pp. 83-127. He writes:

> From practical as well as purely scientific purposes it is necessary to use selection procedures whose errors are measurable. A procedure should be capable of characterization relative to bias and variability. The fundamental procedure satisfying these conditions is simple random sampling, a method in which each individual has an equal chance of being selected. Simple random sampling is performed with the aid of random numbers, while systematic sampling is a variation which proceeds from a random start to select elements at a preset interval.
>
> By breaking the population into subgroups, we may select a sample in stages. If a random sample is selected at each stage, we have a multistage random sample. If a complete count of sampling units is taken at one stage other than the last, we have a stratified sample. If a complete count is made at the last stage, we have a cluster sample. The probability of selecting any subgroup may be made proportionate to some function of the size of the subgroup, and the number of units selected from any subgroup may also be made proportionate to some such function. Proportionate sampling tends to reduce sampling errors. Stratification and clustering can be combined to yield efficient samples, particularly where stratification and/or clustering is based on geographic properties (i.e., in area sampling). Area sampling reduces the complexity of preparing sampling lists and permits the clustering of subjects so that they come in bunches.
>
> In double sampling a first sample can be used to provide information which can in turn be used to design an efficient second sample. Such sampling can also be used to reduce the number of observations required, on the average, for coming to a conclusion. When double sampling is generalized, it yields sequential sampling, a method of drawing one item or set of items at a time and using the data obtained to decide whether to continue sampling or not.
>
> —The ultimate basis for selecting a sampling procedure should be minimization of the cost of getting the sample and the expected cost of errors which may result from using the method. Expert assistance should be employed in making such evaluations.
>
> The sampling chart summarizes in a very brief way the description, advantages, and disadvantages of the various sampling procedures discussed.

I.10. A SELECTED BIBLIOGRAPHY ON RESEARCH DESIGN

ACKOFF, RUSSELL L., *The Design of Social Research*, Chicago: University of Chicago Press, 1953.

BRIDGMAN, P. W., *The Logic of Modern Physics*, New York: Macmillan, 1927.

BROSS, IRWIN D. J., *Design for Decision*, New York: Macmillan, 1953.

CAMPBELL, DONALD T., "Quasi-Experimental Designs for Use in Natural Social Settings," *Psychological Bulletin*, 54, 297-311, 1957.

CHAPIN, F. S., *Experimental Designs in Sociological Research*, New York: Harper, 1947.

CHURCHMAN, C. W., *Theory of Experimental Inference*, New York: Macmillan, 1948.

COCHRAN, W. G., and COX, G. N., *Experimental Designs*, New York: Wiley, 1950.

COHEN, MORRIS, and NAGEL, E., *An Introduction to Logic and Scientific Method*, New York: Harcourt Brace, 1934.

EDWARDS, ALLEN L., *Experimental Design in Psychological Research*, New York: Rinehart & Co., 1950.

FESTINGER, L., and KATZ, DANIEL (eds.), *Research Methods in the Behavioral Sciences*, New York: Dryden Press, 1953.

GOODE, WM. J., and HATT, PAUL K., *Methods in Social Research*, New York: McGraw-Hill, 1952.

HYMAN, HERBERT, *Survey Design and Analysis: Principles, Cases, and Procedures*, Glencoe, Ill.: The Free Press, 1955.

KAPLAN, ABRAHAM, *The Conduct of Inquiry*, San Francisco: Chandler, 1964.

NORTHROP, F. S. C., *The Logic of the Sciences and the Humanities*, New York: Macmillan, 1947.

POPPER, KARL R., *The Logic of Scientific Discovery*, London: Hutchinson & Co., 1959.

RITCHIE, A. D., *Scientific Method: An Inquiry into the Character and Validity of Natural Laws*, New York: Harcourt Brace, 1923.

SELLTIZ, C., DEUTSCH, M., and COOK, S. W., *Research Methods in Social Relations*, rev. in one volume, New York: Holt, Rinehart & Winston, 1959.

WHITEHEAD, A. F., *Science and the Modern World*, New York: Macmillian, 1954.

ZETTERBERG, HANS L., *On Theory and Verification in Sociology*, 2nd rev. ed., Totowa, N.J.: The Bedminster Press, 1963.

PART II

Guides to Statistical Analysis

THIS PART INCLUDES guides that should prove useful to the researcher as he seeks statistical tools to test hypotheses. He may find it necessary to reformulate his initial hypotheses in order to use the most precise statistical test. Qualitative and quantitative variables require appropriate statistics to provide tests of association or of significant differences between groups. In Part II the researcher will find statistical tests organized to deal with these two kinds of variables. Also the question of the probability of normal distribution of the data forces the researcher to make a distinction between parametric and nonparametric statistics in drawing inferences from samples. These distinctions will be set forth in the description of the statistics presented.

No limited set of guides can replace a good text in statistics. However, it is believed that the researcher can find an array of concepts so organized here that he may be able to survey the dimensions of his problem. The most space has been given to the importance of qualitative variables and their statistical treatment. Computation guides have been included for the use of the most commonly used statistical measures.

The bibliography placed at the end of this part has been selected to provide additional information on statistics, tables, and graphic presentation. Each reference enables the reader to follow step-by-step explanations.

II.1. THE IMPERTINENT QUESTIONER: THE SCIENTIST'S GUIDE TO THE STATISTICIAN'S MIND *

WILLIAM LURIE

Instructions for Guide II.1.

This article should sharpen the researcher's awareness of the dimensions of his hypotheses as he prepares to test them. As Lurie puts it: "It is the scientist's responsibility to decide exactly what his hypotheses are, what these hypotheses are about, and how sure he wants to be of their correctness.... And the more the scientist becomes aware of his responsibilities, and takes them into account in his work, so much more accurate and valid will his conclusions be, and so much more properly related to the reality with which he deals."

Prologue

It has become fashionable to ornament science with statistical embellishments. No equation is complete without at least a double summation sign somewhere in it, sub-ij's attach themselves to familiar X's, Y's and Z's; and phrases like "polymodal distribution," "inverse reciprocal correlation," and "multivariate deviations" now can be seen on practically every other page of "The Journal of the Society for Thus-and-So," "The Transactions of the Association for Such-and-Such," and "The Proceedings of the Symposium on Etc., Etc."

But in addition to providing mathematical and linguistic ornamentation for these publications, the statistician, if he is really to assist the scientist, must perform a necessary, but irritatingly annoying task: he must ask the scientist impertinent questions. Indeed, the questions, if bluntly asked, may appear to be not only impertinent but almost indecently prying—because they deal with the foundations of the scientist's thinking. By these questions, unsuspected weaknesses in the foundations may be brought to light, and

* *American Scientist,* March, 1958, 46: 57-61.

the exposure of weaknesses in one's thinking is a rather unpleasant occurrence.

The statistician will, then, if he is wise in the ways of human beings as well as learned in statistics, ask these questions diplomatically, or even not ask them as questions at all. He may well guide the discussion with the scientist in such a way that the answers to the questions will be forthcoming without the questions having been even explicitly asked.

And if happily the scientific and statistical disciplines reside within one mind, and it is the scientist's statistical conscience that asks him these questions, instead of impertinent questioning there is valid scientific soul-searching.

Regardless, then, of whether these questions arise inside or outside the scientist's own mind, what are they? These:

1. With respect to the experiment you are performing, just what are your ideas?
2. With respect to the scientific area to which these ideas refer, just what are they about?
3. How sure do you want to be of the correctness of these ideas?

In order to understand the statistician's reasons for asking these questions, let us first see how the scientist's activities look to the statistician.

From the statistician's point of view, what the scientist does, is: performs experiments and/or makes observations to obtain data relating to *an idea he has* about the organization of *that portion of the world he is interested in,* so that he can decide *whether his idea was correct or not.*

For each of these italicized aspects of the scientist's activity, there is a corresponding question.

Let us, then, examine each of these aspects of the scientist's activities, and the purpose for and consequences of the question concerning it.

An Idea He Has

The impertinent questioner must take the risk of appearing to imply that the scientist is not thinking clearly. And, of course, even an implication to this effect is not calculated to endear the implier to the heart of the implyee. But it is exactly this implication that, perhaps innocently, is associated with the question, "Just what are your ideas?"

Why does the statistician ask this impertinent question? Because it is a precondition for the statistician's being able to help the scientist accomplish his objective. A hazily formulated idea not only can be discussed, at best, with difficulty, but further, it is practically impossible to test its correctness. Therefore, the statistician has a rule, his name for which is: EXPLICIT HYPOTHESIZATION. This rule expresses the requirement that the idea, whose correctness is to be determined by the experiment, should be stated in as clear, detailed and explicit form as possible, preferably before the experiment is conducted. This idea can relate either to the influence of one factor or to the influence of several factors, or to the numerical characterization of a property (or properties) of whatever is being experimented on. In the early stages of an investigation, where what are being sought are the influential factors (i.e. those which, when they are at varying levels, give rise to sufficiently varied results) the idea (or hypothesis) need not be specific, but it must be explicit. The hypothesis can be broad, but it must be explicitly broad:—that is, even though it is not a hypothesis about details, its boundary must be sharply delineated.

For example, "Factors A, B, C, and D individually influence the results, "Factors A and B, acting in conjunction, influence the results differently than would be expected from the effects of A alone and B alone," "Factors A, B, and C, acting in conjunction, etc., etc." Or later in the investigation, and more specifically, "The measurement of the effect of factor A at level a_1, will result in the numerical value $N \pm n$."

To emphasize unmistakably the requirement for Explicit Hypothesization, let us use an obviously exaggerated example dealing with a particular subject: the task of an industrial psychologist who has been given the job of finding out why the accounting clerks are making too many errors in addition. (The problem of deciding how many errors are "too many" is another statistical problem, which will not be considered here.)

The psychologist, for the purposes of this example, may say to himself: "My training as a psychologist tells me that the situation in which a person operates affects his behavior. So let me find out what the situation is that is causing the clerks to make these errors." If the formulation of the psychologist's idea goes no further than this, he can obviously continue to attempt to find out what the situation is, from now on forever, since "The Situation" has no boundaries.

It might, for example, not only include the working circumstances of the clerks, but their home circumstances, their childhood histories, their dream life; and it is seen that the possibilities are unlimited. As then is obvious, the hypothesis has not been sufficiently explicitly formulated, nor the situation covered by it clearly enough delineated, for a decision to be able to be arrived at as to the correctness of the hypothesis.

But now, let the psychologist's statistical conscience awaken, and his ideas begin to crystallize out of their original diffuseness. "The Situation?—Well, to be more specific, let's just consider the office situation. And within the office situation, I'll pick three factors that I believe affect the performance of the clerks. The factors I'm selecting to study for their effects are: Temperature, Humidity, and Noise. And now, my explicit hypothesis: It makes a difference what the levels of temperature, humidity, and noise are with respect to the number of errors in addition made by the accounting clerks." The hypothesis could (and probably should) have been even more explicitly formulated (e.g., including as factors Illumination Level, Desk Space per employee, etc.) but the direction of the path to statistical virtue has been pointed out, and further travel along that path is left to the reader.

Now, assuming that the hypothesis has been sufficiently explicitly formulated, the scientist and statistician can together review the plan (or design) of the experiment, and assure themselves that such data will be obtained as will be sufficient to determine the correctness (or noncorrectness) of the scientist's idea.

That Portion of the World He Is Interested in

Again, the impertinent questioner must be careful in asking: "Just what are your ideas about?" Even though one may admit that his ideas are not as clearly and explicitly formulated as he would like, the question "Just what are your ideas about?" carries with it, to the person being asked, the implication that he isn't clear about the subject-matter of his ideas, surely not a flattering implication. The statistician has a reason for his implied aspersion on the basis of the scientist's self-esteem. The statistician's reason can be stated to the scientist thus: "It's for your own good. If I am to help you decide, on the basis of the experimental facts, whether your ideas are correct or not, I have to know, as explicitly as possible, not only what your ideas are, but *what they are about*. My name for this requirement is: MODEL FORMULATION." Technically, Model Formulation establishes the requirement that a clear differentiation be made as to whether the scientist's ideas are intended to be applicable only to the conditions of the experiment (the narrower range of application) or to conditions (i.e., levels of the factors) other than those specific ones under which the experiment is being conducted (the broader range of application). Why the necessity for this differentiation? Because, when the experimental data have been obtained, the analysis of the data is carried on in different ways, depending on whether the hypotheses are intended to have the broader or narrower range of application.

Let us again, for exemplification, return to our industrial psychologist. And, let us say, his experimental conditions are, for temperature, 40°, 55°, and 70°F.; for humidity, 40, 55, and 70 per cent; and for noise level, 40, 55, and 70 decibels.

It may well make a difference in the way the experimental data are analyzed to arrive at conclusions (i.e., decisions as to correctness of ideas), and whether any conclusions can be arrived at, and, if so, what they are, depending on whether the scientist wants his conclusions to apply only to the three levels of temperature, humidity, and noise level that have been used in the experiment, or also to other (unspecified) temperature, humidity, and noise levels. Data that support narrow conclusions may not be sufficient to support broader conclusions. Therefore, the scientist must have clearly in mind what his hypotheses are about, and whether, consequently, his conclusions will be broad or narrow; and the statistician's effort to assure that the scientist does have this clearly in mind, may well, to the scientist, appear to be impertinent.

Whether His Idea Was Correct or Not

The statistician's third question—"How sure do you want to be of the correctness of your ideas?" is the least impertinent of the three. This question, unlike the other two, does not probe the foundations of the scientist's thinking, but rather requests him to quantify a previously unquantified aspect of it. (In fact, the request is in accordance with the scientist's own predilection for quantitative data.) This aspect is that dealing with levels of assurance, for which ordinary language supplies us with qualitatively descriptive terms (somewhat sure, rather sure, quite sure, extremely sure). But these terms are not sufficiently explicit for scientific use. Therefore, the statistician asks the scientist to decide upon and express his desired level of assurance in quantitative terms, so that it can be determined, by analysis of the quantitative data, whether the desired level of assurance of the conclusions has been achieved. The statistician's name for the choice and quantitative expression of the desired level of assurance is: SIGNIFICANCE LEVEL SELECTION. And how does the statistician help the scientist choose the desired level of assurance? By bringing to the forefront of the scientist's consciousness his already unconscious awareness of the inherent variability of events (i.e., that, because of chance alone, no repetition of an experiment will give exactly the same results); by helping the scientist decide what assurance is desired that the hypothesis has not been "confirmed" just by the operation of chance alone; and by furnishing the mathematical tools to decide, on the basis of the experimental data, whether the desired level of assurance has been attained. Say, for example, in the temperature-humidity-noise level experiment, when all the data have been accumulated, and the scientist is preparing them for analysis so that he may decide whether his hypotheses were correct or not, the statistician will then say to him: "You know, of course, that if you did the experiment over, under as near the same conditions as possible, you'd get slightly, or even somewhat different results. The results might even, just by chance, be different enough to lead you to believe that temperature does affect accuracy, even though it really doesn't. Or even if you didn't do the experiment over again, the particular experiment you've just done might be the one in which the data are such that you'd believe temperature has an effect though it really doesn't. *But I can test these data of yours.* I can assure you that when you state the conclusion, say, that temperature does affect accuracy, you'll have only a 5 per cent, or 1 per cent, or 1/10th of 1 per cent chance of being wrong, as a result of that off chance I told you about. Now—what chance do you want to take? If you select a very small chance of being wrong in saying there is a temperature effect when there really isn't you're taking a bigger chance of saying there isn't a temperature effect when there really might be. I can figure this out for you also. So again, what chance do you want to take?"

When the scientist has selected the chance he is willing to take of being wrong (or what is equivalent, how sure he wants to be that he is correct) in his conclusions, the statistician can analyze the data and tell the scientist what conclusions he can validly draw (i.e., what decisions he can make about the correctness of his ideas).

Epilogue

One final word. *It is the statistician's responsibility to ask these questions, not to answer them.* It is the scientist's responsibility to decide exactly what his hypotheses are, what these hypotheses are about, and how sure he wants to be of their correctness.

The statistician, in asking his impertinent questions, is just explicitly bringing to the scientist's attention, responsibilities that the scientist may not have been aware that he had. And the more the scientist becomes aware of his responsibilities, and takes them into account in his work, so much more accurate and valid will his conclusions be, and so much more properly related to the reality with which he deals.

II.2. A NOTE ON STATISTICAL ANALYSIS IN THE AMERICAN SOCIOLOGICAL REVIEW *

DAVID GOLD

State University of Iowa

Instructions for Guide II.2.

This analysis of statistics used by social scientists provides a basis for evaluating the kinds of statistics most commonly used in research. Note the large importance given to qualitative analysis. It is also significant to learn that "rarely does the sociologist have occasion to deal simultaneously with more than two quantitative variables." This limitation may change with new knowledge about matrices and the use of the computer.

In order to get some notions about the nature of the data and the kinds of statistical analysis that do and do not occur in sociological research, an examination has been made of all articles published in the *American Sociological Review* from 1944 through 1953.

* *American Sociological Review,* June, 1957, 22: 332-33.

Roughly 48 per cent of these articles reported data that conceivably could be subjected to some sort of statistical analysis. This classification uses the broadest possible definition of statistical analysis, assuming that any ordering of statistical data, qualitative or quantitative, represents statistical analysis. Included in the 48 per cent are some reports that present incomplete data for purposes of possible statistical analysis but from which it can be inferred that the investigator has more complete data, which he did not present.[1]

The other 52 per cent of the articles were discussions or studies whose data could not be subjected to any sort of statistical analysis. Included in the 52 per cent are some articles that refer to statistical data and/or the results of statistical analysis in other reports but indicate no statistical manipulation by the writer. The proportion of such "nonstatistical" articles has steadily decreased in the ten-year period examined, from almost two-thirds in 1944 to less than one-third in 1953.

Eleven per cent of the "statistical" articles were strictly in the area of demography, population, and census analysis. The remaining "statistical" articles (37 per cent), a total of 272 reports, run the gamut of sociological research. For the purposes of this investigation, these latter reports were subjected to intensive examination.

In 38 per cent (102 of the 272)[2] of these research reports, no statistical analysis other than presentation of the data in tables was performed. It is significant to note that in all but four of these 102 reports, the investigator was dealing exclusively with qualitative variables.[3] Apparently when dealing with qualitative data the investigator often feels he can do nothing but present the data and reach inferences about the degree and significance of relationships by inspection. However, if he is dealing with quantitative data, the investigator invariably performs some sort of statistical analysis beyond tabular presentation.

With respect to tests of significance, it is perhaps just as well that they are not used. There is widespread confusion between substantive significance and statistical significance as well as questionable legitimacy of application and interpretation in many instances.[4] Sophisticated and rigorous statistical tests are certainly not desirable per se. The research design and the quality of the data must merit such treatment. However, most data, if worth reporting at all, merit some statistical analysis at the descriptive level. The omission of an index of degree of relationship can be serious. In a simple fourfold table, it may seem unnecessary. But often the investigator must compare the relationship displayed in one fourfold table with that in another; and this is not always easy by inspection.

TABLE 1

ARTICLES IN THE *American Sociological Review,* 1944 THROUGH 1953

Nonstatistical		386
Statistical		357
Demographic	85	
Other	272	
Quantitative Data	19	
Qualitative Data	149	
Both	104	
Total *		743

* Articles in the "Notes on Research and Teaching" section were counted if "statistical" but were ignored if "nonstatistical."

In only 7 per cent of the articles does the author use a computed measure of degree of relationship among qualitative variables. In another 29 per cent of the articles, there is a statement that clearly implies an inference about the degree of relationship among qualitative variables but which is based on no computed index of degree. Included here are those cases in which the analyst mistakenly based statements of degree of relationship on tests of significance. It is evident that, on the most elementary descriptive level, there is markedly inadequate statistical analysis of qualitative data.

And qualitative data are by far the most common data with which the sociologist concerns himself. In 55 per cent of the research reports nothing but qualitative data occur. In another 38 per cent there are both qualitative and quantitative data; and in only 7 per cent are quantitative data the only kind that occur. It can additionally be noted that in 23 per cent of the articles not only are qualitative data the only kind that occur, but none of the variables makes up an ordered set of categories.

The proportion of reports in which legitimately quantitative variables actually occur is considerably less than the aforementioned figures would indicate. For included in the "quantitative" classification are scores on tests and some indexes which, in fact, are order statistics only. The possible effects upon substantive conclusions of treating such data as if they represent equal-interval measurement has yet to be systematically examined.

Rarely does the sociologist [in the material here examined] have occasion to deal simultaneously with more than two quantitative variables. During the ten-year period there appeared only eight reports in which multiple and/or partial correlation was used; in addition, there were four reports involving the use of factor analysis.[5] There were no instances in which the investigator confined himself to tabular presentation only when dealing with three or more quantitative variables. On the other hand, in 27 per cent (73) of the articles there appeared some statement or direct question concerning the nature of the relationship among three or more qualitative variables but no accompanying statistical analysis involving more than two variables. That is, not even the joint frequencies for more than two variables simultaneously were presented.

It seems clear that in sociological research most variables are of the nature of manifold classification or order statistics rather than quantitative or continuous. We count the number of cases that fall into each of a set of categories that, not too infrequently, are not even mutually exclusive. More often than not there is no particularly meaningful way in which such categories can be rank ordered.

The emphasis in the development of applied statistics has been on techniques for the analysis of data that represent strict quantitative measurement, i.e., with fixed units of magnitude. These research reports seem to indicate that what the sociologist most needs are appropriate measures of association, measures of differences between contingency tables, descriptive measures that will perform a task somewhat analogous to multiple and partial correlation. In other words, he needs statistical techniques for describing the nature of the relationship among qualitative variables.

FOOTNOTES

1. A question can, of course, be raised concerning the reliability of this content analysis. All the coding and classification were done by the writer only.
2. All the following per cents refer to this base of 272.
3. Any variable that was operationally treated in terms of nominal classification

(a set of two or more categories) or ordinal measurement only (ranks) was classified as qualitative.

4. Hanan C. Selvin, "A Critique of Statistical Tests in Survey Research," paper presented at the annual meeting of the American Sociological Society, September, 1956.

5. A change has occurred here. Greater use of multiple and partial correlation, analysis of variance, and factor analysis is being made. An analysis of the 54 articles in the *American Sociological Review* for 1963 shows trends as reported by David Gold except for an increase in statistical analysis. Sixty per cent show use of statistical analysis, still highly qualitative in character.   D. C. M.

II.3. THE IDEA OF PROPERTY-SPACE IN SOCIAL RESEARCH *

ALLEN H. BARTON

Instructions for Use of Guide II.3.

This guide presents a technique of classifying qualitative data so that associations may be discovered. Arranging data in "property-space" is particularly useful in permitting the effects of various background variables to be compared, while other variables are held constant in each case. The concept of property space is valuable because it becomes a way of thinking about qualitative data and the way in which relations may be ascertained. Hans Zeisel, *Say It With Figures,* rev. 4th ed.; New York: Harpers, 1957, presents a more elaborate description of causal analysis and the role of cross tabulation for the reader who wishes additional knowledge. The more advanced student should consult Herbert Hyman, *Survey Design and Analysis: Principles, Cases, and Procedures,* Glencoe, Illinois: The Free Press, 1955. See also the selected readings on causal models and multivariate analysis in the bibliography at the end of Part II.

Everyone is familiar with the idea of indicating location in space by means of coordinates. Every point on this page can be described by two numbers: its distance from the left-hand side and its distance from the bottom (or from any other pair of axes we choose). The location of any point on the earth's surface can be indicated by giving its latitude and longitude, using as base lines the equator and the Greenwich meridian.

* Reprinted by permission from Paul F. Lazarsfeld and Morris Rosenberg (eds.), *The Language of Social Research* (Glencoe, Ill.: The Free Press, 1955), pp. 40-44.

Other properties besides location in physical space can likewise be indicated by coordinates. A man can be characterized by his scores on tests of mathematical and linguistic ability, just as by his latitude and longitude. These two scores locate him in a "property-space" with the two dimensions of mathematical ability and linguistic ability. We can chart this property-space on paper by using mathematics score as one axis and linguistic score for the other, just as we can chart the earth's surface. Of course in the latter case we are making a spatial representation of actual spatial dimensions, only on a smaller scale. In the former our distances on paper represent the numbers of correct answers to questions given by people taking tests, or in a larger sense, the ability of their minds to perform certain tasks.

The dimensions on which we "locate" people in property-space can be of different kinds. Most psychological test scores are for all practical purposes *continuous variables,* but they usually do not have equal intervals or a meaningful zero point. They provide only a relative ordering of people. Once we have located a representative sample of the United States population in our mathematical-linguistic property-space, we can say that a man is in the fifth percentile of the population in mathematical ability and in the fortieth in linguistic ability. Sometimes social scientists do work with continuous variables that do have a zero-point and equal intervals, at least formally; age, income, size of community, number of hours spent watching television.

More often, probably, the dimensions will be qualitative properties, which locate cases in one of a number of classes, like "State of birth," "military rank," or "occupation." State of birth locates everyone born in the continental U.S. in one of 51 *unordered classes* (counting District of Columbia). Military rank locates members of the armed forces in what is by definition a set of *rank-ordered classes,* ranging from buck private up to five-star general. Occupations in themselves do not necessarily form a set of ranked classes, although some of them are specifically defined in terms of degree of "skill." We might simply list them arbitrarily, as in alphabetical order. Or we might draw upon outside information about them— for example average income, as known from census data, or prestige status, as discovered through surveys—to arrange them in one or another rank-order.

The simplest type of property by which an object can be characterized is a *dichotomous attribute,* such as voter/nonvoter, white/ nonwhite, male/female, or Democrat/Republican. It is always possible to simplify a more complex property by reducing the number of classes that are distinguished. A continuous variable can be cut up to form a set of ranked classes, like income brackets or age levels. A set of ranked classes, in turn, can be simplified by combining all those above a certain point into one class and all those below into a second class, forming a dichotomy. This is done when we reduce the military hierarchy to the distinction between officers and enlisted men, or the income brackets to above or below a certain amount. By picking out one aspect of a set of unordered classes we can sometimes order them into a dichotomy, as when we classify states as east or west of the Mississippi, or occupations as manual or nonmanual.

When we chart the property-space formed by two qualitative characteristics the result is not, of course, a continuous plane, but an array of cells each representing one combination of values on two properties. For example, a study of the 1952 election described people's "political position" in October 1952 in terms of the two dimensions of "usual party affiliations" and "degree of political interest." If one asks Americans what their usual party affiliation is almost everyone falls into three categories: Republicans, Democrats, and independents. These are natural divisions. Degree of interest on the other hand can be divided into any number of ranked categories we please, depending on the alternatives we offer the respondent. In the present case they could rate themselves as having high, medium, or low interest. These two trichotomous dimensions then define a ninefold property-space as shown in Table 1.

TABLE 1

A QUALITATIVE PROPERTY-SPACE OF POLITICAL POSITION

		USUAL PARTY AFFILIATION		
		Republican	Democratic	Independent
DEGREE OF	High			
POLITICAL	Medium			
INTEREST	Low			

We can locate a person within this property-space by giving as coordinates his usual party affiliation and his degree of political interest.

TABLE 2

A THREE-DIMENSIONAL ATTRIBUTE-SPACE LAID OUT
IN TWO DIMENSIONS

FATHER MANUAL
OCCUPATION

Son's Occupation

SON'S		Manual	Nonmanual
PARTY			
	Democrat		
	Republican		

FATHER NONMANUAL
OCCUPATION

Son's Occupation

SON'S		Manual	Nonmanual
PARTY			
	Democrat		
	Republican		

There is no reason why we cannot characterize objects by as many properties as we want. We can add a test in historical knowledge to tests in mathematics and language, and characterize our subjects by three coordinates. These can still be presented in the form of a physical model, by using a box in which everyone is located by distance from the left-hand side, from the front, and from the bottom. If we add a fourth test, for instance, of reading speed, we can give our subjects four coordinates and locate them in a four-dimensional property-space. Thus we can say that someone is in the fifth percentile of the U.S. population in mathematics, the fortieth in language skill, the sixtieth in historical knowledge, and the twenty-ninth in reading speed. We can no longer represent this by a physical model, but we can perform mathematical operations on the four coordinates just as well as on two or three.

In dealing with qualitative property-spaces which have limited numbers of categories on each dimension, we can still chart the property-space on paper even though it is three-dimensional or even higher-dimensional. Let us take the two dimensions of occupation, dichotomized as manual/nonmanual, and political preference, dichotomized as Democratic/Republican. These give us a fourfold table. If we add the dimension of father's occupation, again dichotomized as manual/nonmanual, we now have a "two-story" fourfold table: occupation and party of sons of manual workers and occupation and party of sons of nonmanually employed people. This can be physically represented by a cube with eight cells, with the original fourfold table repeated on both the "first floor" and the "second floor." If we want to represent this cube on a flat piece of paper, all we have to do is to lay the two "stories" side by side, as an architect would two floor plans. (See Table 2 on page 68.)

Now suppose that we ask a fourth question, for example, the father's usual party, again dichotomized as Democratic/Republican. Our property-space then becomes a four-dimensional "cube." But we can still lay out each level on this fourth dimension on paper just as we did those on the third. (See Table 3 on page 70.)

The combination of dichotomous attributes produces a type of property-space that may be labeled "dichotomous attribute-space." [1] Position in a dichotomous attribute-space can be indicated as a response-pattern of plus and minus signs, where we have assigned these values (arbitrarily or otherwise) to the two sides of each dichotomy and arranged the dimensions in some order. Thus a Democratic manual worker, whose father was a Democratic manual worker, might be indicated by the coordinates $(++++)$. A Republican nonmanually employed person, whose father was a Democratic manual worker, would have the coordinates $(--++)$, and so on. (This system of notation is often used in "political score-sheets" that show how congressmen voted on a series of bills, a plus sign showing a "correct" vote and a minus sign a "wrong" vote, in terms of a given political viewpoint or economic interest.)

If we are particularly interested in one of the dimensions as a

TABLE 3

A Four-Dimensional Attribute-Space Laid Out in Two Dimensions

	FATHER MANUAL OCCUPATION				FATHER NONMANUAL OCCUPATION		
	Son's Occupation				Son's Occupation		
		Manual	Nonmanual			Manual	Nonmanual
FATHER DEMOCRAT	Son Democrat				Son Democrat		
	Republican				Republican		
FATHER REPUBLICAN	Son Democrat				Son Democrat		
	Republican				Republican		

70

criterion or dependent variable, we may present a dichotomous attribute-space in abbreviated form by showing only the "background" factors as dimensions in the chart, and filling in each cell with a figure showing the per cent who are "positive" on the criterion behavior. No information is lost since the attribute is a dichotomy, and all those not positive are classified as "negative" on the attribute. It is as if we had raised three-dimensional bars from the two-dimensional chart of background characteristics with a height proportional to the positive answers on the criterion behavior, and then replaced them with figures indicating their height just as altitudes are shown on a flat map. Thus Table 3 could be presented as an eightfold table showing the dimensions of father's occupation, father's party, and son's occupation; the cells would be filled in with figures showing "per cent Democrat" (or vice versa). (See Table 4.)

TABLE 4

ABBREVIATED PRESENTATION OF A FOUR-DIMENSIONAL ATTRIBUTE-SPACE

FATHER'S OCCUPATION

	Manual		Nonmanual	
	SON'S OCCUPATION		SON'S OCCUPATION	
	Manual	Nonmanual	Manual	Nonmanual
Democratic	___% Dem.	___% Dem.	___% Dem.	___% Dem.
Republican	___% Dem.	___% Dem.	___% Dem.	___% Dem.

FATHER'S PARTY

Such tables are particularly useful in permitting the effects of the various background variables to be compared, holding the others constant in each case.[2]

To suggest how far the use of very high-dimension property-spaces has actually developed in social research, we need only note that the results of each interview in a survey are normally punched on an IBM card containing 80 columns, each with twelve rows. Such a card provides for an 80-dimensional property-space, with each property having twelve classes. In practice one never uses all eighty dimensions simultaneously to characterize a respondent; however, they are all available to use in whatever smaller combinations we select. If we consider each position in the 80 by 12 matrix as representing a dichotomous attribute (each can either be punched or not punched), we have the possibility of locating each respondent in a dichotomous attribute-space of 960 dimensions.

FOOTNOTES

1. This has special characteristics that are used in latent-structure analysis, but this will not be discussed here. A dichotomous system is also equivalent to a binary number system, or an "off/on" system of information, as used in computing machines and in communication theory.

2. Many concrete examples can be found in chap. VI in Hans Zeisel, *Say It With Figures* (New York: Harper, 1947).

II.4. SUMMARY OF COMMON MEASURES OF ASSOCIATION *

Instructions for Use of Guide II.4.

Statistical methods enable us to study and to describe precisely averages, differences, and relationships. The number of statistical tests has risen considerably in the last thirty years and has become so large that not even a professional statistician can keep all of them at his fingertips. As these tests have become more numerous so have the kinds of hypotheses that can be tested by statistical procedures.

Common questions that the researcher often asks are:

Is there a significant difference between these two (or more) groups on this variable? What confidence can I have that observed differences did not occur by chance?

Is there an association between these two (or more) variables? If so, how close is the association?

To ascertain significance of differences and the existence of possible associations between variables, the most common statistics

* From Allen L. Edwards, *Statistical Analysis,* 1946, pp. 127-28 and A. L. Edwards, *Statistical Methods for the Behavioral Sciences,* New York: Holt, Rinehart, & Winston, Inc., 1958.

used include: t, z, X^2, r, r_s, and F. Consult the bibliography, Guide II.11 for a statistical text describing these measures. Note that computation guides have been included in this handbook for the very useful statistics, t, r, X^2, and r_s.

Guide II.4, which follows, summarizes common measures of association. Since a major object of scientific inquiry is to discover relationships, these measures become standard equipment in the training of the scientist who uses statistical tests to ascertain relationships.

a. Pearson product-moment r: For measuring relationships between two variables when both are continuous and the relationship is rectilinear. The coefficient of correlation is most reliable when based upon a large number of pairs of observations. An *r* based upon 15 pairs of observations would have to be at least .64 to indicate that the correlation in the population from which the sample was drawn was not zero, for example, whereas the same inference might be made for an *r* of .18 if the sample consisted of 200 cases.

b. The correlation ratio: For measuring relationships between two variables that are related in a curvilinear fashion. The correlation ratio, unlike the correlation coefficient, is overestimated when the number of class intervals of X is large so that but a few cases are found in each class. Obviously, if only a single case were present in each column, then the variance of the means of the columns would be as great as the total variance of Y, and the correlation ratio would be 1.00. However, if N is sufficiently large and the grouping of X is in terms of 8 to 10 intervals, each interval is apt to have a sufficient number of cases in it to make the obtained correlation ratio approximately accurate.

c. Biserial r: For measuring relationships when one variable is recorded in terms of a dichotomy and the other is continuous. Biserial *r* assumes that the individuals in each of the two categories represent a complete distribution (i.e., not just the two extremes), that the dichotomized variable is really continuous and normally distributed, and that the relationship between the two variables is rectilinear.

d. Point biserial r: For measuring the relationship between a truly dichotomous variable and a continuous variable.

e. Phi coefficient: For measuring the relationship between two variables that are truly dichotomus. Cf. with Yule's Q for appropriate use.

f. Pearson r estimated by ϕ and tetrachoric r: For measuring the relationship between two variables, when each one is recorded in terms of a dichotomy. It is assumed that both variables are essentially continuous and normally distributed and that the measures in each of the categories represent a complete distribution, and that the relationship is rectilinear.

g. Contingency coefficient: For measuring the relationship between two variables that can be classified in two or more categories, but when the categories themselves are not quantitative.

h. Rank difference coefficient: For measuring the relationship between two variables, each of which is arranged in terms of rank order.

i. Multiple correlation coefficient: For measuring the maximum relationship that may be obtained between a combination of several variables and some other one variable.

j. Partial correlation coefficient: For measuring the relationship between two variables with the effects of a third (or several others) held constant.

k. Coefficient of concordance: For measuring the degree of agreement among m sets of n ranks. If we have a group of n objects ranked by each of m judges, the coefficient of concordance tells us the degree of agreement among the m sets of ranks.

II.5. FOUR LEVELS OF MEASUREMENT AND THE STATISTICS APPROPRIATE TO EACH LEVEL

Instructions for Use of Guide II.5.

In Part III many sociometric scales have been included to measure social variables. These scales may be *nominal, ordinal, interval,* and *ratio* types.

A Nominal or Classificatory Scale refers to a level of measurement when numbers or other symbols are used simply to classify an object, person, or characteristic. Example: Folkways, Mores, Laws.

The Ordinal or Ranking Scale refers to a level of measurement when objects in various categories of a scale stand in some kind of *relation* to the categories. Given a group of equivalence classes, if the relation greater than holds between some but not all pairs of classes we have a partially ordered scale. If the relation greater than holds for all pairs of classes so that a complete rank ordering of classes arises, we have an ordinal scale. Example: Socioeconomic status as conceived by Warner in his ranking from Lower Lower to Upper Upper.

The Interval Scale refers to a level of measurement when a scale has all the characteristics of an ordinal scale, and when in addition the distances between any two numbers on the scale are of known size. Then, measurement considerably stronger than ordinality has been achieved. Example: Thurstone's Equal Appearing Interval Scale.

The Ratio Scale refers to a level of measurement when a scale has all the characteristics of an interval scale and in addition has a true zero point as its origin. The ratio of any two scale points is independent of the unit of measurement. Example: Centigrade temperature scale.

Four Levels of Measurement and the Statistics Appropriate to Each Level *

Scale	Defining Relations	Examples of Appropriate Statistics	Appropriate Statistical Tests
Nominal	(1) Equivalence	Mode Frequency Continency coefficient	Nonparametric test
Ordinal	(1) Equivalence (2) Greater than	Median Percentile Spearman r_s Kendall T Kendall W	Nonparametric test
Interval	(1) Equivalence (3) Greater than (3) Known ratio of any two intervals	Mean Standard deviation Pearson product-moment correlation Multiple product-moment correlation	Nonparametric and parametric test
Ratio	(1) Equivalence (2) Greater than (3) Known ratio of any two intervals (4) Known ratio of any two scale values	Geometric mean Coefficient of variation	Nonparametric and parametric tests

* By permission from *Nonparametric Statistics for the Behavioral Sciences* by Sidney Siegel. Copyright 1956 by McGraw-Hill Book Co., Inc.

Each of these scales has defining relations that make particular statistical tests appropriate. Nominal and ordinal scales require nonparametric tests; only interval and ratio scales may permit use of parametric tests. Since most indexes and scales are ordinal, the nonparametric test is of especial importance. It is necessary to match the appropriate statistic with the defining characteristics of the scale. The guide summarizes these relations between type of scale and appropriate statistic.

II.6. NONPARAMETRIC STATISTICAL TESTS APPROPRIATE TO VARIOUS TYPES OF SCALES

Instructions for Use of Guide II.6.

In the development of modern statistical methods, the first techniques of inference that appeared were those that made many assumptions about the nature of the population from which the scores were drawn. Since population values are "parameters" these statistical techniques are called *parametric*. For example, a technique of inference may be based on the assumption that the scores were drawn from a normally distributed population. Or the technique of inference may be based on the assumption that both sets of scores were drawn from populations having the same variance (σ^2) or spread of scores. Such techniques produce conclusions that contain qualifications, i.e., "If the assumptions regarding the shape of the population(s) are valid, then we may conclude that...."

More recently a large number of techniques of inference have been developed that do not make stringent assumptions about parameters. These newer nonparametric techniques are "distribution free," so that "Regardless of the shape of the population(s), we may conclude that...."

In the computation of parametric tests, we add, divide, and multiply the scores from samples. When these arithmetic processes are used on scores that are not truly numerical, they naturally introduce distortions in those data and thus throw doubt on conclusions from the test. Thus it is permissible to use the parametric techniques only with scores that are truly numerical. The mean and standard deviation are the central concepts of position and dispersion. Many nonparametric tests, on the other hand, focus on the order or ranking

NONPARAMETRIC STATISTICAL TEST *†

| LEVEL OF MEASURE-MENT | One-Sample Case | Two-Sample Case | | k-Sample Case | | NONPARAMETRIC MEASURE OF CORRELATION |
| | Col. 1 | Col. 2 | Col. 3 | Col. 4 | Col. 5 | Col. 6 |
	(Chap. 4)	Related Samples (Chap. 5)	Independent Samples (Chap. 6)	Related Samples (Chap. 7)	Independent Samples (Chap. 8)	(Chap. 9)
Nominal	Binomial test, pp. 36-42 χ^2 one-sample test pp. 42-47	McNemar test for the significance of changes, pp. 63-67	Fisher exact probability test, pp. 96-104 χ^2 test for two independent samples, pp. 104-11	Cochran Q test, pp. 161-66	χ^2 test for k independent samples, pp. 175-79	Contingency coefficient: C, pp. 196-202
Ordinal	Kolmogorov-Smirnov one-sample test, pp. 47-52 One-sample runs test, pp. 52-58	Sign test, pp. 68-75 Wilcoxon matched-pairs signed-ranks test, pp. 75-83 ‡	Median test, pp. 111-16 Mann-Whitney U test, pp. 116-27 Kolmogorov-Smirnov two-sample test, pp. 127-36 Wald-Wolfowitz runs test, pp. 136-45 Moses test of extreme reactions, pp. 145-52	Friedman two-way analysis of variance by ranks, pp. 166-72	Extension of the median test, pp. 179-84 Kruskal-Wallis one-way analysis of variance by ranks, pp. 184-93	Spearman rank correlation coefficient: r_s, pp. 202-13 Kendall rank correlation coefficient: r, pp. 213-23 Kendall partial rank correlation coefficient: $r_{xy \cdot z}$, pp. 223-29 Kendall coefficient of concordance: W, pp. 229-38
Interval		Walsh test, pp. 83-87 Randomization test for matched pairs, pp. 88-92	Randomization test for two independent samples, pp. 152-56			

* Each column lists, cumulatively downward, the tests applicable to the given level of measurement. For example, in the case of k related samples, when ordinal measurement has been achieved both the Friedman two-way analysis of variance and the Cochran Q test are applicable.

† For use of this table, consult Sidney Siegel, *Nonparametric Statistics for the Behavioral Sciences* (New York: McGraw-Hill Book Co., 1956).

‡ The Wilcoxon test requires ordinal measurement not only within pairs, as is required for the sign test, but also of the differences between pairs. See the discussion on pp. 75-76.

of the scores, not on their "numerical" values. The advantages of order statistics for data in the behavioral sciences are especially pronounced since so many "numerical" scores are numerical in appearance only.

Guide II.6 presents a wide range of various nonparametric statistical tests. Note that each row divides the tests into those appropriate for nominal, ordinal, and interval scales. The first column contains those tests that may be used when one wishes to determine whether a single sample is from a specified sort of population. Columns 2 and 3 contain tests that may be used when one wishes to compare the scores obtained from two samples—one set considers tests for two related samples, while the other considers tests for two independent samples. Columns 4 and 5 are devoted to significance tests for k (3 or more) samples; one of these presents tests for k related samples and the other presents tests for k independent samples. Column 6 gives nonparametric measures of association and the tests of significance that are useful with some of these.

The field of statistics has developed to the extent that we now have, for almost all research designs, alternative statistical tests that might be used in order to come to a decision about a hypothesis. Having alternative tests, the researcher has two choices—read carefully about criteria to follow in choosing among various tests applicable to a given research design or get advice from a professional statistician. Preferably, he should do both. In order to use Guide II.6 intelligently, the researcher should note where his problem falls within the table and then consult Sidney Siegel, *Nonparametric Statistics,* New York: McGraw-Hill, 1956.

II.7. COMPUTATION GUIDES

Instructions for Use of Computation Guide II.7.

The computation guides that follow describe procedures for computing four statistics commonly needed by research workers in the behavioral sciences. Statistics t and r are parametric statistics, assuming randomness and normality of the populations; X^2 and r_s are nonparametric or "distribution free," only randomness is generally assumed.

The computation design for the t test of the significance of the difference between two means is for the case of two independent samples. This is the test commonly used to test the difference between two means because we are often dealing with small samples, and we cannot assume that our data and values of *t* derived from them are normally distributed as are the parameters of large samples of 500 or more observations. However, it is assumed that the observations are drawn from normally distributed populations. The computation design for *r,* Pearson's product-moment coefficient of correlation, is useful when the number of cases is relatively large and the correlation chart is desired as a substitute for machine calculation. Pearson's *r* is for measuring relationships between two variables when both are continuous and the relationship is rectilinear. Both *t* and *r* may be used when the scores under analysis result from measurement in the strength of at least an *interval scale.*

The computation design for X^2 is for testing significance of association between two attributes; for the general *r X s* case and for the special 2 *X* 2 table. This is the most widely used statistic for use with qualitative variables. The Spearman rank order coefficient r_s is the nonparametric statistic corresponding to the parametric Pearsonian *r.* This statistic is based on two sets of rankings of the same set of items. The rank order coefficient is not limited by the restrictions of normality and linearity imposed on the product-moment r. While X^2 is a test of the *existence* of a possible association, r_s provides a measure of the *degree of relationship* between two sets of rankings. Both X^2 and r_s may be used when the scores under analysis result from measurements of *ordinal* or *nominal scales.*

II.7.a. *t* Test of Significance between Two Means of Independent Samples

Computation Design for *t* Test of the Difference between Two Means, for Two Independent Samples *

$$from\ S_1: \overline{X}_1 = \Sigma X_{1i}/N_1$$
$$\Sigma x_1{}^2 = \Sigma X_{1i}{}^2 - (\Sigma X_{1i})^2/N_1$$

$$from\ S_2: \overline{X}_2 = \Sigma X_{2i}/N_2$$
$$\Sigma x_2{}^2 = \Sigma X_{2i}{}^2 - (\Sigma X_{2i})^2/N_2$$

Continued on page 80.

* From Morris Zelditch, Jr., *A Basic Course in Sociological Statistics* (New York: Holt, Rinehart & Winston, Inc., 1959), p. 245.

1. H_0:

2. $s_{\bar{x}1 - \bar{x}2} = \sqrt{\left(\dfrac{\Sigma x_1{}^2 + \Sigma x_2{}^2}{N_1 + N_2 - 2}\right)\left(\dfrac{1}{N_1} + \dfrac{1}{N_2}\right)}$

   $=$

3. $t = \dfrac{\overline{X}_1 - \overline{X}_2}{s_{\bar{x}1 - \bar{x}2}} =$

4. d.f. $= N_1 + N_2 - 2 =$

5. $P =$

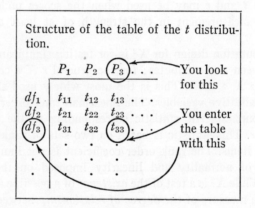

Structure of the table of the t distribution.

1. Formulate the null hypothesis you wish to test. This will determine whether you are to make a two-sided or one-sided test. The chief null hypotheses are $\mu_1 = \mu_2$ (two-sided), $\mu_1 \leqq \mu_2$, or $\mu_1 \geqq \mu_2$ (both one-sided). Write the hypothesis on line 1.

2. Compute the standard error of the difference by pooling estimates of the sums of squares. Enter on line 2.

3. Assume that both samples are normally and independently distributed; assume also that they have equal variances; then the distribution of t, which is the difference between the means divided by the estimated standard error of the difference, follows the t distribution with $N_1 + N_2 - 2$ degrees of freedom. Enter t on line 3 and d.f. on line 4.

4. With the value of t and d.f. you enter the table of t. You are looking for P, the probability that a value of t this large or larger

would have been obtained by chance if the null hypothesis were true. P will be shown along the head of the table, d.f. down the side, and the values of t will be shown in the body of the table. The probability shown will be two-tailed (i.e. the *sum* of the probability to the right of t and to the left of $-t$) ; if the hypothesis is one-sided, use one-half the tabled probability.

5. If P is equal to, or less than, 0.05, reject the null hypothesis. (Set the level of significance at 0.01 if you prefer greater certainty.) If P is greater than 0.05, accept the null hypothesis.

II.7.b. Pearsonian r to Measure Linear Correlation between Two Variables

Instructions for Calculation of r from Coded Group Data by Means of a Correlation Chart *

After the scatter diagram has been completed, and the distribution has been judged to be rectilinear, the data are then transferred to some standard product-moment correlation chart. It is much cheaper, quicker, and more reliable to use a printed correlation chart than it is to lay one out by hand. The correlation chart that will be used in the present discussion was devised by Professor F. Stuart Chapin, formerly of the University of Minnesota.[1]

The following instructions summarize the various steps to be observed in computing a coefficient of correlation with this type of chart:

1. The class-intervals for both the X- and Y-variables should be written in the spaces at the top and left-hand side of the correlation chart and the number of cases recorded in the proper cells. The frequencies for the two variables should also be entered on the chart. This operation involves merely a transferral of the essential data from the scatter diagram to the correlation chart. In selecting the zero-intervals for the two variables, an attempt should be made to choose intervals in which the means of the respective distributions are most likely to occur. In this problem, 69 was chosen to represent the zero-interval for the X-variable and 140 to 149 for the Y-variable.

* Calvin F. Schmid in Pauline V. Young, *Scientific Social Surveys and Research* (3rd ed.; Englewood Cliffs, N.J.: Prentice-Hall, 1949), pp. 287-90. By permission of Prentice-Hall, Inc.

Y \ X	-10	-9	-8	-7	-6	-5	-4	-3	-2	-1	0	+1	+2	+3	+4	+5	+6	+7	+8	+9	+10
			61	62	63	64	65	66	67	68	69	70	71	72	73	74	75	76	77		
+10	100	90	80	70	60	50	40	30	20	10	0	10	20	30	40	50	60	70	80	90	100
+9	90	81	72	63	54	45	36	27	18	9	0	9	18	27	36	45	54	63	72	81	90
+8	80	72	64	56	48	40	32	24	16	8	0	8	16	24	32	40	48	56	64	72	80
+7	70	63	56	49	42	35	28	21	14	7	0	7	14	21	28	35	42	49	56	63	70
+6 200-209	60	54	48	42	36	30	24	18	12	6	0 *(1)*	6	12	18	24	30 *(1)*	36	42	48	54	60
+5 190-199	50	45	40	35	30	25	20	15	10	5	0	5 *(1)*	10	15	20	25	30	35	40	45	50
+4 180-189	40	36	32	28	24	20	16	12	8	4	0 *(1)*	4 *(2)*	8	12 *(1)*	16 *(4)*	20 *(3)*	24	28	32	36	40
+3 170-179	30	27	24	21	18	15	12	9	6	3 *(1)*	0 *(3)*	3 *(3)*	6 *(2)*	9 *(2)*	12 *(1)*	15 *(2)*	18 *(1)*	21	24	27	30
+2 160-169	20	18	16	14	12	10	8	6	4 *(4)*	2 *(5)*	0 *(7)*	2 *(8)*	4 *(9)*	6 *(3)*	8 *(2)*	10	12	14	16 *(1)*	18	20
+1 150-159	10	9	8	7	6	5 *(1)*	4 *(2)*	3 *(4)*	2 *(6)*	1 *(4)*	0 *(11)*	1 *(9)*	2 *(3)*	3 *(4)*	4 *(3)*	5	6	7	8	9	10
0 140-149	0	0	0	0	0	0 *(1)*	0 *(5)*	0 *(2)*	0 *(20)*	0 *(-8 +)*	0 *(12)*	0 *(9)*	0 *(4)*	0 *(4)*	0	0	0 *(1)*	0	0	0	0
-1 130-139	10	9	8	7	6	5 *(2)*	4 *(5)*	3 *(12)*	2 *(7)*	1 *(7)*	0 *(5)*	1 *(3)*	2 *(1)*	3	4	5	6	7	8	9	10
-2 120-129	20	18	16 *(1)*	14	12 *(3)*	10 *(4)*	8 *(4)*	6 *(5)*	4 *(4)*	2 *(4)*	0 *(4)*	2	4 *(1)*	6	8	10	12	14	16	18	20
-3 110-119	30	27	24	21	18 *(1)*	15 *(1)*	12 *(1)*	9 *(6)*	6 *(2)*	3 *(3)*	0 *(1)*	3	6	9	12	15	18	21	24	27	30
-4 100-109	40	36	32	28	24	20 *(1)*	16	12	8	4	0	4	8	12	16	20	24	28	32	36	40
-5 90-99	50	45	40 *(1)*	35	30	25	20	15	10	5	0	5	10	15	20	25	30	35	40	45	50
-6	60	54	48	42	36	30	24	18	12	6	0	6	12	18	24	30	36	42	48	54	60
-7	70	63	56	49	42	35	28	21	14	7	0	7	14	21	28	35	42	49	56	63	70
-8	80	72	64	56	48	40	32	24	16	8	0	8	16	24	32	40	48	56	64	72	80
-9	90	81	72	63	54	45	36	27	18	9	0	9	18	27	36	45	54	63	72	81	90
-10	100	90	80	70	60	50	40	30	20	10	0	10	20	30	40	50	60	70	80	90	100
f			2	0	4	6	11	19	27	42	41	38	27	22	15	8	2	0	1		
d_x	10-	9-	8-	7-	6-	5-	4-	3-	2-	1-	0	1+	2+	3+	4+	5+	6+	7+	8+	9+	10+
fd_x			-16	0	-24	-30	-44	-57	-54	-42	Σ267	38	54	66	60	40	12	0	8	+277	
fd_x^2	100	81	64 128	49 0	36 144	25 150	16 176	9 171	4 108	1 42	0	38	108	198	240	200	72	0	64 64	81	100

Correlation Chart by F. Stuart Chapin

f	d_y	fd_y	fd_y^2	Σfd_{xy}^+	Σfd_{xy}^-
	+10		100		
	+9		81		
	+8		64		
	+7		49		
3	+6	18	108	42	
1	+5	5	25	10	
11	+4	44	176	144	
15	+3	45	135	99	6
39	+2	78	156	160	8
47	+1	47	47	39	41
66	0	237	0		
42	-1	-42	42	54	14
30	-2	-60	120	178	6
9	-3	-27	81	66	
1	-4	-4	16	16	
1	-5	-5	25	40	
	-6	Σ -138	36		
	-7		49		
	-8		64		
	-9		81		
	-10		100		

N = 265

$\Sigma fd_y = +99$

$\Sigma fd_y^2 = 931$

$\Sigma fd_x = +11$

$\Sigma fd_x^2 = 1839$

$\Sigma fd_{xy}^+ = 848$

$\Sigma fd_{xy}^- = 75$

$\Sigma fd_{xy} = +773$

X Height
Y Weight

$r = +.59973$

$S.E._r = .039$

$$r = \frac{N\Sigma fd_{xy} - [\Sigma fd_x][\Sigma fd_y]}{\sqrt{N\Sigma fd_x^2 - [\Sigma fd_x]^2} \cdot \sqrt{N\Sigma fd_y^2 - [\Sigma fd_y]^2}} = \frac{265[773] - [11][99]}{\sqrt{265[1839] - [11]^2} \cdot \sqrt{265[931] - [99]^2}}$$

$$= \frac{204,845 - 1,089}{\sqrt{487,335 - 121} \cdot \sqrt{246,715 - 9801}}$$

$$= \frac{203,756}{\sqrt{487,214} \cdot \sqrt{236,914}}$$

$$= \frac{203,756}{339,746.53} = +.59973 \text{ or } .60$$

COMPUTED BY _____ DATE _____

2. For the X-variable determine the products of (f) (d_x) and record them in the fd_x row. Multiply (f) (d_y) for the Y-variable and enter in the fd_y column. Care should be taken to observe signs. Determine the algebraic sums of the fd_x row and the fd_y column. In the chart on pages 82-83 it will be observed that $\Sigma fd_x = +11$ and $\Sigma fd_y = +99$.

3. The respective values of $fd_x{}^2$ are next obtained, as are also the values of $fd_y{}^2$, and recorded on the chart. Add the $fd_x{}^2$ row and the $fd_y{}^2$ column. In the problem, $\Sigma fd_x{}^2 = 1{,}839$ and $\Sigma fd_y{}^2 = 931$. It will be recalled that the second and third steps are identical with those used in computing the standard deviation.

4. The fourth operation is different from anything that has thus far been discussed. First, note the small figures printed in the upper left-hand corner of each cell. Second, observe the signs for each of the quadrants indicated in the center of the field of the chart. The lower left-hand quadrant and the upper right-hand quadrant are plus $(+)$ and the other two are minus $(-)$. Multiply the number of cases in each cell by the corresponding printed figure in the cell, observing signs. The products are entered in either the $\Sigma fd_{xy} +$ or the $\Sigma fd_{xy} -$ column, depending on the sign. Let us illustrate this step by performing the computations in the row 130 to 139 in the chart on pages 82-83. Multiply each of the frequencies in the row designated by the class-interval 130 to 139 by the small printed figures in each of the corresponding cells. The products for the numbers located in the plus quadrant are as follows: (4) $(2) = 8$; (3) $(5) = 15$; (2) $(12) = 24$; and (1) $(7) = 7$. The sum of these products, which is 54, is entered in the $\Sigma fd_{xy} +$ column. The products of the numbers for this row that are located in the minus quadrant are: (3) $(1) = -3$; (2) $(3) = -6$; and (1) $(5) = -5$. By adding these products together we have -14, which is recorded in the $\Sigma fd_{xy} -$ column. The figures in each of the columns are added and entered on the chart. The next step is to determine the algebraic sum of $\Sigma fd_{xy} +$ and $\Sigma fd_{yx} -$. In the problem the figures are: $848 - 75 = 773$.

5. This completes all the preliminary computations on the chart. The final step is to substitute in the formula on the right side of the chart and proceed with the calculations. It will be observed from the chart that the proper substitutions have been made in the formula and the coefficient of correlation has been computed for the illustrative problem. The coefficient of correlation between height and weight for this sample of 265 men students is $r = +.60$.

FOOTNOTE

1. All of the printed forms for computing the coefficient of correlation are very similar. A few of the better known charts are: (1) Thurstone (published by C. H. Stoelting Company, Chicago); (2) Otis (World Book Company, New York); (3) Cureton and Dunlop (Psychological Corporation, New York); (4) Tryon (University of California); (5) Ruch-Stoddard (University of Iowa); (6) Holzinger (University of Chicago); (7) Dvorak (David McKay Co., New York); (8) Kelley (World Book Company, New York); and (9) Durost-Walker (World Book Company).

II.7.c. χ^2 Test of Association

Computation Design for χ^2 for Testing Significance of Association between
Two Attributes; for the General $r \times s$ Case and
for the Special 2×2 *

n_{11}	n_{12}	$n_{13} \ldots n_{1s}$		$n_1.$
n_{21}	n_{22}	$n_{23} \ldots n_{2s}$		$n_2.$
n_{31}	n_{32}	$n_{33} \ldots n_{3s}$		$n_3.$
.	.	.	.	.
.	.	.	.	.
.	.	.	.	.
n_{r1}	n_{r2}	$n_{r3} \ldots n_{rs}$		$n_r.$
$n_{.1}$	$n_{.2}$	$n_{.3} \ldots n_{.s}$		N

1	2	3	4	5
O	E	$O - E$	$(O - E)^2$	$(O - E)^2/E$
n_{11}	$n_1.n_{.1}/N$			
n_{12}	$n_1.n_{.2}/N$			
n_{13}	$n_1.n_{.3}/N$			
.	.			
.	.			
n_{rs}	$n_r.n_{.s}/N$			

$$\chi^2 = \Sigma[(O - E)^2/E]$$
$$\text{d.f.} = (r - 1)(s - 1)$$

1. Enter the observed frequencies in column 1.

2. Calculate the expected values, E, as follows: find the marginal in the row containing the cell ij and the marginal in the column

* From Morris Zelditch, Jr., *op. cit.*, p. 290.

containing the cell, and multiply them together, giving $n_i.n_j$; then divide by N, the total number of observations in the table, giving $n_i.n_j/N$, and enter in column 2.

3. Subtract the expected values from the observed, column 2 from 1, and enter the result in column 3.

4. Square the differences obtained and enter in column 4.

5. Divide each entry in column 4 by the expected values in column 2 and enter in column 5.

6. Add up column 5. This gives you χ^2.

7. To find the number of degrees of freedom with which you enter the table, take one less than the number of rows times one less than the number of columns $(r-1)(s-1)$.

Special treatment of the 2 × 2 table

1. For the 2 × 2 table, or whenever you have only 1 degree of freedom, you must use a correction for continuity; this involves taking 0.5, from the absolute value of the difference between observed and expected, i.e.

$$|n_{ij} - n_i n_j/N| - 0.5.$$

2. You do not need to use the format for the general $r \times s$ above; you can calculate χ^2 directly from the formula below, using the letters in the 2 × 2 below for reference to cells. The correction is built into the formula.

a	b	$a+b$
c	d	$c+d$

$$a+c \quad b+d \quad N$$

$$\chi^2_{1 \text{ d.f.}} = \frac{N(|ad-bc|-N/2)^2}{(a+c)(b+d)(a+b)(c+d)}$$

II.7.d. Spearman's Rank Correlation

Computation Design for Spearman Rank Correlation Coefficient, r_s *

K_i designates an ordered position. K_{xi} designates the position of the ith observation in an array of the X variable; K_{yi} designates

* From Morris Zelditch, Jr., *op. cit.*, p. 326.

the position of the *same* observation in the Y array. If, for example, the first observation, O_1, is first in the X array and fourth in the Y array, the first row of the layout form below should read

$$K_{x1} = 1, K_{y1} = 4, K_{x1} - K_{y1} = -3, (K_{x1} - K_{y1})^2 = 9$$

(1) O_i	(2) K_{xi}	(3) K_{yi}	(4) d	(5) d^2
O_1	K_{x1}	K_{y1}	$K_{x1} - K_{y1}$	$(K_{x1} - K_{y1})^2$
O_2	K_{x2}	K_{y2}	$K_{x2} - K_{y2}$	$(K_{x2} - K_{y2})^2$
.	.	.	.	.
.	.	.	.	.
.	.	.	.	.
O_N	K_{xN}	K_{yN}	$K_{xN} - K_{yN}$	$(K_{xN} - K_{yN})$

$$\Sigma(K_{xi} - K_{yi})^2 = \Sigma d^2 =$$

$$r_s = 1 - \frac{6\Sigma d^2}{N^2(N - 1)} =$$

$$t = r_s \sqrt{\frac{N - 2}{1 - r_s^2}} = \qquad , \text{d.f.} = N - 2.$$

1. Form an array of the observations on the X variable. (Start with the "best," "smallest," "highest." You may choose the starting point at will, but you must be consistent on both X and Y, or the sign of r_s will be meaningless.) Order the observations on the variable Y in the same manner.

2. Replace the X value of each observation by its rank in the X array and the Y value of each observation by its rank in the Y array. In column 2 at the right enter ranks of the observations on the X variable and in column 3 enter ranks of the observations on the Y variable. Ranks in the same row must be for the *same* observation.

3. Take the difference between ranks and enter in column 4.

4. Square these differences, enter in column 5, and sum column 5.

5. Compute r_s from the formula shown above.

6. For $N > 10$, to test $H_0: \rho_s = 0$, use t, computed from the formula shown above with $(N - 2)$ d.f. (ρ_s [read "rho sub-s"] is the population parameter corresponding to r_s.)

II.8. A BIBLIOGRAPHY OF STATISTICAL GUIDES

The following books are especially valuable as reference books when the researcher is seeking a readable step-by-step explanation or procedure. The selections are based on the simplicity of the description and the inclusion of illustrative examples.

1. AIKEN, HERBERT, and COLTON, RAYMOND R. *An Outline of Statistical Methods,* New York: Barnes & Noble, 1960. (A guide to elementary statistics.)
2. EDWARDS, ALLEN. *Statistical Methods for the Behavioral Sciences,* New York: Rinehart and Co., 1954. (Statistical techniques and methods presented for the student with a minimum amount of mathematical knowledge. The emphasis is on parametric methods but nonparametric methods also are integrated into the text.)
3. FREUND, JOHN E., LIVERMORE, PAUL E., and MILLER, IRVIN. *Manual of Experimental Statistics,* Englewood Cliffs, N.J.: Prentice-Hall, 1960. (Presents in outline form the most frequently used statistical techniques, including appropriate computing formulas and completely worked-out examples of each method.)
4. MARK, MARY LOUISE. *Statistics in the Making: A Primer in Statistical Survey Method,* Columbus, Ohio: Ohio State University Bureau of Business Research, 1958. (Shows how to produce statistical tables of scientific quality.)
5. MAXWELL, ALBERT E. *Analyzing Qualitative Data,* New York: John Wiley & Sons, 1961. (The book, which might have been given the title χ^2 tests, aims at providing the research worker with a simple but up-to-date account of statistical techniques available for the analysis of qualitative data.)
6. MORONEY, M. J. *Facts from Figures,* Baltimore: Penguin Books, 1954. (Lucid explanation of the background of statistics, well illustrated.)
7. MUELLER, JOHN H., and SCHUESSLER, KARL F. *Statistical Reasoning in Sociology,* Boston: Houghton Mifflin, 1961. (Emphasis is placed on reasons supporting statistical analysis.)
8. SCHMID, CALVIN F. *Handbook of Graphic Presentation,* New York: Ronald, 1954. (Methods for presenting social statistics in a visual manner.)
9. SMITH, G. MILTON. *A Simplified Guide to Statistics for Psychology and Education,* 3rd ed., New York: Holt, Rinehart & Winston, 1962. (Integrates most commonly used tools.)
10. WALKER, HELEN M. *Mathematics Essential for Elementary Statistics: A Self-Teaching Manual,* New York: Henry Holt, 1951.

(Material permits student to proceed with mathematical training by self instruction.)

11. ZEISEL, HANS. *Say It with Figures,* New York: Harper, 1957. (A guide to the assembly and interpretation of social statistics.)

12. ZELDITCH, MORRIS, JR. *A Basic Course in Sociological Statistics: A Textbook and Workbook Combined,* New York: Henry Holt, 1959. (Has step-by-step computation guides for all basic statistics, well illustrated.)

II.9. A SPECIALIZED BIBLIOGRAPHIC SECTION FOR THE ADVANCED STUDENT

SELECTED READINGS ON CASUAL MODELS AND MULTIVARIATE ANALYSIS

HUBERT M. BLALOCK, JR., "Correlational Analysis and Causal Inferences," *American Anthropologist,* August, 1960, 62: 624-31.

———, "Correlation and Causality: the Multivariate Case," *Social Forces,* March, 1961, 39: 246-51.

———, "Evaluating the Relative Importance of Variables," *Amer. Sociol. Rev.,* December, 1961, 26: 866-74.

———, "Spuriousness versus Intervening Variables: The Problem of Temporal Sequences," *Social Forces,* May, 1962, 40: 330-34.

———, "Further Observations on Asymmetric Causal Models," *Amer. Sociol. Rev.,* August, 1962, 27: 542-45.

———, "Four-Variable Causal Models and Partial Correlation," *Amer. J. Sociol.,* September, 1962, 48: 182-94.

PETER M. BLAU, "Determining the Dependent Variable in Certain Correlations," *Public Opinion Quarterly,* Spring, 1955, 19: 100-105.

HERBERT HYMAN, *Survey Design and Analysis: Principles, Cases, and Procedures,* Glencoe, Ill.: The Free Press, 1955, pp. 242-329 (chaps. 6 and 7).

PATRICIA KENDALL and PAUL LAZARSFELD, "Problems of Survey Analysis," in R. K. Merton and P. Lazarsfeld (eds.), *Continuities in Social Research,* Glencoe, Ill.: The Free Press, 1950, pp. 133-96.

PAUL F. LAZARSFELD, "Interpretation of Statistical Relations as a Research Operation," in P. Lazarsfeld and M. Rosenberg (eds.), *The Language of Social Research,* Glencoe, Ill.: The Free Press, 1955, pp. 115-25.

S. NOWAK, "Some Problems of Causal Interpretation of Statistical Relationships," *Philosophy of Science,* January, 1960, 27: 23-38.

KENNETH POLK, "A Note on Asymmetric Causal Models," *Amer. Sociol. Rev.,* August, 1962, 27: 539-42.

GUY H. ORCUTT, "Actions, Consequences and Causal Relations," *The Review of Economics and Statistics*, 1952, 34: 305-14.

W. S. ROBINSON, "Asymmetric Causal Models: Comments on Polk and Blalock," *Amer. Sociol. Rev.*, August, 1962, 27: 545-48.

ARNOLD M. ROSE, "A Weakness of Partial Correlation in Sociological Studies," *Amer. Sociol. Rev.*, August, 1949, 14: 536-39.

HERBERT A. SIMON, "Causal Ordering and Identifiability," in W. C. Hood and T. C. Koopmans (eds.), *Studies in Econometric Methods*, New York: Wiley, 1953, pp. 49-74.

———, "Spurious Correlation: A Causal Interpretation," *J. Amer. Stat. Assoc.*, September, 1954, 49: 467-79.

———, *Models of Man: Social and Rational*, New York: Wiley, 1957, pp. 37-49.

HERMAN WOLD, "Casual Inference from Observational Data," *Journal of the Royal Statistical Society*, Series A, Part I, 1956, 119: 28-60.

———, and L. JUREEN, *Demand Analysis: A Study in Econometrics*, New York: Wiley, 1953.

PART III

Selected Sociometric Scales and Indexes

Introduction

There are literally thousands of scales and indexes to measure social variables. Social scientists have often elected to construct new measures even when scales of high reliability and validity have been available. This practice is wasteful of time, energy, and money. In addition, it makes replication and accumulation of research findings difficult if not impossible. The selection of scales to be found in this handbook was based on such criteria as validity, reliability, and utility. The variables most commonly used in social measurement were studied and measures for them were sought. Those with the highest reliability and validity were selected. It is hoped that this handbook will encourage greater use of these scales or stimulate the search for better ones.

In general, three groups of variable factors need to be observed and measured in any research design that seeks to test a basic hypothesis or social relationship.

First, there is the dependent variable, the effect we wish to observe and describe.

Second, there is the independent variable that has been designated as the causal factor. Sometimes this factor must be broken down into the component parts that operate more or less as a unit pattern.

Third, there are intervening or other independent variables that must be controlled lest they obscure the relationship we wish to measure by use of experimental design.

Sociometric scales have been constructed in substantial numbers to permit quantitative description of these factors in human relations.

Three areas of social measurement can be identified. These are:

1. Psychometric and social psychological scales: psychological measurements including intelligence scales, personality tests and scales, attitude tests and scales.

Examples of these scales that are included in this part are the Minnesota Multiphasic Personality Inventory, the Authoritarian Personality (F) Scale, Morale and Job Satisfaction Scales, as well as attitude scales to measure wants and satisfactions, social insight, community attitudes, and labor-management attitudes.

2. Demographic Scales: measurements of the forms or results of social behavior in large units such as the community, state, or nation.

Examples in this part include community rating scales, community services activity, citizen political activity, and a community solidarity index.

3. Sociometric Scales: measurements of the social structure and process.*

Examples in this part include sociometric tests to measure informal friendship constellations, measurements of social participation, of social distance, and of group cohesiveness. Other scales are provided to assess marital adjustment and group dimensions. The measurement of social status is of such crucial importance that a number of scales are included, such as *Alba Edwards' Socioeconomic Scale, Warner's Revised Occupational Scale, and Evaluated Participation Method for Social Class, Hatt-North Occupational Prestige Scores,* and the *Sewell* and *Chapin Social-Status Scales.*

If you do not find a scale that fits your particular research interest consult the inventory of measures used by researchers represented in the *American Sociological Review* during 1951-60. This inventory has been placed at the end of Part III.

Scale construction yields four types of scales: the *nominal* scale, consisting simply of distinguishable categories with no implication of "more" or "less"; the ordinal scale, on which positions can be identified in a rank order but with no implication as to the distance between positions; the *interval* scale, which has equal distance between any two adjacent positions on the continuum; and the *ratio* scale, which has not only equal intervals but an absolute zero.

The ideal scale is a ratio scale, but with the possible exception of the procedures for measuring certain psychophysical phenomena none of the measurement techniques currently used fits the requirements for a ratio scale. The nominal scale permits neither rank

* Cf. F. Stuart Chapin, *Experimental Designs in Sociological Research* (New York: Harper & Bros., 1947), chap. VI, Sociometric Scales, pp. 140-64. This chapter summarizes rationale for scales and contains a compilation of selected scales.

ordering nor a metric scale. It is so elemental as a classification scheme that such scales are generally regarded as first approximations toward the quantification of a social variable. The result is that ordinal and interval scales are the most frequent types in use. There is considerable disagreement over whether an ordinal or interval scale provides the most appropriate model for social data. Some writers have taken the view (see David Gold in this handbook, pp. 61-64) that few, if any, of the techniques now in use provide data that can be considered as appropriate to more than ordinal scales. Others believe that various types of scales may properly be treated as conforming to interval scales. Still others have taken the position that, although most of the measurements used do not go beyond ordinal scales, little harm is done in applying statistics to them that are appropriate to interval scales.

The result is that statistics appropriate to interval scales continue to be widely used in the analysis of social data whether the assumptions are met or not. However, there is also an increasing use of statistics that are specifically appropriate to ordinal scales. The statistical tools included in Part II of the handbook are for the use of the ordinal and interval scales included in this section.

The selection of a good scale involves weighing a number of criteria. The most important single consideration is validity. Does the scale measure what it purports to measure? How much and what kind of evidence is available? Does the scale fit the problem selected for study?

Other considerations include its reliability, its precision, its simplicity and ease of administration. In recent years there has been considerable emphasis on unidimensionality. The Guttman technique enables the researcher to identify and construct scales of a single dimension. This may be very important in increasing the precision and predictability of a given variable. However, two qualifications must be kept in mind. Such a scale may not be the most effective either for measuring attitudes toward complex objects or for making predictions about behavior in relation to such objects. It must also be remembered that a given scale may be unidimensional for one group of individuals but not for another.

The scales assembled in this part include those constructed by arbitrary or judgmental ranking, by item analysis techniques, by Thurstone's equal-appearing interval method, by Guttman's technique of scale analysis, and by factor analysis.[1] Regardless of the method used in construction, what the researcher seeks is the scale that best fits his problem, has the highest reliability and validity, is precise, and is relatively easy to apply.[2] When he has made his selection he must be aware of the statistical techniques he may subsequently apply. Generally, he will be using nonparametric statistics for ordinal scales and parametric statistics for interval scales and for those ordinal scales that do not deviate too far from the assumptions of randomness and normal distribution.

FOOTNOTES

1. An excellent handbook of scale construction is Allen L. Edwards, *Techniques of Attitude Scale Construction* (New York: Appleton-Century-Crofts, 1957). Cf. W. S. Torgerson, *Theory and Methods of Scaling* (New York: John Wiley & Sons, 1958).

2. For an excellent discussion of these criteria, see Paul F. Lazarsfeld and Morris Rosenberg, *The Language of Social Research* (Glencoe, Ill.: The Free Press, 1955); Hans Zeisel, *Say It with Figures* (New York: Harper & Bros., 1957), pp. 91-127.

SECTION A

Social Status

Social class or status is one of the most important variables in social research. The socioeconomic position of the person affects his chances for education, income, occupation, marriage, health, friends, and even life expectancy. The variable has proved difficult to measure in a pluralistic, equalitarian, and fluid society such as exists in the United States. However, many researchers have tried to identify the social strata and to measure them. There are six scales presented here for the researcher's choice. These are:

1. Alba M. Edwards' Social-Economic Grouping of Occupations
2. The Revised Occupational Rating Scale from Warner, Meeker, and Eells's Index of Status Characteristics
3. Hatt-North Occupational Prestige Ratings
4. Warner's Evaluated Participation Method of Social Class Measurements
5. Chapin's Social Status (Living Room) Scale, Revised 1952
6. Sewell's Short Form of the Farm Socioeconomic Status Scale

Choose Edwards' socioeconomic grouping if a relatively broad classification is satisfactory for your problem. This grouping makes it possible to use the United States Census for all kinds of comparative purposes.

Choose the Warner, Meeker, and Eells's Occupational Rating Scale if a more precise scale is needed. Note how it differentiates each of the Edwards' classifications into graduated, more precise rankings.

Choose the Hatt-North Occupational Prestige Ratings if the problem requires a greater range of ratings. The prestige rankings probably are less reliable and valid than the gradations in the Warner Occupational Scale. They rest on subjective assessments while the Warner rankings have undergone empirical tests of various kinds. However, prestige rankings offer the opportunity of making finer distinctions. Note the range of Warner's Occupation Scale is 1–7, the Hatt-North range is 33–96.

Choose Warner's Evaluated Participation Method of Social Class Measurement if the study involves careful analysis of social processes within a community context. The use of this scale requires considerable time and effort.

Choose Chapin's Social Status Scale for family studies. It is quick, reliable, valid, and well standardized.

Choose Sewell's Short Form of the Farm Socioeconomic Status Scale for studies in rural life.

INDEX: ALBA M. EDWARDS' SOCIAL-ECONOMIC GROUPING OF OCCUPATIONS

VARIABLE MEASURED: Socioeconomic Position

DESCRIPTION: Occupations are classified into six major groups with each group purported to have a somewhat distinct economic standard of life and to exhibit intellectual and social similarities. The two major dimensions for the ranking order are income and education.

WHERE PUBLISHED: Alba M. Edwards, *Comparative Occupation Statistics for the United States,* United States Government Printing Office, 1934, pp. 164-69.

RELIABILITY: Occupational Grouping shows high comparability with similar occupational ranking systems such as Barr-Taussig, Beckman Goodenough and Anderson, Centers, etc.

VALIDITY: Major Occupational groups can be ranked on the two dimensions of income and education with relatively high correspondence as shown for the following occupational groups.

Occupational Group	Adults with Some College Education (1957) (a) Percentage	Median (1959) Income (b) Male Workers
Professional, technical, and kindred workers	78.7	$6,725
Business managers, officials, and proprietors	40.6	6,315
Clerical and kindred workers	30.2	4,904
Craftsman, foreman, and kindred workers	14.7	5,355
Operatives and kindred workers	9.0	4,281
Laborers, except farm and mine	8.3	3,150

(a) *Current Population Reports,* Series P-20 No. 83, Bureau of the Census, August, 1958, p. 18.
(b) *Current Population Reports,* Series P-60 No. 35, Bureau of the Census, January, 1961, pp. 41-42.

UTILITY: This is the most widely used scale of social-economic groupings of gainful workers in the United States. It is the basis on which the United States Census has grouped workers since 1930 in the decennial census.

The universe of gainful workers is fully enumerated every ten years. Any research worker can check his sample against enumeration parameters and can draw generalizations with high confidence.

RESEARCH APPLICATIONS: H. Dewey Anderson and Percy E. Davidson, *Occupational Trends in the United States,* Stanford: Stanford University Press, 1940.
———, *Occupational Mobility in an American Community,* Stanford: Stanford University Press, 1937.
F. W. Taussig and C. S. Joslyn, *American Business Leaders,* New York: Macmillan, 1932.
W. Lloyd Warner and James C. Abegglen, *Occupational Mobility in American Business and Industry, 1928-1952,* Minneapolis: University of Minnesota Press, 1955.
Percy E. Davidson and Dewey Anderson, *Ballots and the Democratic Class Struggle,* Stanford: Stanford University Press, 1943.
A. J. Jaffe and R. O. Carleton, *Occupational Mobility in the United States, 1930-1960,* New York: Columbia University Press, 1954.
Seymour Martin Lipset and Reinhard Bendix, *Social Mobility and Industrial Society,* Berkeley: University of California Press, 1959.

SOCIAL-ECONOMIC GROUPING OF OCCUPATIONS

After *Alba M. Edwards*

(Present United States Census Classification
of Occupational Groups)

1. Professional, technical, and kindred workers
2. Business managers, officials, and proprietors
   a. Nonfarm managers, officials, and proprietors
   b. Farm owners and managers
3. Clerical and sales workers
   a. Clerical and kindred workers
   b. Sales workers
4. Craftsmen, foremen, and kindred workers
5. Operatives and kindred workers

6. Unskilled, service, and domestic workers
   a. Private household workers
   b. Service workers, except private household
   c. Farm laborers, unpaid family workers
   d. Laborers, except farm and mine

INDEX: REVISED OCCUPATIONAL RATING SCALE FROM W. L. WARNER, M. MEEKER, AND K. EELLS'S INDEX OF STATUS CHARACTERISTICS

VARIABLE MEASURED: Social Class Position according to a seven point rating.

DESCRIPTION: The rating of occupations is one measure included in the Index of Status Characteristics. The Index is composed of four status characteristics: Occupation, Source of Income, House Type, and Dwelling Area. Each of these is rated on a seven point scale, and this rating is then weighted according to its separate contributions to the total Index. The weighted ratings are totaled to yield the scores that are appropriate to the various classes. The scores on the Index of Status Characteristics range from 12 to 84. The ranges are calculated by validating preliminary scores using the Evaluated Participation method of determining social class position. Occupation is the single measure most highly correlated with class position.

WHERE PUBLISHED: W. Lloyd Warner, Marchia Meeker, and Kenneth Eells, *Social Class in America,* Chicago: Science Research Associates, 1949, pp. 121-59. The occupational rating scale is shown on pp. 140-41.

VALIDITY OF INDEX OF STATUS CHARACTERISTICS:
1. Accuracy in prediction: 85 per cent of the Old Americans were placed correctly or within one point. Not as valid for ethnics.
2. Correlation with the Evaluative Participation Method as reported by Warner, *et. al.,* on p. 168.

Occupation	$r = .91$
Source of Income	$r = .85$
House Type	$r = .85$
Dwelling Area	$r = .82$
I.S.C. (all four measures)	$r = .97$

3. Comparative Study by John L. Haer.
   Five indexes of social stratification were compared and evaluated by examining their capacities for predicting variables that have been shown in previous studies to be related to measures of

stratification. These five indexes include Centers' class identification question, an open end question, occupation, education, and Warner's Index of Status Characteristics. An overall comparison reveals that coefficients are higher for the Index of Status Characteristics than for other indexes in 18 out of 22 comparisons. Its greater efficiency may be due to the fact that it is a composite index that provides a continuous series of ranks. These features make it possible to discern minute variations in relation to other variables. John L. Haer, "Predictive Utility of Five Indices of Social Stratification," *American Sociological Review*, October, 1957, 22: 541-46.

VALIDITY OF THE OCCUPATION SCALE: Joseph A. Kahl and James A. Davis selected 19 single measures of socioeconomic status and measured their intercorrelations. They report a product moment correlation of .74 between occupation (Warner) and status of friends, and a multiple correlation of .80 between occupation plus education and status of friends—". . . our data agree with Warner's that occupation (as he measures it) is the best predictor of either social participation or the whole socioeconomic cluster represented by the general factor identified by factor analysis." "A Comparison of Indexes of Socio-Economic Status," *American Sociological Review*, June, 1955, 20: 317-25.

Stanley A. Hetzler reports the following coefficients between seven rating scales and ratings of social class and social position.

Rating Scales	Social Class	Social Position
Occupational Prestige	.69	.57
Residential Area	.54	.46
Family Background	.53	.48
Personal Influence	.49	.52
Dwelling Unit	.47	.39
Family Wealth	.45	.45
Personal Income	.34	.44

The four rating scales showing the highest coefficients were occupational prestige, family background, residential area, and personal influence. The multiple correlation of these four scales with social class is .75; with social position it is .68. "An Investigation of the Distinctiveness of Social Classes," *American Sociological Review*, October, 1953, 18: 493-97. *See also* J. L. Haer "A Test of the Unidimensionality of the Index of Status Characteristics," *Social Forces*, 1955, 34: 56-58.

UTILITY: The Index of Status Characteristics presents a comparatively objective means of determining social class position. The limits defined for the various seven point ratings are sufficiently precise to eliminate to a great degree any subjective judgment. All one needs to know is a person's name, occupation, and address; the source of income can generally be derived from the occupation, and the house type and dwelling area can be evaluated through the address. This eliminates extensive, time-consuming interviewing.

The Occupation Scale is the best single predictor of social class position within a seven point range. The high correlation it exhibits with the evaluative participative method of social class position ($r = .91$) commends occupation as a single dimension. Researchers will achieve a high degree of predictive efficiency by use of the one scale. Cf. Hollingshead's use of a two factor index of social position in August B. Hollingshead and Frederick C. Redlich, *Social Class and Mental Illness: A Community Study*, New York: John Wiley & Sons, 1958, pp. 390-91.

RESEARCH APPLICATIONS: W. Lloyd Warner and Associates, *Democracy in Jonesville*, New York: Harper & Bros., 1949.
Gregory P. Stone and William H. Form, "The Local Community Clothing Market: A Study of the Social and Social Psychological Contexts of Shopping," *Technical Bulletin 247*, East Lansing, Michigan: Michigan State University, June, 1955.
Howard E. Freeman and Ozie G. Simmons, "Social Class and Post-Hospital Performance Levels," *American Sociological Review*, 1959, 24: 345-51.
Robert J. Havighurst and Allison Davis, "A Comparison of the Chicago and Harvard Studies of Social Class Differences in Child Rearing," *American Sociological Review*, August, 1955, 20: 438-42.
Gregory P. Stone and William H. Form, "Instabilities in Status: The Problem of Hierarchy in the Community Study of Status Arrangements," *American Sociological Review*, April, 1953, 18: 149-62.
Martha Sturm White, "Social Class, Child Rearing Practices and Child Behavior," *American Sociological Review*, December, 1957, 22: 704-12.
Edwin D. Lawson and Walter E. Bock, "Correlations of Indexes of Families' Socio-Economic Status," *Social Forces*, December, 1960, 39: 149-52.

WARNER, MEEKER, EELLS'S REVISED SCALE FOR RATING OCCUPATION

Rating Assigned to Occupation	Professionals	Proprietors and Managers	Business Men	Clerks and Kindred Workers, Etc.	Manual Workers	Protective and Service Workers	Farmers
1	Lawyers, doctors, dentists, engineers, judges, high-school superintendents, veterinarians, ministers (graduated from divinity school), chemists, etc., with postgraduate training, architects	Businesses valued at $75,000 and over	Regional and divisional managers of large financial and industrial enterprises	Certified Public Accountants			Gentlemen farmers
2	High-school teachers, trained nurses, chiropractors, undertakers, ministers (some training), newspaper editors, librarians (graduate)	Businesses valued at $20,000 to $75,000	Assistant managers and office and department managers of large businesses, assistants to executives, etc.	Accountants, salesmen of real estate and insurance, postmasters			Large farm owners, farm owners

WARNER, MEEKER, EELLS'S REVISED SCALE FOR RATING OCCUPATION—*Continued*

Rating Assigned to Occupation	Professionals	Proprietors and Managers	Business Men	Clerks and Kindred Workers, Etc.	Manual Workers	Protective and Service Workers	Farmers
3	Social workers, grade-school teachers, optometrists, librarians (not graduate), undertaker's assistants, ministers (no training)	Businesses valued at $5,000 to $20,000	All minor officials of businesses	Auto salesmen, bank clerks and cashiers, postal clerks, secretaries to executives, supervisors of railroad, telephone, etc., justices of the peace	Contractors		
4		Businesses valued at $2,000 to $5,000		Stenographers, bookkeepers, rural mail clerks, railroad ticket agents, sales people in dry goods stores, etc.	Factory foreman, electricians, plumbers, carpenters, watchmakers (own business)	Dry cleaners, butchers, sheriffs, railroad engineers and conductors	
5		Businesses valued at $500 to $2,000		Dime store clerks, hardware salesmen, beauty operators, telephone operators	Carpenters, plumbers, electricians (apprentice), timekeepers, linemen, telephone or telegraph, radio repairmen, medium skilled workers	Barbers, firemen, butcher's apprentices, practical nurses, policemen, seamstresses, cooks in restaurant, bartenders	Tenant farmers

6	Businesses valued at less than $500	Moulders, semi-skilled workers, assistants to carpenter, etc.	Baggage men, night police-men and watchmen, taxi and truck drivers, gas station attendants, waitresses in restaurants	Small tenant farmers, laborers
7		Heavy labor, migrant work, odd-job men, miners	Janitors, scrubwomen, newsboys	Migrant farm laborers

INDEX: HATT-NORTH OCCUPATIONAL PRESTIGE RATINGS

VARIABLE MEASURED: Stratification is measured through occupational prestige and esteem.

DESCRIPTION: A nationwide cross-section of Americans (National Opinion Research Center Sample of 2,930) were asked to rate the standing of ninety occupations. These occupations were chosen from a wide range of white collar and manual occupations.

Respondents were asked—"For each job mentioned, please pick out the statement that best gives your own personal opinion of the general standing that such a job has: 1. *Excellent* standing, 2. *Good* standing, 3. *Average* standing, 4. *Somewhat below average* standing, 5. *Poor* standing. I don't know where to place that one." Ranking the ninety occupations was made possible by a procedure devised to translate the percentage ratings on each of the jobs into a single general score. When the "Don't Know" answers were excluded, the scoring theoretically allowed a maximum of 100 points for any job receiving only "excellent" ratings and a minimum of 20 points for work that was unanimously rated as poor. The actual range became 33-96.

WHERE PUBLISHED: Paul K. Hatt and C. C. North, "Jobs and Occupations: A Popular Evaluation," *Opinion News,* September, 1947, pp. 3-13.

RELIABILITY: Reliability of raters is known to be highest in the higher and lower extremes of the prestige continuum and least reliable in the midrange. Social stratification of subjects has an effect on judgments in this field. Reliability is also lowered whenever the respondent is asked to rate unfamiliar occupations.

VALIDITY: Numerous prestige studies exist, and correspondence between independent samples of respondents is quite high.

For an excellent comparative analysis see Lawrence Thomas, *The Occupational Structure and Education,* Prentice-Hall, 1956, pp. 181-82.

Hatt later reexamined his own data to discover whether occupational prestige could be considered as a single dimension. The Guttman scaling technique was employed and responses were examined. They were not scalable, but occupational subgroups or families all proved to be scalable or to have reproducibilities high enough to consider them so. These occupational families and situs are shown:

1. Political	2. Professional	
National	Free Professions	Applied Sciences
Local	Pure Sciences	Community Professionals

3. Business
   Big Business
   Small Business
   Labor Organization
   White-collar Employees

4. Recreation and Aesthetics
   High Arts
   Journalism and Radio
   Recreation

5. Agriculture
   Farming
   Employed on Farms

6. Manual Work
   Skilled Mechanics
   Construction Trades
   Outdoor Work
   Factory Work
   Unskilled Labor

7. Military
   Army
   Navy
   Marine Corps
   Coast Guard

8. Service
   "Official Community"
   "Unofficial Community
   Personnel"

The researcher who is working with subgroups should be aware of these occupational situs. For further information see Paul K. Hatt, "Occupation and Social Stratification," *American Journal of Sociology,* May, 1950, 55: 538-43.

Theodore Caplow also insists that occupational prestige ranking is not unidimensional. See his *Sociology of Work,* Minneapolis: University of Minnesota Press, 1954, pp. 33-57.

RESEARCH APPLICATIONS: Peter M. Blau, "Occupational Bias and Mobility," *American Sociological Review,* August, 1957, 22: 392-99.

Alfred C. Clarke, "The Use of Leisure and Its Relation to Levels of Occupational Prestige," *American Sociological Review,* June, 1956, 21: 301-7.

Evelyn Ellis, "Social Psychological Correlates of Upward Social Mobility among Unmarried Career Women," *American Sociological Review,* October, 1952, 17: 558-63.

La Mar T. Empey, "Social Class and Occupational Aspirations: A Comparison of Absolute and Relative Measurement," *American Sociological Review,* December, 1956, 21: 703-9.

A. Inkeles and P. Rossi, "National Comparisons of Occupational Prestige," *American Journal of Sociology,* 1956, 61: 329-39.

Ward S. Mason and Neal Gross, "Intra-Occupational Prestige Differentiation: The School Superintendency," *American Sociological Review,* June, 1955, 20: 326-31.

Albert J. Reiss, Jr., Otis Dudley Duncan, Paul K. Hatt, and Cecil C. North, *Occupations and Social Status,* New York: The Free Press of Glencoe, 1961.

Leonard Reissman, "Levels of Aspiration and Social Class," *American Sociological Review,* June, 1953, 18: 233-42.

W. H. Sewell, A. O. Haller, and M. A. Straus, "Social Status and Educational and Occupational Aspiration," *American Sociological Review,* February, 1957, 22: 67-73.

C. F. Westoff, P. C. Sagi, and E. L. Kelly, "Fertility through Twenty Years of Marriage: A Study in Predictive Possibilities," *American Sociological Review,* October, 1958, 23: 549-56.

OCCUPATIONAL RATINGS

Paul K. Hatt and C. C. North

Occupation	*Score*
U.S. Supreme Court Justice	96
Physician	93
State Governor	93
Cabinet member in the federal government	92
Diplomat in the U.S. Foreign Service	92
Mayor of a large city	90
College professor	89
Scientist	89
United States Representative in Congress	89
Banker	88
Government scientist	88
County judge	87
Head of a department in a state government	87
Minister	87
Architect	86
Chemist	86
Dentist	86
Lawyer	86
Member of the board of directors of a large corporation	86
Nuclear physicist	86
Priest	86
Psychologist	85
Civil engineer	84
Airline pilot	83
Artist who paints pictures that are exhibited in galleries	83
Owner of factory that employs about 100 people	82
Sociologist	82
Accountant for a large business	81
Biologist	81

OCCUPATIONAL RATINGS—(Continued)

Paul K. Hatt and C. C. North

Occupation	Score
Musician in a symphony orchestra	81
Author of novels	80
Captain in the regular army	80
Building contractor	79
Economist	79
Instructor in the public schools	79
Public school teacher	78
County agricultural agent	77
Railroad engineer	77
Farm owner and operator	76
Official of an international labor union	75
Radio announcer	75
Newspaper columnist	74
Owner-operator of a printing shop	74
Electrician	73
Trained machinist	73
Welfare worker for a city government	73
Undertaker	72
Reporter on a daily newspaper	71
Manager of a small store in a city	69
Bookkeeper	68
Insurance agent	68
Tenant farmer—one who owns livestock and machinery and manages the farm	68
Traveling salesman for a wholesale concern	68
Playground director	67
Policeman	67
Railroad conductor	67
Mail carrier	66
Carpenter	65
Automobile repairman	63
Plumber	63
Garage mechanic	62
Local official of a labor union	62
Owner-operator of a lunch stand	62
Corporal in the regular army	60
Machine operator in a factory	60
Barber	59

OCCUPATIONAL RATINGS—(Continued)

Paul K. Hatt and C. C. North

Occupation	Score
Clerk in a store	58
Fisherman who owns his own boat	58
Streetcar motorman	58
Milk routeman	54
Restaurant cook	54
Truck driver	54
Lumberjack	53
Filling station attendant	52
Singer in a nightclub	52
Farmhand	50
Coal miner	49
Taxi driver	49
Railroad section hand	48
Restaurant waiter	48
Dock worker	47
Night watchman	47
Clothes presser in a laundry	46
Soda fountain clerk	45
Bartender	44
Janitor	44
Share cropper—one who owns no livestock or equipment and does not manage farm	40
Garbage collector	35
Street sweeper	34
Shoe shiner	33
AVERAGE	69.8

INDEX: WARNER'S EVALUATED PARTICIPATION METHOD OF SOCIAL CLASS MEASUREMENT

VARIABLE MEASURED: Identifies the social-class group with which the individual actually is found to participate in community living.

DESCRIPTION: Extensive interviews of socially aware persons are conducted. From these the social configuration in the community is determined and the families or persons are placed within the classes. Six techniques of utilization of interview material are used—rating by matched agreements, rating by symbolic placement, rating by status reputation, rating by comparison, rating by simple assignment to a class, rating by institutional membership. This is a method more than a scale, but it yields a measurement of social class and produces a nominal scale.

WHERE PUBLISHED: W. Lloyd Warner, M. Meeker, and K. Eells, *Social Class in America* (Chicago: Science Research Associates, 1949), pp. 3-117.

RELIABILITY: For matched agreements of 10 judges on 340 persons representing 7 occupational categories: 95 per cent agreement. See p. 65.

VALIDITY: Correlations of Evaluative Participation Placements with occupation $(r = .91)$; with source of income $(r = .85)$; with house type $(r = .85)$; with dwelling area $(r = .82)$.

STANDARD RANKING: Many cities show six classes—Upper-upper, Lower-upper, Upper-middle, Lower-middle, Upper-lower, Lower-lower.

UTILITY: While the method takes a great deal of time and discerning skill, it does give a careful measure of evaluated class participation.

RESEARCH APPLICATIONS: A. B. Hollingshead, *Elmtown's Youth*, New York: John Wiley, 1949.
W. L. Warner, *Democracy in Jonesville*, New York: Harper's, 1949.
W. L. Warner and Paul S. Lunt, *The Social Life of a Modern Community*, Yankee City Series, Yale University Press, 1941.
Irwin W. Goffman, "Status Consistency and Preference for Change in Power Distribution," *American Sociological Review*, June, 1957, 22: 275-81.
Gregory P. Stone and William H. Form, "Instabilities in Status: The Problem of Hierarchy in the Community Study of Status Arrangements," *American Sociological Review*, April, 1953, 18: 149-62.

MEASURING STATUS BY THE
METHOD OF EVALUATED PARTICIPATION

W. L. Warner, Marchia Meeker, Kenneth Eells

The method of Evaluated Participation (E.P.) comprises six rating techniques. These are: (1) Rating by Matched Agreements, (2) Rating by Symbolic Placement, (3) Rating by Status Reputation, (4) Rating by Comparison, (5) Rating by Simple Assignment to a Class, and (6) Rating by Institutional Membership.

These techniques rest on the propositions that those who interact as the social system of a community evaluate the participation of

MASTER LIST OF SOCIAL-CLASS CONFIGURATIONS

Class	Carleton (Church member)	Withington (Church member)	Davis (Doctor)	Little (School girl)	Brown (Teacher)	Towne (Politician)
Above the Common Man I. U	Group One—the highest. People so high up they're social history around here. People who feel secure	The fancy crowd. The wealthy and prominent Federated Church people	The 400. The Society Class. The 398's who think they're 400's. Federated Church people	The High Class. The No. 1 Class	Upper Stratum. People with family and money	The Top Families. The Federated Church people
II. UM	Group Two. People who are working to get somewhere	Strictly middle class. People a notch or two below the fancy crowd	The fringe of society - - - - - - The upper-middle class	My class. Second highest class - - - - - - Higher-middle - - - - - - Middle-middle	"Upper-middle"	The solid people but don't go in for social things. The Methodist Church
Common Man III. LM	Third Group. More religious than intelligent	Working people. "Baptists"	The working class	Low-middle	Lower, but middle status	The plain, common people. Like most of the Baptists
IV. UL	The Fourth Group. At the bottom of the pile	Very Low. People with a persecution complex	→	Higher-lower	Lower class	The little people. The real poor people, but honest and fine
Below the Common Man V. LL	→	→	The lulus. People just like animals, not worth a damn	The lowest class	Canal renters. Older Poles. The people back of the tannery	The poor, but not respectable

112

Class		Other Informants
Above the Common Man	I. U	A group founded on wealth and ancient family
		People who look down on everyone else in town
		Snobs
		The silk stockings
		The landed gentry
		The aristocrats
		The Mainstreeters
		People who are in everything
		The community leaders
		Working hard to get in the 400
		Above average, but not tops
	II. UM	Not in the top group, but good substantial people
		The level just below the top group
		Prominent but not tops
		The strivers
		Good common people
		People with nice families but don't rate socially
		Nobodies (socially) but nice
		People just below the Country Club crowd
		Top of the common people
Common Man	III. LM	Average people
		Ordinary people
		Working people, but superior
		Top of the working people
		Not poor and not well off
	IV. UL	The Mill people
		The poor but honest
		Poor people, but nothing the matter with them
		The little people
		The younger Poles
		Poor but hard working
		Poor but respectable
		"We're poor (UL) but not as poor as a lot of people (LL)"
Below the Common Man	V. LL	The poor and unfortunate
		The chronic reliefers
		Tobacco road
		Poor whites
		Hillbillies
		River rats
		Peckerwoods
		Dirty and immoral
		(Those who) live like pigs
		People who scrape the bottom
		Goddamn yellow hammers

those around them, that the place where an individual participates is evaluated, and that the members of the community are explicitly or implicitly aware of the ranking and translate their evaluations of such social participation into social-class ratings that can be communicated to the investigator.

The Method of Matched Agreements will be illustrated. For precise instructions the analyst should refer to *Social Class in America* by Warner, Meeker, and Eells. There are four steps connected with the Technique of Matched Agreements. These are:

1. Rank orders are abstracted from the interviews of those who contributed this kind of information.
2. The several levels of each informant are compared for agreement and disagreement to establish the class system of the community.
3. The names of citizens assigned to the several classes are compared for the amount of agreement among the rank orders in placing people.
4. The agreements and disagreements for the several levels are counted to determine the degree of consistency in placement.

Social Class configurations are social maps of the informant's understanding of the social stratification of his city. As such they are evaluated schemes of who is, and who is not, who. The table on pages 112-13 is a social-class configuration of a medium-sized midwestern city. Note the nomenclature of various informants.

INDEX: CHAPIN'S SOCIAL STATUS (LIVING ROOM) SCALE, REVISED 1952

VARIABLE MEASURED: A family's socioeconomic position on the social class or social status scale.

DESCRIPTION: The scale attempts to measure social status by checking selected items in the interviewee's living room. The 21 question index contains four groupings: fixed features; standard furniture; furnishings and cultural resources; condition, or the distinctive personality of the living room, and aesthetic atmosphere. There are 17 questions on the items in the room and 4 on the condition of the room. A direction sheet is included with the check sheet.

WHERE PUBLISHED: F. Stuart Chapin, *Contemporary American Institutions*. New York: Harper & Bros., 1935, pp. 373-97.

RELIABILITY: $r = .90 \pm .03$ to $.99 \pm .004$.

VALIDITY: Living Room Scale score and occupation r = .57 to .58
Living Room Scale and income r = .39 to .65
Living Room Scale and participation r = .60 to .62

STANDARD SCORES:

Class		Range in Scores	Examples
Upper:	1. Upper part	250 and over	Professional, physician
	2. Lower part	200-249	Small-town banker
Middle:	1. Upper part	150-99	Factory manager
	2. Lower part	100-149	Skilled trades
Lower:	1. Upper part	50-99	Unemployed semiskilled
	2. Lower part	0-49	Unemployed unskilled

Tentative norms were established in 1942.

UTILITY: This is an objective scale that does not require a great amount of questioning or judgment on the part of the interviewer. It is simple to use, since all the user must do is check the items present and later multiply these checks by the respective weights. The time necessary is about 15 or 20 minutes.

The disadvantage of the scale lies in its questionable stability over a long period of time. As our culture changes, the possessions expected of the various classes may change correspondingly. The scale should be periodically revised to take into account new cultural developments that affect those possessions one expects to find in various status living rooms.

This scale is designed for use in experimental work wherever it is important to control the factors of social status and in child welfare work wherever it is desired to have an objective check on foster home standards.

RESEARCH APPLICATIONS: F. Stuart Chapin, "The Effects of Slum Clearance and Re-housing on Families and Community Relationships in Minneapolis," *American Journal of Sociology*, March, 1938, pp. 744-63.

F. Stuart Chapin and J. A. Jahn, "The Advantages of Work Relief over Direct Relief in Maintaining Morale in St. Paul in 1939," *American Journal of Sociology*, July, 1940, pp. 13-22.

G. A. Lundberg and Margaret Lansing, "The Sociography of Some Community Relations," *American Sociological Review*, June, 1937, pp. 318-35.

Walter T. Martin, "A Consideration of Differences in the Extent and Location of the Formal Associational Activities of Rural-Urban Fringe Residents," *American Sociological Review*, December, 1952, 17: 687-94.

THE SOCAL STATUS SCALE, REVISED, 1952

Visitor's Name _____

Schedule Number_____Date____

Family Name_____

Street Address_____

Town and State_____

Race _____

For original standardization or reliability and validity, which still holds, see F. Stuart Chapin, *Contemporary American Institutions,* Harper, 1935, or W. C. Brown (Dubuque, Iowa), 1948. Mean scores by occupational groups, as of 1950, are as follows: I. Professional, and II. Managerial and Proprietary, 177 (upper limit 607); III. Clerical, 147; IV. Skilled, 117; V. Semiskilled, 87; VI. Unskilled, 57.

Directions to Visitor

1. The following list of items is for the guidance of the recorder. Not all the features listed may be found in any one home. Entries on the schedules should, however, follow the order and numbering indicated. Weights appear (in parentheses) after the names of the items. Disregard these weights in recording. Only when the list is finally checked should the individual items be multiplied by these weights and the sum of the weighted scores be computed, and then only after leaving the home. All information is confidential.

2. Where the family has no real living room, but uses the room at night as a bedroom, or during the day as a kitchen or as a dining room, or as both, in addition to using the room as the chief gathering place of the family, please note this fact clearly and describe for what purposes the room is used. Scores corrected for these uses are as follows: (1) used as dining room, deduct 6 (but if a dining alcove is structurally built in, assign *no* penalty score); (2) used as kitchen, deduct 9; (3) used as bedroom or dining room and kitchen combined, deduct 12; (4) used as bedroom, dining room, and kitchen combined, deduct 15.

3. If the item you are scoring is present, enter the figure 1 on the *dotted* part of the line. If more than one item is present, write 2, 3, 4, etc., as the case may be. If the item is not present, enter a zero. Each division of each of the twenty items should have a number (0, 1, 2, 3, 4, etc.) entered opposite it. *Be sure that each item gets some number.* Leave no dotted line blank. A blank line means an oversight on your part.

4. Disregard figures in parentheses until all schedules are finished.

5. Always enter color of each family (white or Negro; specify if any other) below town and state.
6. Descriptions of items in Parts I and II.

    (1) Hardwood floors are usually made of narrow boards. Verify your own judgment by asking the occupant.

    (2) A large rug is one covering the entire floor area except a border of about 12 inches. (Usually a 9 x 12-foot rug.)

    (3) A drape is a covering over a window or windows. The drape may be either at the side of the window or across the top. Each draped window gets one point. Where the drape covers more than one window, give the question as many points as there are windows covered by the drape.

    (4) Only a real fireplace (one in which a coal, wood, or other fire, including gas, can be built) gets a number.

    (6) A library table is any table not used for serving meals. (Exclude such small tables as end tables, card tables, etc.) If a library table is used as a personal-social desk, number it either as a library table or as a personal desk, *but not as both.*

    (7) Armchairs include rocking chairs with arms.

    (8) Piano bench: a chair or stool does not get a point.

    (9) See No. 6. A personal-social desk is a writing desk.

    (10) If no bookcase is seen, be sure to ask if there is one in another room. Be sure to record any bookcase, whether in living room or in any other room, *except* professional library of doctor, lawyer, clergyman, teacher.

    (11) Sewing machine must be in living room in order to be marked minus two points. If outside living room, mark zero.

    (13) Alarm clock: same as No. 11.

    (14) Number of different periodicals *regularly bought* or *subscribed* to. Always get answer to this question by asking.

    (15) Newspapers: same as No. 14.

    (16) Telephone: to be recorded whether in living room or in some other room. Always ask concerning the telephone if you do not see one.

    (17) Radio and/or television: to be recorded whether in living room or in some other room. Always ask regarding these.

    (18) It is possible for a room to be both (*a*) spotted or stained and (*b*) dusty. In this case each gets *one* check.

    (20) "In good repair" means in good condition and not obviously patched up; therefore *only one* of the parts (*a, b,* or *c*) gets a check.

    (21) *Only one* of the parts (*a, b,* or *c*) gets a check.

Part I. Material Equipment and Cultural Expression of the Living Room of the Home

1. Floor,

    softwood (6) _____

    hardwood (10) _____

2. Large rug or wall-to-wall carpet (8) _____

3. Windows with shades and curtains, or with Venetian blinds and drapes (each window 2) _____

4. Fireplace with 3 or more utensils (8) _____

5. Artificial light,

    electric (8) _____

    kerosene (−2) _____

6. Library table (8) _____

7. Armchairs (8 each) _____

8. Piano bench (4) _____

9. Desk: personal-social (8) _____

10. Bookcases with books (8 each) _____

11. Sewing machine (−2) _____

12. Couch pillows (2 each) _____

13. Alarm clock (−2) _____

14. Periodicals (8 each) _____

15. Newspapers (8 each) _____

16. Telephone (8) _____

17. Radio (2), television (6); both (8) _____

Score on Part I _____

Part II. Condition of Articles in Living Room

18. Cleanliness of room and furnishings

    a. Spotted or stained (−4) _____

    b. Dusty (−2) _____

    c. Spotless and dustless (+2) _____

19. Orderliness of room and furnishings

    a. Articles strewn about in disorder (−2) _____

    b. Articles in place or in usable order (+2) _____

20. Condition of repair of articles and furnishings

    a. Broken, scratched, frayed, ripped, or torn (−4) _____

    b. Articles or furnishings patched up (−2) _____

    c. Articles or furnishings in good repair and well kept (+2) _____

21. Record your general impression of good taste

    a. Bizarre, clashing, inharmonious, or offensive (−4) _____

    b. Drab, monotonous, neutral, inoffensive (−2) _____

    c. Attractive in a positive way, harmonious, quiet and restful (+2) _____

    Score on Part II _____

    Total score,* Parts I and II _____

* With penalties deducted.

INDEX: SEWELL'S SHORT FORM OF THE FARM SOCIOECONOMIC STATUS SCALE

VARIABLE MEASURED: The socioeconomic status of farm families.

DESCRIPTION: There are 14 items including construction of house, room-person ratio, lighting facilities, water piped into house, power washer, refrigerator, radio, telephone, automobile, church or Sunday School, and wife attends church or Sunday School. These items can be classified as first measuring the material possessions (6 items), the cultural possessions (6 items), and last measuring the social participation (2 items). This short form scale was adapted from an original scale including 39 items. The correlation between the long and short form is .95.

WHERE PUBLISHED: William H. Sewell, "A Short Form of the Farm Family Socioeconomic Status Scale," *Rural Sociology,* Vol. 8, No. 2, June, 1943.

RELIABILITY: $r = .81$ to .87.

VALIDITY:

Scale Scores Correlated with	257 Family Sample	800 Family Sample
Chapin, Social Status Scale, 1933	0.82	*
Dickins revision of Chapin Scale	0.82	*
Clark Rural Home Equipment Scale	0.71	*
Experimental Scale	0.97	0.96
Cash Income per annum	0.37	0.63
Net Wealth per family	0.57	0.55
Expenditures for living per family	0.52	0.63
Total money value of living per annum	0.51	0.67

* Scores on these scales were not available for this sample. These coefficients are reported in William H. Sewell, "The Development of a Sociometric Scale," *Sociometry,* V (September, 1940), 279-97.

STANDARD SCORES: Mean Scores on the Short Scale for Various
Tenure Groups in the 3 Samples.

Tenure Status	Oklahoma	Louisiana	Kansas
Owner	61.4	61.5	71.8
Tenant	54.9	53.7	65.8
Cropper	—	50.9	—
Laborer	50.0	47.1	60.4

UTILITY: Short Scale is composed of only 14 items. A family can be
rated on the average in 5 minutes. The questions can be so formulated
that they can be answered by school children and others away from
home.

RESEARCH APPLICATION: George A. Dale, "Correlations of Scores
Secured by Interview with Scores Based on Observation for the
Sewell Farm Family Socioeconomic Status Scale," *Rural Sociology,*
September, 1954, 19: 291. (Correlation of $r = .894$ secured.)

FARM FAMILY SOCIOECONOMIC STATUS SCALE

(Short Form)

Score

_____ 1. Construction of house:
Brick, stucco, etc., or painted frame   Unpainted frame or other
Score: (5)   (3)

_____ 2. Room-person ratio:
Number of rooms _____ + Number of persons _____ = _____
Ratio: Below 1.00   1.00-1.99   2.00 and up
Score: (3)   (5)   (7)

_____ 3. Lighting facilities:

	Electric	Gas, mantle, or pressure	Oil lamps, other, or none
Score:	(8)	(6)	(3)

_____ 4. Water piped into house?   Y (8)   N (4)

_____ 5. Power washer?   Y (6)   N (3)

_____ 6. Refrigerator:

	Mechanical	Ice	Other or none
Score:	(8)	(6)	(3)

_____ 7. Radio?   Y (6)   N (3)

_____ 8. Telephone?   Y (6)   N (3)

_____ 9. Automobile? (Other than truck)   Y (5)   N (2)

_____ 10. Family takes daily newspaper?   Y (6)   N (3)

_____ 11. Wife's education:

Grades completed:	0-7	8	9-11	12	13 and up
Score:	(2)	(4)	(6)	(7)	(8)

_____ 12. Husband's education:

Grades completed:	0-7	8	9-11	12	13 and up
Score:	(3)	(5)	(6)	(7)	(8)

_____ 13. Husband attends church or Sunday school?   Y (5)   N (2)
(¼ of meetings)

_____ 14. Wife attends church or Sunday school?   Y (5)   N (2)
(¼ of meetings)

_____ Scale Score

Group Structure and Dynamics

This section contains five scales, each of which measures a different variable relating to group structure and dynamics. Hemphill's Index of Group Dimensions, which ascertains thirteen dimensions of a group, is the most ambitious attempt to measure the structural properties of groups. Bales's Interactional Process Analysis is a nominal scale, widely used to assess the characteristics of personal interaction in problem-solving groups. Seashore's Group Cohesiveness Index provides a measure of the strength of a group to maintain its identity and to persist. The Sociometry Scales of Sociometric Choice and Sociometric Preference reveal the interpersonal attractions of members in groups. These scales may be widely adapted to suit many different kinds of situations. They are useful not only to a researcher seeking basic relationships, but also to the action researcher or social worker. New groupings of individuals can be quickly arranged and new measurements of morale or productivity can be made. The Bogardus Social Distance Scale may also be adapted to many different purposes. The social distance between two persons, person and group, or between groups can be measured in such diverse situations as that involving an outgroup member and a country, a community, or an organization.

INDEX: HEMPHILL'S INDEX OF GROUP DIMENSIONS

VARIABLE MEASURED: The index is designed to measure group dimensions or characteristics.

DESCRIPTION: The index is built upon thirteen comparatively independent group dimensions: autonomy, control, flexibility, hedonic tone, homogeneity, intimacy, participation, permeability, polarization, potency, stability, stratification, and viscidity. The 150 items are answered on a five-point scale. The dimensions were selected from a list of group adjectives used by authorities. Items were suggested from a free-response type questionnaire administered to 500 individuals, and 5 judges then put the items into the dimensional categories.

WHERE PUBLISHED: John K. Hemphill, *Group Dimensions: A Manual for Their Measurement*, Research Monograph Number 87, Columbus, Ohio: Bureau of Business Research, Ohio State University, 1956.

RELIABILITY: Split-half reliabilities range from .59 to .87. The relationship between an item and high-low categories ranges from .03 to .78 with a median of .36 on the keyed items and from .01 to .36 with a median of .12 on the randomly selected items. Intercorrelation of dimension scores ranges from —.54 to .81, with most within +.29 (which has a .01 significance level). Agreement between different reporters of the same group ranges from .53 to .74.

VALIDITY: The dimension scores describing the characteristics of two quite different groups vary accordingly, while those describing the characteristics of two similar groups are quite similar.

UTILITY: The index can be useful in studying the relationships between the behavior of leaders and characteristics of groups in which they function. Although fairly long, it is comparatively easy to administer and score.

RESEARCH APPLICATIONS: Validation and Reliability studies on 200 descriptions of 35 groups. John K. Hemphill and Charles M. Westie, "The Measurement of Group Dimensions," *The Journal of Psychology*, April, 1950, 29: 325-42.
V. J. Bentz, "Leadership: A Study of Social Interaction," unpublished report, Bureau of Business Research, Ohio State University.
M. Seeman, "A Sociological Approach to Leadership: The Case of the School Executive," unpublished report, Bureau of Business Research, Ohio State University.

GROUP DIMENSIONS DESCRIPTIONS QUESTIONNAIRE

Directions:

Record your answer to each of the items on the answer sheet for the group you are describing. Make no marks on the question booklet itself.

In considering each item go through the following steps:

1. Read the item carefully.

2. Think about how well the item tells something about the group you are describing.

3. Find the number on the answer sheet that corresponds with the number of the item you are considering.

4. After each number on the answer sheet you will find five pairs of dotted lines lettered A, B, C, D, or E.

If the item you are considering tells something about the group that is definitely true blacken the space between the pair of dotted lines headed by A.

If the item you are considering tells something that is mostly true, blacken the space between the pair of lines headed by B.

If the item tells something that is to an equal degree both true and false, or you are undecided about whether it is true or false, blacken the space between the pair of lines headed by C.

If the item you are considering tells something that is mostly false, blacken the space between the pair of lines headed by D.

If the item you are considering tells something about the group that is definitely false, blacken the space between the pair of dotted lines headed by E.

5. When blackening the space between a pair of lines, fill in all the space with a heavy black line. If you should make an error in marking your answer, erase thoroughly the mark you made and then indicate the correct answer.

6. In rare cases where you believe that an item does not apply at all to the group or you feel that you do not have sufficient information to make any judgment concerning what the item tells about the group, leave that item blank.

7. After you have completed one item, proceed to the next one in order. You may have as long as you need to complete your description. Be sure the number on the answer sheet corresponds with the number of the item being answered in the booklet.

Questions:

The questions that follow make it possible to describe objectively certain characteristics of social groups. The items simply describe characteristics of groups; they do not judge whether the characteristic is desirable or undesirable. Therefore, in no way are the questions to be considered a "test" either of the groups or of the person answering the questions. We simply want an objective description of what the group is like.

1. The group has well understood but unwritten rules concerning member conduct.

2. Members fear to express their real opinions.
3. The only way a member may leave the group is to be expelled.
4. No explanation need be given by a member wishing to be absent from the group.
5. An individual's membership can be dropped should he fail to live up to the standards of the group.
6. Members of the group work under close supervision.
7. Only certain kinds of ideas may be expressed freely within the group.
8. A member may leave the group by resigning at any time he wishes.
9. A request made by a member to leave the group can be refused.
10. A member has to think twice before speaking in the group's meetings.
11. Members are occasionally forced to resign.
12. The members of the group are subject to strict discipline.
13. The group is rapidly increasing in size.
14. Members are constantly leaving the group.
15. There is a large turnover of members within the group.
16. Members are constantly dropping out of the group but new members replace them.
17. During the entire time of the group's existence no member has left.
18. Each member's personal life is known to other members of the group.
19. Members of the group lend each other money.
20. A member has the chance to get to know all other members of the group.
21. Members are not in close enough contact to develop likes or dislikes for one another.
22. Members of the group do small favors for one another.
23. All members know each other very well.
24. Each member of the group knows all other members by their first names.
25. Members are in daily contact either outside or within the group.
26. Members of the group are personal friends.
27. Certain members discuss personal affairs among themselves.
28. Members of the group know the family backgrounds of other members of the group.
29. Members address each other by their first names.
30. The group is made up of individuals who do not know each other well.
31. The opinions of all members are considered as equal.

32. The group's officers hold a higher status in the group than other members.
33. The older members of the group are granted special privileges.
34. The group is controlled by the actions of a few members.
35. Every member of the group enjoys the same group privileges.
36. Experienced members are in charge of the group.
37. Certain problems are discussed only among the group's officers.
38. Certain members have more influence on the group than others.
39. Each member of the group has as much power as any other member.
40. An individual's standing in the group is determined only by how much he gets done.
41. Certain members of the group hold definite office in the group.
42. The original members of the group are given special privileges.
43. Personal dissatisfaction with the group is too small to be brought up.
44. Members continually grumble about the work they do for the group.
45. The group does its work with no great vim, vigor, or pleasure.
46. A feeling of failure prevails in the group.
47. There are frequent intervals of laughter during group meetings.
48. The group works independently of other groups.
49. The group has support from outside.
50. The group is an active representative of a larger group.
51. The group's activities are influenced by a larger group of which it is a part.
52. People outside the group decide on what work the group is to do.
53. The group follows the examples set by other groups.
54. The group is one of many similar groups that form one large organization.
55. The things the group does are approved by a group higher up.
56. The group joins with other groups in carrying out its activities.
57. The group is a small part of a larger group.
58. The group is under outside pressure.
59. Members are disciplined by an outside group.
60. Plans of the group are made by other groups above it.
61. The members allow nothing to interfere with the progress of the group.
62. Members gain a feeling of being honored by being recognized as one of the group.
63. Membership in the group is a way of acquiring general social status.
64. Failure of the group would mean little to individual members.

65. The activities of the group take up less than ten per cent of each member's waking time.
66. Members gain in prestige among outsiders by joining the group.
67. A mistake by one member of the group might result in hardship for all.
68. The activities of the group take up over ninety per cent of each member's waking time.
69. Membership in the group serves as an aid to vocational advancement.
70. Failure of the group would mean nothing to most members.
71. Each member would lose his self-respect if the group should fail.
72. Membership in the group gives members a feeling of superiority.
73. The activities of the group take up over half the time each member is awake.
74. Failure of the group would lead to embarrassment for members.
75. Members are not rewarded for effort put out for the group.
76. There are two or three members of the group who generally take the same side on any group issue.
77. Certain members are hostile to other members.
78. There is constant bickering among members of the group.
79. Members know that each one looks out for the other one as well as for himself.
80. Certain members of the group have no respect for other members.
81. Certain members of the group are considered uncooperative.
82. There is a constant tendency toward conniving against one another among parts of the group.
83. Members of the group work together as a team.
84. Certain members of the group are responsible for petty quarrels and some animosity among other members.
85. There are tensions among subgroups that tend to interfere with the group's activities.
86. Certain members appear to be incapable of working as part of the group.
87. There is an undercurrent of feeling among members that tends to pull the group apart.
88. Anyone who has sufficient interest in the group to attend its meetings is considered a member.
89. The group engages in membership drives.
90. New members are welcomed to the group on the basis "the more the merrier."
91. A new member may join only after an old member resigns.
92. A college degree is required for membership in the group.
93. A person may enter the group by expressing a desire to join.
94. Anyone desiring to enter the group is welcome.

95. Membership is open to anyone willing to further the purpose of the group.
96. Prospective members are carefully examined before they enter the group.
97. No applicants for membership in the group are turned down.
98. No special training is required for membership in the group.
99. Membership depends upon the amount of education an individual has.
100. People interested in joining the group are asked to submit references which are checked.
101. There is a high degree of participation on the part of members.
102. If a member of the group is not productive he is not encouraged to remain.
103. Work of the group is left to those who are considered most capable for the job.
104. Members are interested in the group but not all of them want to work.
105. The group has a reputation for not getting much done.
106. Each member of the group is on one or more active committees.
107. The work of the group is well divided among members.
108. Every member of the group does not have a job to do.
109. The work of the group is frequently interrupted by having nothing to do.
110. There are long periods during which the group does nothing.
111. The group is directed toward one particular goal.
112. The group divides its efforts among several purposes.
113. The group operates with sets of conflicting plans.
114. The group has only one main purpose.
115. The group knows exactly what it has to get done.
116. The group is working toward many different goals.
117. The group does many things that are not directly related to its main purpose.
118. Each member of the group has a clear idea of the group's goals.
119. The objective of the group is specific.
120. Certain members meet for one thing and others for a different thing.
121. The group has major purposes which to some degree are in conflict.
122. The objectives of the group have never been clearly recognized
123. The group is very informal.
124. A list of rules and regulations is given to each member.
125. The group has meetings at regularly scheduled times.
126. The group is organized along semimilitary lines.
127. The group's meetings are not planned or organized.

128. The group has an organization chart.
129. The group has rules to guide its activities.
130. The group is staffed according to a table of organization.
131. The group keeps a list of names of members.
132. Group meetings are conducted according to "Robert's Rules of Order."
133. There is a recognized right and wrong way of going about group activities.
134. Most matters that come up before the group are voted upon.
135. The group meets at any place that happens to be handy.
136. The members of the group vary in amount of ambition.
137. Members of the group are from the same social class.
138. Some members are interested in altogether different things than other members.
139. The group contains members with widely varying backgrounds.
140. The group contains whites and Negroes.
141. Members of the group are all about the same ages.
142. A few members of the group have greater ability than others.
143. A number of religious beliefs are represented by members of the group.
144. Members of the group vary greatly in social background.
145. All members of the group are of the same sex.
146. The ages of members range over a period of at least 20 years.
147. Members come into the group with quite different family backgrounds.
148. Members of the group vary widely in amount of experience.
149. Members vary in the number of years they have been in the group.
150. The group includes members of different races.

SCORING KEY AND DIRECTIONS FOR SCORING

A subject's score for a particular dimension is the sum of the item scores for that dimension. For example, the raw score for the dimension "Control" is the sum of the scores for items 1 to 12 inclusive. The total (raw) score for this dimension can range from 12 to 60.

Occasionally a respondent may fail to indicate his answer. Such omissions are scored as C responses (neither true nor false). However, if the number of omitted items exceeds half the total number of items assigned to a given dimension, no score for that dimension is assigned. In general, experience has shown that few respondents deliberately omit items.

The answers are marked on a separate answer sheet (IBM Answer Sheet No. 1100 A 3870). A separate blank answer sheet may be used for preparing a scoring key for each dimension.

SCORING KEYS

Control	A	B	C	D	E
1	5	4	3	2	1
2	5	4	3	2	1
3	5	4	3	2	1
4	1	2	3	4	5
5	5	4	3	2	1
6	5	4	3	2	1
7	5	4	3	2	1
8	1	2	3	4	5
9	5	4	3	2	1
10	5	4	3	2	1
11	5	4	3	2	1
12	5	4	3	2	1

Stability	A	B	C	D	E
13	1	2	3	4	5
14	1	2	3	4	5
15	1	2	3	4	5
16	1	2	3	4	5
17	5	4	3	2	1

Intimacy	A	B	C	D	E
18	5	4	3	2	1
19	5	4	3	2	1
20	5	4	3	2	1
21	1	2	3	4	5
22	5	4	3	2	1
23	5	4	3	2	1
24	5	4	3	2	1
25	5	4	3	2	1
26	5	4	3	2	1
27	5	4	3	2	1
28	5	4	3	2	1
29	5	4	3	2	1
30	1	2	3	4	5

Stratification	A	B	C	D	E
31	1	2	3	4	5
32	5	4	3	2	1
33	5	4	3	2	1
34	5	4	3	2	1
35	1	2	3	4	5
36	5	4	3	2	1
37	5	4	3	2	1
38	5	4	3	2	1

Stratification	A	B	C	D	E
39	1	2	3	4	5
40	5	4	3	2	1
41	5	4	3	2	1
42	5	4	3	2	1

Hedonic Tone	A	B	C	D	E
43	5	4	3	2	1
44	1	2	3	4	5
45	1	2	3	4	5
46	1	2	3	4	5
47	5	4	3	2	1

Autonomy	A	B	C	D	E
48	5	4	3	2	1
49	1	2	3	4	5
50	1	2	3	4	5
51	1	2	3	4	5
52	1	2	3	4	5
53	1	2	3	4	5
54	1	2	3	4	5
55	1	2	3	4	5
56	1	2	3	4	5
57	1	2	3	4	5
58	1	2	3	4	5
59	1	2	3	4	5
60	1	2	3	4	5

Potency	A	B	C	D	E
61	5	4	3	2	1
62	5	4	3	2	1
63	5	4	3	2	1
64	1	2	3	4	5
65	1	2	3	4	5
66	5	4	3	2	1
67	5	4	3	2	1
68	5	4	3	2	1
69	5	4	3	2	1
70	1	2	3	4	5
71	5	4	3	2	1
72	5	4	3	2	1
73	5	4	3	2	1
74	5	4	3	2	1
75	1	2	3	4	5

Viscidity	A	B	C	D	E
76	1	2	3	4	5
77	1	2	3	4	5
78	1	2	3	4	5
79	5	4	3	2	1
80	1	2	3	4	5
81	1	2	3	4	5
82	1	2	3	4	5
83	5	4	3	2	1
84	1	2	3	4	5
85	1	2	3	4	5
86	1	2	3	4	5
87	1	2	3	4	5

Polarization	A	B	C	D	E
111	5	4	3	2	1
112	1	2	3	4	5
113	1	2	3	4	5
114	5	4	3	2	1
115	5	4	3	2	1
116	1	2	3	4	5
117	1	2	3	4	5
118	5	4	3	2	1
119	5	4	3	2	1
120	1	2	3	4	5
121	1	2	3	4	5
122	1	2	3	4	5

Permeability	A	B	C	D	E
88	5	4	3	2	1
89	5	4	3	2	1
90	5	4	3	2	1
91	1	2	3	4	5
92	1	2	3	4	5
93	5	4	3	2	1
94	5	4	3	2	1
95	5	4	3	2	1
96	1	2	3	4	5
97	5	4	3	2	1
98	5	4	3	2	1
99	1	2	3	4	5
100	1	2	3	4	5

Flexibility	A	B	C	D	E
123	5	4	3	2	1
124	1	2	3	4	5
125	1	2	3	4	5
126	1	2	3	4	5
127	5	4	3	2	1
128	1	2	3	4	5
129	1	2	3	4	5
130	1	2	3	4	5
131	1	2	3	4	5
132	1	2	3	4	5
133	1	2	3	4	5
134	1	2	3	4	5
135	5	4	3	2	1

Participation	A	B	C	D	E
101	5	4	3	2	1
102	5	4	3	2	1
103	1	2	3	4	5
104	1	2	3	4	5
105	1	2	3	4	5
106	5	4	3	2	1
107	5	4	3	2	1
108	1	2	3	4	5
109	1	2	3	4	5
110	1	2	3	4	5

Homogeneity	A	B	C	D	E
136	5	4	3	2	1
137	1	2	3	4	5
138	1	2	3	4	5
139	1	2	3	4	5
140	1	2	3	4	5
141	5	4	3	2	1
142	1	2	3	4	5
143	1	2	3	4	5
144	1	2	3	4	5
145	5	4	3	2	1
146	1	2	3	4	5
147	1	2	3	4	5
148	1	2	3	4	5
149	1	2	3	4	5
150	1	2	3	4	5

GROUP DIMENSIONS PROFILE AND FACE SHEET

Name _____ Age _____ Date _____

Name of group _____

Length of your membership _____ No. of group members _____

General purpose of the group _____

Dimension		*Stanine Score* 1 2 3 4 5 6 7 8 9
A	Autonomy	. . . .
B	Control	. . . .
C	Flexibility	. . . .
D	Hedonic Tone	. . . .
E	Homogeneity	. . . .
F	Intimacy	. . . .
G	Participation	. . . .
H	Permeability	. . . .
I	Polarization	. . . .
J	Potency	. . . .
K	Stability	. . . .
L	Stratification	. . . .
M	Viscidity	. . . .

INDEX: BALES'S INTERACTION PROCESS ANALYSIS

VARIABLE MEASURED: Group Interaction.

DESCRIPTION: This index consists of twelve categories—shows solidarity, shows tension release, agrees, gives suggestion, gives opinion, gives orientation, asks for orientation, asks for opinion, asks for suggestion, disagrees, shows tension, shows antagonism. Scoring is made by designating each person in the group with a number. All interaction is analyzed according to the category and marked in the fashion of 1-5 or 1-0 as the interaction takes place. After observation a summary or profile can be constructed and inferences made to describe the underlying workings of the group.

WHERE PUBLISHED: R. F. Bales, *Interaction Process Analysis: A Method for the Study of Small Groups,* Cambridge, Mass.: Addison-Wesley, 1950.

RELIABILITY: With competent and trained observers an inter-observer correlation of between .75 and .95 can be obtained.

VALIDITY: Face validity.

UTILITY: A general purpose, standard set of categories well suited for the observation and analysis of small groups. The chief disadvantage is that the training of observers requires long practice. Frequent retraining is also necessary.

RESEARCH APPLICATIONS: See the bibliography of small group research in A. Paul Hare, Edgar F. Borgatta, and Robert F. Bales (eds.), *Small Groups: Studies in Social Interaction,* New York: Alfred A. Knopf, 1955.

1	SHOWS SOLIDARITY, raises other's status, gives help, reward:					
2	SHOWS TENSION RELEASE, jokes, laughs, shows satisfaction:					
3	AGREES, shows passive acceptance, understands, concurs, complies:					
4	GIVES SUGGESTION, direction, implying autonomy for other:					
5	GIVES OPINION, evaluation, analysis, expresses feeling, wish:					
6	GIVES ORIENTATION, information, repeats, clarifies, confirms:					
7	ASKS FOR ORIENTATION, information, repetition, confirmation:					
8	ASKS FOR OPINION, evaluation, analysis, expression of feeling:					
9	ASKS FOR SUGGESTION, direction, possible ways of action:					
10	DISAGREES, shows passive rejection, formality, withholds help:					
11	SHOWS TENSION, asks for help, withdraws "Out of Field":					
12	SHOWS ANTAGONISM, deflates other's status, defends or asserts self:					

PERCENT: O

Prepared for use with
Interaction Process Analysis
by Robert F. Bales
PRINTED IN U.S.A.

INTERACTION SCORING FORM
Published by
ADDISON-WESLEY PRESS, INC.
Cambridge 42, Mass.

Group _____

Date _____

Observer _____

INDEX: SEASHORE'S GROUP COHESIVENESS INDEX

VARIABLE MEASURED: The index measures group cohesiveness, defined as attraction to the group or resistance to leaving.

DESCRIPTION: The test consists of three questions: "Do you feel that you are really a part of your work group?" "If you had a chance to do the same kind of work for the same pay, in another work group, how would you feel about moving?" and "How does your work group compare with other work groups at Midwest on each of the following points?"—The way the men get along together, the way the men stick together, and the way the men help each other on the job. The first two questions can be answered by five degrees, while the three items of the third question are answered by four degrees.

WHERE PUBLISHED: Stanley E. Seashore, *Group Cohesiveness in the Industrial Work Group,* Ann Arbor: Survey Research Center, Institute for Social Research, University of Michigan, 1954.

RELIABILITY: Intercorrelations among mean scale values for the groups on scales comprising the index of cohesiveness ranged from .15 to .70.

VALIDITY: The variance found between groups on this scale was significant beyond the .001 level.

UTILITY: As the questions are phrased, the index is especially set up for an industrial situation. It can probably, with a few changes, be adapted to almost any situation where an index of group cohesiveness is required. The test takes very little time to administer. The subject should be assured that his replies will be kept confidential.

RESEARCH APPLICATIONS: The study of 228 section-shift groups in a company manufacturing heavy machinery, described in the aforementioned Seashore article.

INDEX OF GROUP COHESIVENESS

"Do you feel that you are really a part of your work group?"

- ☐ Really a part of my work group
- ☐ Included in most ways
- ☐ Included in some ways, but not in others
- ☐ Don't feel I really belong
- ☐ Don't work with any one group of people
  - ☐ Not Ascertained

"If you had a chance to do the same kind of work for the same pay, in another work group, how would you feel about moving?"

- ☐ Would want very much to move
- ☐ Would rather move than stay where I am
- ☐ Would make no difference to me
- ☐ Would rather stay where I am than move
- ☐ Would want very much to stay where I am
  - ☐ Not Ascertained

"How does your work group compare with other work groups at Midwest on each of the following points?"

	Better than most	About the same as most	Not as good as most	Not ascertained
The way the men get along together	☐	☐	☐	☐
The way the men stick together	☐	☐	☐	☐
The way the men help each other on the job	☐	☐	☐	☐

INDEX: SOCIOMETRY SCALES OF SOCIOMETRIC CHOICE
AND SOCIOMETRIC PREFERENCE

VARIABLE MEASURED: The degree to which individuals are accepted in a group, relationships that exist among individuals, and structure of the group.

DESCRIPTION: Results are most satisfactory for small cohesive groups. The sociometric technique consists of asking each individual in a group to state with whom among the members of the group he would prefer to associate for specific activities or in particular situations. Criteria (selected areas that should include different aspects of possible association: work, play, visiting) range in number from 1 to 8 or more; and choices, from 1 to as many as desired by the researcher.

WHERE PUBLISHED: J. L. Moreno *Who Shall Survive?* Beacon, N.Y.: Beacon House, 1934.

RELIABILITY: Loeb's correlation between odd-even items $r = .65$ to $.85$

Loeb's correlation between split-halves $r = .53$ to $.85$

Mary L. Northway between general criteria $r = .64$ to $.84$

Mary L. Northway between skill criteria $r = .37$ to $.50$

Correlations between scores on tests given at different times $r = .74$

Constancy of choice (actual preference on 1st test repeated later on) $r = .69$

VALIDITY: Eugene Byrd comparison of sociometric choice with actual choice and then an 8-week interval retest shows $r = .76, .80, .89$. See Eugene Byrd, "A Study of Validity and Constancy of Choices in a Sociometric Test," *Sociometry,* 1946, 9: 21.

N. Gronlund comparison of judgment of teachers vs. testing shows $r = .59$. See N. Gronlund, *Accuracies of Teachers' Judgments concerning the Sociometric Status of Sixth Grade Pupils,* Sociometry Monograph No. 25, Beacon, N.Y.: Beacon House, 1951.

(For discussion of reliability and validity, see Mary L. Northway, *A Primer of Sociometry,* Toronto: University of Toronto Press, 1952, pp. 16-20. Also cf. Stuart C. Dodd and Louise H. Klein, " 'Likeratings' in the Prediction of Human Behavior," *Language and Speech,* April-June, 1962, 5: 54-66.

STANDARD SCORES: None.

RESEARCH APPLICATION: J. L. Moreno, *Who Shall Survive? A New Approach to the Problem of Human Relationships,* Beacon, N.Y.: Beacon House, 1934. See also J. L. Moreno, *Sociometry and the Science of Man,* Beacon House, 1956.

Helen H. Jennings, *Leadership and Isolation: A Study of Personality in Interpersonal Relations,* 2nd ed., New York: David McKay Co., 1950.

Urie Bronfenbrenner, *The Measurement of Sociometric Status, Structure and Development,* Sociometry Monograph No. 6, Beacon House, 1945.

Fred Massarik, Robert Tannenbaum, Murray Rahane, and Irving Weschler, "Sociometric Choice and Organizational Effectiveness: A Multi-Relational Approach," *Sociometry,* August, 1953, pp. 211-38; or see their *Leadership and Organization,* McGraw-Hill, 1961, pp. 346-70.

Leslie D. Zeleny, "Selection of Compatible Flying Partners," *American Journal of Sociology,* March, 1947, 52: 424-31.

John H. Jacobs, "The Application of Sociometry to Industry," *Sociometry,* May, 1945, pp. 181-98.

George A. Lundberg and Lenore Dickson, "Inter-Ethnic Relations in a High School Population," *American Journal of Sociology,* July, 1952, 57: 1-10.

Harrison White, "Management Conflict and Sociometric Structure," *American Journal of Sociology,* September, 1961, 67: 185-99.

For an excellent review of the literature on "Measures of Sociometric Structure" see M. Glanzer and R. Glaser, "Techniques for the Study of Group Structure and Behavior: I. Analysis of Structure," *Psychological Bulletin,* September, 1959, 56: 317-32. Cf. J. L. Moreno, "Contributions of Sociometry to Research Methodology in Sociology," *American Sociological Review,* June, 1947, 12: 287-92.

SPONTANEOUS CHOICE TEST

Opposite each name check how you feel about persons in your group.

	Like	Dislike	Indifferent
Mary J.			
James F.			
John J.			
Etc.			

141

SOCIOMETRIC PREFERENCE TEST

Choose five persons you would most like to work with.* Mark 1st, 2nd, 3rd, 4th, 5th choice.

Mary J.	
James F.	
John J.	
Sam E.	
Etc.	

* Many criteria may be employed. For example, to have in a discussion group, to have in your neighborhood, to play bridge with, to work on a project with, etc.

INDEX: BOGARDUS SOCIAL DISTANCE SCALE

VARIABLE MEASURED: The social distance or degree of social acceptance that exists between given persons and certain social groups. The scale may be adapted to measure the social distance between two persons or between two or more social groups. The method has been applied to racial distance, regional distance, sex distance, age distance, parent-child distance, educational distance, class distance, occupational distance, religious distance, international distance.

DESCRIPTION: Typically, a group of persons are asked to rank a series of social types with respect to the degrees of social distance on seven attributes starting with *acceptance to close kinship by marriage* and concluding with *would exclude from my country.* One hundred persons acting as judges have identified these seven attributes among 60 as those ordered on a continuant of social distance.

WHERE PUBLISHED: Best source is Emory S. Bogardus, *Social Distance,* Yellow Springs, Ohio: Antioch Press, 1959; Emory S. Bogardus, *Immigration and Race Attitudes,* Boston: D. C. Heath, 1928; E. S. Bogardus, "A Social Distance Scale," *Sociology and Social Research,* Jan.-Feb., 1933, 265-71. Excellent instructions may be found in William J. Goode and Paul K. Hatt, *Methods in Social Research,* New York: McGraw-Hill, 1952, pp. 26, 245-49.

RELIABILITY: Split-half reliability coefficients reported at .90 or higher in repeated tests by Eugene L. Hartley and Ruth E. Hartley.

VALIDITY: Theodore Newcomb reports high validity if we use "agreement with other scales that in certain particulars are more exact." Application of the known-group method is advocated in determination of validity. This involves finding groups known to be favorable toward some of the ethnic types and unfavorable toward others. If the responses of these groups fit the requisite pattern, evidence for validity may be accepted. For full discussion see E. S. Bogardus, *Social Distance,* Yellow Springs, Ohio: Antioch Press, 1959, pp. 92-95.

SCORING: A variety of scoring methods has been used. A simple method that has been found to be as reliable as the more complex ones is that of counting the numbers of the "nearest column" that is checked. That is, if the racial distance quotient, *RDQ,* of a number of persons is desired, then the arithmetic mean of the total number of the "nearest columns" that are checked by all the subjects for each race is obtained. If the *RDQ* of a person is sought, then the arithmetic mean of the total numbers of the "nearest column" for each race is obtained.

STANDARD SCORES: Racial Distance Quotients Given Racial Groups in 1956 by 2,053 selected persons throughout the United States.

1.	Americans (U.S. White)	1.08
2.	Canadians	1.16
3.	English	1.23
4.	French	1.47
5.	Irish	1.56
6.	Swedish	1.57
7.	Scots	1.60
8.	Germans	1.61
9.	Hollanders	1.63
10.	Norwegians	1.56
11.	Finns	1.80
12.	Italians	1.89
13.	Poles	2.07
14.	Spanish	2.08
15.	Greeks	2.09
16.	Jews	2.15
17.	Czechs	2.22
18.	Armenians	2.33
19.	Japanese Americans	2.34
20.	Indians (**American**)	2.35
21.	Filipinos	2.46
22.	Mexican Americans	2.51
23.	Turks	2.52
24.	Russians	2.56
25.	Chinese	2.68
26.	Japanese	2.70
27.	Negroes	2.74
28.	Mexicans	2.79
29.	Indians (from India)	2.80
30.	Koreans	2.83

Arithmetic Mean of 61,590 Racial Reactions   2.08.

UTILITY: The Bogardus Scale may be used to estimate the amount of potential and real conflict existing between any cultural groups, anywhere in the industrial, political, racial, religious, and other phases of life. It also helps to determine the extent of the trend toward conflict or toward cooperation between groups. The test is easy to administer and to score. It can be adapted easily to other problems of social distance.

A good illustration of such an adaptation is to be found in the Mock

Table for a Scale to Measure the Attractiveness of Different Communities. See William J. Goode and Paul K. Hatt, *Methods in Social Research,* New York: McGraw-Hill, 1952, p. 248. The fullest description of applications is to be found in Emory S. Bogardus, *Social Distance,* Yellow Springs, Ohio: Antioch Press, 1959.

RESEARCH APPLICATIONS: Barber, Bernard. *Social Stratification.* New York: Harcourt, Brace & Co., 1957.

Bardis, Panos D. "Social Distance among Foreign Students," *Sociology and Social Research,* 41: 112-15.

―――. "Social Distance in a Greek Metropolitan City," *Social Science,* April, 1962, 37: 108-111.

Best, W. H., and Sohner, C. P. "Social Distance Methodology in the Measurement of Political Attitudes," *Sociology and Social Research,* 40: 266-70.

―――. "Social Distance and Politics," *Sociology and Social Research,* 40: 339-42.

Biesanz, J., and Biesanz, M. "Social Distance in the Youth Hostel Movement," *Sociology and Social Research,* 25: 237-45.

Binnewies, W. G. "A Method of Studying Rural Social Distance," *Sociology and Social Research,* 10: 239-42.

Bogardus, Emory S. *Sociometry,* X: 306-11; *International Journal of Opinion and Attitude Research,* I: 55-62; *American Sociological Review,* 16: 48-53; *Journal of Educational Sociology,* 3: 497-502; *Survey Graphic,* IX: 169-70, 206, 208; *Journal of Applied Sociology,* 9: 216-26; *Sociology and Social Research,* 12: 173-78; 13: 73-81; 13: 171-75; 14: 174-80; 17: 167-73; 17: 265-71; 18: 67-73; 20: 473-77; 22: 462-76; 24: 69-75; 32: 723-27; 32: 798-802; 32: 882-87; 33: 291-95; 36: 40-47; *The Urban Community,* ed. by E. W. Burgess. Chicago: The University of Chicago Press, 1927. Pp. 48-54.

Bradway, John S. "Social Distance Between Lawyers and Social Workers," *Sociology and Social Research,* 14: 516-24.

Briggs, Arthur E. "Social Distance Between Lawyers and Doctors," *Sociology and Social Research,* 13: 156-63.

Brooks, Lee M. "Racial Distance as Affected by Education," *Sociology and Social Research,* 21: 128-33.

Campbell, Donald T. "The Bogardus Social Distance Scale," *Sociology and Social Research,* 36: 322-25.

Catapusan, Benicio T. "Social Distance in the Philippines," *Sociology and Social Distance,* 38: 309-12.

Dodd, Stuart C. "A Social Distance Test in the Near East," *American Journal of Sociology,* September, 1935, XLI: 194-204.

―――, and Nehnevajsa, J. "Physical Dimensions of Social Distance," *Sociology and Social Research,* 38: 287-92.

Duncan, W. L. "Parent-Child Isolations," *The Family*, 10: 115-18.

DuVall, Everett W. "Child-Parent Social Distance," *Sociology and Social Research*, 21: 458-63.

Eisenstadt, S. N. *From Generation to Generation: Age Groups and the Social Structure*. Glencoe: The Free Press, 1956.

Ellefsen, J. B. "Social Distance Attitudes of Negro College Students," *Phylon*, 17: 79-83.

Ellis, Robert A. "Social Status and Social Distance," *Sociology and Social Distance*, 40: 240-46.

Franklin, Clay. "The Effect of the Format Upon the Scale Values of the Bogardus Social Distance Scale," *Research Studies of the State College of Washington*, 18: 117-20.

Gleason, George. "Social Distance in Russia," *Sociology and Social Research*, 17: 37-43.

Grace, H. A., and Neuhaus, J. O. "Information and Social Distance as Predictors of Hostility Toward Nations," *Journal of Abnormal and Social Psychology*, 1952, 47: 540-45.

Greifer, Julian L. "Attitudes to the Stranger," *American Sociological Review*, December, 1945, 10: 739-45.

Gurnee, H., and Baker, E. "Social Distances of Some Common Social Relationships," *Journal of Abnormal and Social Psychology*, 1938, 33: 265-69.

Halbwachs, M. *The Psychology of Social Classes*. Glencoe: The Free Press, 1958.

Hamren, Vandyce. "Social Farness Between the A.F. of L. and the C.I.O.," *Sociology and Social Research*, 24: 442-52.

———. "Social Nearness Between the A.F. of L. and the C.I.O.," *Sociology and Social Research*, 26: 232-40.

Hartley, Eugene L. *Problems in Prejudice*. New York: Columbia University Press, 1946.

———, and Hartley, Ruth E. *Fundamentals of Social Psychology*. New York: Alfred A. Knopf, 1952. Pp. 431-43.

Hunt, Chester L. "Social Distance in the Philippines," *Sociology and Social Research*, 40: 253-60.

Hypes, E. L. "The Social Distance Score Card as a Teaching Device," *Social Forces*, December, 1928, 7: 234-37.

Jameson, S. H. "Social Distance between Welfare Organizations," *Sociology and Social Research*, 5: 230-43.

———. "Social Nearness among Welfare Organizations," *Sociology and Social Research*, 15: 322-33.

Kahl, Joseph A. *The American Class Structure*. New York: Rinehart & Co., 1957.

Koch, H. L. "Study of Some Factors Conditioning the Social Distance between the Sexes," *Journal of Social Psychology*, 20: 79-107.

Krout, M. H. "Periodic Change in Social Distance; A Study in the Shifting Bases of Perception," *Sociology and Social Research*, 27: 339-51.

Lambert, W. E. "Comparison of French and American Modes of Response to the Bogardus Social Distance Scale, *Social Forces*, 31: 155-60.

McDonagh, Edward C. "Social Distance between China and Japan," *Sociology and Social Research*, 22: 131-36.

———. "Asiatic Stereotypes and National Distance," *Sociology and Social Research*, 22: 474-78.

———. "Military Social Distance," *Sociology and Social Research*, 29: 289-96.

McKenzie, R. D. "Spatial Distance and Community Organization Pattern," *Social Forces*, 5: 623-27.

———. "Spatial Distance," *Sociology and Social Research*, 13: 536-44.

McMath, Ella M. "A Girl without a Country," *Journal of Applied Sociology*, 11: 65-71.

Martin, R. R. "Sudden Change in Social Distance," *Sociology and Social Research*, 22: 53-56.

Mitchell, Roy. "An Ethnic Distance Study in Buffalo," *Sociology and Social Research*, 40: 35-40.

Mowrer, E. R. *Domestic Discord*. Chicago: The University of Chicago Press, 1928, Ch. III.

Neprash, J. A. "Minority Group Contacts and Social Distance," *Phylon*, 14: 207-12.

Newcomb, Theodore M. *Social Psychology*. New York: Holt, Rinehart & Winston, 1950. Pp. 154-75.

Nimkoff, M. F. "Parent-Child Conflict," *Sociology and Social Research*, 12: 446-58.

———. "Parent-Child Conflict," *Sociology and Social Research*, 14: 135-50.

North, C. C. *Social Differentiation*. Chapel Hill: University of North Carolina Press, 1926.

Owen, John E. "Social Distance in England," *Sociology and Social Research*, 30: 460-65.

Parish, Helen R. "Social Nearness between Latin America and the United States," *Sociology and Social Research*, 19: 253-58.

Park, R. E. "The Concept of Social Distance," *Journal of Applied Sociology*, 8: 339-44.

Pettigrew, Thomas F. "Social Distance Attitudes of South African Students," *Social Forces*, March, 1960, 38: 246-53.

Poole, W. C., Jr. "Distance in Sociology," *American Journal of Sociology*, 33: 99-104.

Poole, W. C., Jr. "Social Distance and Social Pathology," *Sociology and Social Research,* 12: 268-72.

———. "Social Distance and Personal Distance," *Journal of Applied Sociology,* 11: 114-20.

———. "The Social Distance Margin Reviewed," *Sociology and Social Research,* 13: 49-54.

———, and Poole, Harriet K. "Laws of Social Distance," *Journal of Applied Sociology,* 11: 365-69.

Prothro, E. T., and Miles, O. K. "Social Distance in the Deep South as Measured by a Revised Bogardus Scale," *Journal of Social Psychology,* 37: 171-74.

Runner, Jessie R. "Social Distance in Adolescent Relationships," *American Journal of Sociology,* 43: 428-39.

Sartain, A. I., and Bell, Harold V., Jr. "An Evaluation of the Bogardus Scale of Social Distance by the Method of Equal-Appearing Intervals," *Journal of Social Psychology,* 29: 85-91.

Sarvis, Guy W. "Social Distance in Religion," *The Christian Century,* 49: 1331-33.

Schenk, Q. F., and Romney, A. K. "Some Differential Attitudes among Adolescent Groups as Revealed by Bogardus' Social Distance Scale," *Sociology and Social Research,* 35: 38-45.

Schnetz, Alfred. "The Stranger," *The American Journal of Sociology,* 49: 499-508.

Schroff, Ruth. "Charting Social Distance," *Sociology and Social Research,* 14: 567-70.

Seymour, J. G. "Rural Social Distance of Normal School Students," *Sociology and Social Research,* 14: 238-48.

Sherif, Muzafer and Sherif, Carolyn W. *An Outline of Social Psychology.* New York: Harper & Bros., 1956. Pp. 659-78.

Shideler, Ernest. "The Social Distance Margin," *Sociology and Social Research,* 12: 243-52.

Sorokin, P. *Social Mobility.* New York: Harper & Bros., 1927, Ch. VI, "Occupational Stratification."

Stephenson, C. M., and Wilcox, Carol G. "Social Distance Variations of College Students," *Sociology and Social Research,* 39: 240-41.

Turbeville, Gus. "A Social Distance Study of Duluth, Minnesota," *Sociology and Social Research,* 18: 420-30.

Van der Berghe, Pierre L. "Distance Mechanisms of Stratification," *Sociology and Social Research,* Jan.-Feb., 1960, 44: 155-64.

Westie, F. R. "Negro-White Status Differentials and Social Distance," *American Sociological Review,* October, 1952, 17: 550-58.

Westie, Frank R., and Westie, Margaret L. "The Social Distance Pyramid: Relationships between Caste and Class," *American Journal of Sociology,* 63: 190-96.

————. "Social Distance Scales, a Tool for the Study of Stratification," *Sociology and Social Research*, 43: 251-58.

Wood, Margaret Mary. *Paths of Loneliness*. New York: Columbia University Press, 1953.

Zeligs, Rose, and Hendrickson, G. "Checking the Social Distance Technique through Personal Interviews," *Sociology and Social Research*, 18: 420-30.

Ziegler, George H. "Social Farness between Hindus and Moslems, *Sociology and Social Research*, 33: 188-95.

Interesting adaptations of the social distance scale are found in:

Westie, Frank R. "A Technique for the Measurement of Race Attitudes," *American Sociological Review*, February, 1953, 18: 73-78.

DeFleur, M. L., and Westie, Frank R. "Verbal Attitudes and Overt Acts: An Experiment on the Salience of Attitudes," *American Sociological Review*, December, 1958, 23: 667-73.

BOGARDUS RACIAL DISTANCE SCALE

(Race is defined here largely as a cultural group.)

1. Remember to give your *first feeling reactions* in every case.
2. Give your reactions to each race as a *group*. Do not give your reactions to the best or to the worst members that you have known, but think of the picture or stereotype that you have of the whole race.
3. Put a cross after each race in as many of the seven rows as your feelings dictate.

Category	English	Swedes	Poles	Koreans	Etc.
1. To close kinship by marriage					
2. To my club as personal chums					
3. To my street as neighbors					
4. To employment in my occupation					
5. To citizenship in my country					
6. As visitors only to my country					
7. Would exclude from my country					

Morale and Job Satisfaction

Morale has been viewed as a global concept and also as a set of specific dimensions. The Minnesota (Rundquist-Sletto) Survey of Opinions (General Adjustment and Morale Scales) is a Likert-type scale that was carefully constructed to tap a general variable. Use the Short Form of the Minnesota Scale of General Adjustment and Morale when the problem calls for an overall assessment of morale. Use the Long Form to assess specific attitudes toward personal inferiority, family, law, conservatism, and education, in addition to morale and general adjustment.

Many social scientists believe that morale is a meaningful concept only when the separate dimensions of morale have been identified. Scale analysis has shown repeatedly that morale is composed of many dimensions. The S.R.A. Employee Morale Inventory is a diagnostic tool that was constructed by including dimensions of job morale. This is the most widely used instrument for diagnosis of employee morale problems. Item analysis was used in its construction. Use the S.R.A. Employee Morale Inventory if you are seeking to diagnose morale problems in work organizations. Norms are available that make possible departmental and interorganizational comparisons. This is probably the best standardized of all sociometric scales.

Nancy Morse and associates have constructed a set of subscales to measure intrinsic job satisfaction, pride in performance, company involvement, and financial and job status. Use the Morse Scales if short scales are needed to tap these dimensions.

Guttman type scales insure that the factor in the scale has been demonstrated to be of one dimension only in the respondent population. The military morale scales are of this type, the reproducibility coefficients providing evidence for the response pattern. Use these scales for military or organizational research of any kind by substituting appropriate units in place of Air Force, Air Site, and Air Craft and Warning Stations (A.C.&W.). Check scalability by Guttman methods for your respondents. The probability is high that these items will scale for any respondent sample to which they would logically apply.

The Brayfield and Rothe Index of Job Satisfaction has been constructed by applying Thurstone's Method of Equal Appearing Intervals and combining Likert's Scoring system that gives an intensity measure. This scale fits two important criteria: a continuum of interval measures and an intensity measure. Use the Brayfield and Rothe Index when a precise general measure of job satisfaction is desired.

INDEX: SHORT FORM OF THE MINNESOTA SURVEY OF OPINIONS (GENERAL ADJUSTMENT AND MORALE SCALES)

VARIABLE MEASURED: Individual morale and general adjustment.

DESCRIPTION: This short form is taken from the Minnesota Scale for the Survey of Opinions that consists of 132 items. The short form consists of only 31 of the most discriminating items. These items are taken from the seven scales that make up the Minnesota Scale for the Survey of Opinions. These scales are the morale scale, the general adjustment scale, inferiority scale, family scale, law scale, conservatism, and education scale.

WHERE PUBLISHED: Edward A. Rundquist and Raymond F. Sletto, *Personality in the Depression,* Child Welfare Monograph Series No. 12. Minneapolis: University of Minnesota Press. Copyright 1936 by the University of Minnesota.

RELIABILITY: Split-half reliability in the .80's may be expected for the adjustment *score* and the total morale *score*. Split-half reliability coefficients for the general adjustment *scale* range from .686 to .821 with high school seniors as the lowest correlation and an all male group as the highest correlation. The females on the same basis range from .686 to .836. Reliability of actual scores from test to retest was measured over a sixty day period. The average changes were 4.03 for 68 General College men and 5.03 for 68 General College women. Test-retest *r*'s are .793 for men and .668 for women.

VALIDITY: Validity for the general adjustment scale was determined by 2 general methods: (1) relating it to those outside variables that imply maladjustment and (2) relating it to scores on the other 6 scales. An extensive report of validity is included in *Personality in the Depression*, pp. 226-41.

UTILITY: This short form is presented to assist those who may wish to obtain a measure of general adjustment and morale without administering the entire survey. It consists of only 31 items in the questionnaire and can be administered in 15 to 20 minutes. There are 16 items in the general adjustment scale and 22 items in the morale scale, both scales included in the 31 item survey. The Long Form of the Survey takes 30 to 40 minutes.

RESEARCH APPLICATION: D. C. Miller, "Morale of College Trained Adults," *American Sociological Review*, December, 1940, 5: 880-89.
————, "Economic Factors in the Morale of College Trained Adults," *American Journal of Sociology*, September, 1941, 47: 139-57.

SCORING INSTRUCTIONS FOR THE SHORT FORM MINNESOTA SCALE FOR THE SURVEY OF OPINIONS

Administration

The Survey requires between 15 and 20 minutes for all to complete it. Although the printed directions on the Survey are self-explanatory, it is advisable to read the directions aloud while the subjects are reading them silently. To secure frankness and cooperation, it is well to assure the group that their opinions are valued, will be held in complete confidence, and will not affect their grades in any course or their standing with their employers or other persons of responsibility. They may be directed to fill in all the information items (name, age, sex, etc.) or to omit those that the examiner does not require for research or counseling purposes.

Scoring

The five alternative responses to each item are weighted from 1 to 5 in scoring. The sum of the scores in the extreme lefthand column is the adjustment score; the sum of the next column is the score on the acceptable morale items; the sum of the next is the score on the unacceptable morale items. To obtain the total morale score, add the total scores on acceptable and unacceptable items.

Norms

The scoring norms in the table permit conversion of raw scores into standard scores. These norms are based on the scores of 1,000 young people, 500 of each sex. The standardization group included 400 college students, 200 high school seniors, and 400 youth employed and unemployed persons in continuation classes at high school level. The distribution of paternal occupation for the standardization group approximates the census distribution of occupations and indicates that it is composed of a fairly representative sample of young persons between the ages of sixteen and twenty-five years. No significant differences between the scores of high school and college students were found, and the norms are adequate for both groups.

The standard scores given in the table were obtained by the McCall T-Score technique, which expresses scores in tenths of standard deviation units from the mean score for the standardization group. *The mean raw score of the standardization group becomes the standard score of 50.* A standard score of 60 is one standard deviation higher than the mean; a standard score of 40 is one standard deviation below the mean. Response weights to items have been so assigned that a high standard score is unfavorable.

To illustrate the use of the table, suppose an individual makes the same raw scores—say 57—on the morale, economic conservatism, and education scales. We find 57 in the raw score column. Reading to the right, we observe that the individual's standard scores are 50 on the morale scale, 40 on the economic conservatism scale, and 60 on the education scale. These scores indicate that the individual is average, that he is conservative in his economic views (one standard deviation below the mean), and that his estimate of the value of education is relatively unfavorable (one standard deviation above the mean).

Standard Score Equivalents for Raw Scores
(*Based on Standardization Group of 1,000*)

Raw Score	M	I	F	L	EC	E	GA
110							
109					91		
108					90		
107							
106					88		
105					87		
104					86		
103					85		
102			92		84		
101		86	91		83		
100		85	90		82		
99		84	89		81		
98		83	88		80		
97		82	87		79		
96		81	86		78		
95	90	80	85		77		
94	89	79	84		76		
93	88	78	84		75		
92	87	77	83		74		
91	86	76	82		73	96	
90	85	75	81	84	72	95	
89	83	74	80	82	71	94	
88	82	73	79	81	70	93	
87	81	72	78	80	69	92	
86	80	71	77	79	68	90	
85	79	70	76	78	67	89	
84	78	68	75	77	66	88	
83	77	67	74	76	65	87	
82	76	66	73	75	64	86	
81	75	65	73	74	63	85	
80	74	64	72	73	62	84	
79	73	63	71	72	61	83	
78	72	62	70	71	60	82	
77	71	61	69	70	59	81	
76	70	60	68	69	58	80	
75	69	59	67	67	57	79	
74	68	58	66	66	56	78	
73	67	57	65	65	56	77	
72	66	56	64	64	55	76	
71	65	55	63	63	54	75	
70	63	54	62	62	53	74	89
69	62	53	62	61	52	73	87
68	61	52	61	60	51	72	86
67	60	51	60	59	50	71	85
66	59	50	59	58	49	69	83
65	58	49	58	57	48	68	82
64	57	48	57	56	47	67	81
63	56	47	56	55	46	66	79

Raw Score	M	I	F	L	EC	E	GA
62	55	46	55	53	45	65	78
61	54	45	54	52	44	64	77
60	53	44	53	51	43	63	76
59	52	43	52	50	42	62	74
58	51	42	51	49	41	61	73
57	50	41	51	48	40	60	72
56	49	40	50	47	39	59	70
55	48	39	49	46	38	58	69
54	47	37	48	45	37	57	68
53	46	36	47	44	36	56	66
52	45	35	46	43	35	55	65
51	43	34	45	42	34	54	64
50	42	33	44	41	33	53	62
49	41	32	43	39	32	52	61
48	40	31	42	38	31	51	60
47	39	30	41	37	30	49	58
46	38	29	40	36	29	48	57
45	37	28	40	35	28	47	56
44	36	27	39	34	27	46	54
43	35	26	38	33	26	45	53
42	34	25	37	32	25	44	52
41	33	24	36	31	24	43	50
40	32	23	35	30	23	42	49
39	31	22	34	29	22	41	48
38	30	21	33	28	21	40	47
37	29	20	32	27	20	39	45
36	28	19	31	26	19	38	44
35	27	18	30	24	18	37	43
34	26	17	29	23	17	36	41
33	25	16	29	22	16	35	40
32	23	15	28	21	15	34	39
31	22	14	27	20	14	33	37
30	21	13	26	19	13	32	36
29	20	12	25	18	12	31	35
28	19	11	24	17	11	30	33
27	18	10	23	16	10	28	32
26	17	9	22	15	9	27	31
25						26	29
24						25	28
23						24	27
22						23	25
21							24
20							23
19							21
18							20
17							19
16							17

*M–Morale; I–Inferiority; F–Family; L–Law; EC–Economic Conservatism; GA–General Adjustment.

MINNESOTA SURVEY OF OPINION (SHORT FORM)

E. A. Rundquist and R. F. Sletto, Institute of Child Welfare,
University of Minnesota

Name _____ Age _____ Sex _____ Date _____
     (Last)   (First)

The following pages contain a number of statements about which there is no general agreement. People differ widely in the way they feel about each item. There are no right answers. The purpose of the survey is to see how different groups feel about each item. We should like your honest opinion on each of these statements.

READ EACH ITEM CAREFULLY AND UNDERLINE QUICKLY THE PHRASE THAT BEST EXPRESSES YOUR FEELING ABOUT THE STATEMENT. Wherever possible, let your own personal experience determine your answer. Do not spend much time on any item. If in doubt, underline the phrase that seems most nearly to express your present feeling about the statement. WORK RAPIDLY. Be sure to answer every item.

1. TIMES ARE GETTING BETTER.
Strongly agree [1] Agree [2] Undecided [3]
Disagree [4] Strongly disagree [5]

2. ANY MAN WITH ABILITY AND WILLINGNESS TO WORK HARD HAS A GOOD CHANCE OF BEING SUCCESSFUL.
Strongly agree [1] Agree [2] Undecided [3]
Disagree [4] Strongly disagree [5]

3. IT IS DIFFICULT TO SAY THE RIGHT THING AT THE RIGHT TIME.
Strongly agree [5] Agree [4] Undecided [3]
Disagree [2] Strongly disagree [1]

4. MOST PEOPLE CAN BE TRUSTED.
Strongly agree [1] Agree [2] Undecided [3]
Disagree [4] Strongly disagree [5]

5. HIGH SCHOOLS ARE TOO IMPRACTICAL.
   Strongly agree [5]   Agree [4]   Undecided [3]
   Disagree [2]   Strongly disagree [1]

6. A PERSON CAN PLAN HIS FUTURE SO
   THAT EVERYTHING WILL COME OUT
   ALL RIGHT IN THE LONG RUN.
   Strongly agree [1]   Agree [2]   Undecided [3]
   Disagree [4]   Strongly disagree [5]

7. NO ONE CARES MUCH WHAT HAPPENS
   TO YOU.
   Strongly agree [5]   Agree [4]   Undecided [3]
   Disagree [2]   Strongly disagree [1]

8. SUCCESS IS MORE DEPENDENT ON LUCK
   THAN ON REAL ABILITY.
   Strongly agree [5]   Agree [4]   Undecided [3]
   Disagree [2]   Strongly disagree [1]

9. IF OUR ECONOMIC SYSTEM WERE JUST,
   THERE WOULD BE MUCH LESS CRIME.
   Strongly agree [5]   Agree [4]   Undecided [3]
   Disagree [2]   Strongly disagree [1]

10. A MAN DOES NOT HAVE TO PRETEND
    HE IS SMARTER THAN HE REALLY IS
    TO "GET BY."
    Strongly agree [1]   Agree [2]   Undecided [3]
    Disagree [4]   Strongly disagree [5]

11. LAWS ARE SO OFTEN MADE FOR THE
    BENEFIT OF SMALL SELFISH GROUPS
    THAT A MAN CANNOT RESPECT THE
    LAW.
    Strongly agree [5]   Agree [4]   Undecided [3]
    Disagree [2]   Strongly disagree [1]

12. ONE SELDOM WORRIES SO MUCH AS TO
    BECOME VERY MISERABLE.
    Strongly agree [1]   Agree [2]   Undecided [3]
    Disagree [4]   Strongly disagree [5]

13. THE FUTURE LOOKS VERY BLACK.
    Strongly agree [5]   Agree [4]   Undecided [3]
    Disagree [2]   Strongly disagree [1]

14. REAL FRIENDS ARE AS EASY TO FIND AS EVER.
Strongly agree [1]   Agree [2]   Undecided [3]
Disagree [4]   Strongly disagree [5]

_____

15. POVERTY IS CHIEFLY A RESULT OF IN-JUSTICE IN THE DISTRIBUTION OF WEALTH.
Strongly agree [5]   Agree [4]   Undecided [3]
Disagree [2]   Strongly disagree [1]

_____

16. IT IS DIFFICULT TO THINK CLEARLY THESE DAYS.
Strongly agree [5]   Agree [4]   Undecided [3]
Disagree [2]   Strongly disagree [1]

_____

17. THERE IS LITTLE CHANCE FOR AD-VANCEMENT IN INDUSTRY AND BUSI-NESS UNLESS A MAN HAS UNFAIR PULL.
Strongly agree [5]   Agree [4]   Undecided [3]
Disagree [2]   Strongly disagree [1]

_____   _____

18. IT DOES NOT TAKE LONG TO GET OVER FEELING GLOOMY.
Strongly agree [1]   Agree [2]   Undecided [3]
Disagree [4]   Strongly disagree [5]

_____

19. THE YOUNG MAN OF TODAY CAN EX-PECT MUCH OF THE FUTURE.
Strongly agree [1]   Agree [2]   Undecided [3]
Disagree [4]   Strongly disagree [5]

_____   _____

20. IT IS GREAT TO BE LIVING IN THESE EXCITING TIMES.
Strongly agree [1]   Agree [2]   Undecided [3]
Disagree [4]   Strongly disagree [5]

_____

21. LIFE IS JUST ONE WORRY AFTER AN-OTHER.
Strongly agree [5]   Agree [4]   Undecided [3]
Disagree [2]   Strongly disagree [1]

_____   _____

22. THE DAY IS NOT LONG ENOUGH TO DO ONE'S WORK WELL AND HAVE ANY TIME FOR FUN.
Strongly agree [5]   Agree [4]   Undecided [3]
Disagree [2]   Strongly disagree [1]

_____

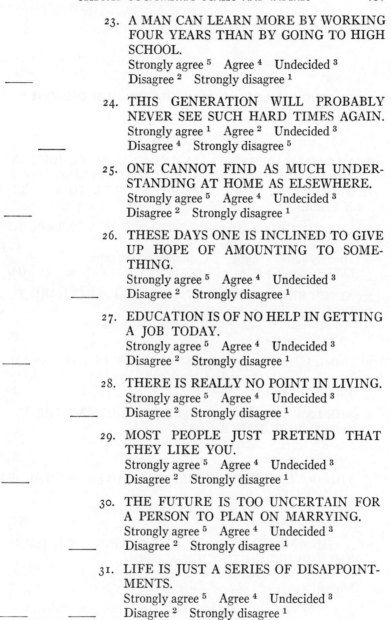

23. A MAN CAN LEARN MORE BY WORKING FOUR YEARS THAN BY GOING TO HIGH SCHOOL.
Strongly agree [5]   Agree [4]   Undecided [3]
Disagree [2]   Strongly disagree [1]

24. THIS GENERATION WILL PROBABLY NEVER SEE SUCH HARD TIMES AGAIN.
Strongly agree [1]   Agree [2]   Undecided [3]
Disagree [4]   Strongly disagree [5]

25. ONE CANNOT FIND AS MUCH UNDERSTANDING AT HOME AS ELSEWHERE.
Strongly agree [5]   Agree [4]   Undecided [3]
Disagree [2]   Strongly disagree [1]

26. THESE DAYS ONE IS INCLINED TO GIVE UP HOPE OF AMOUNTING TO SOMETHING.
Strongly agree [5]   Agree [4]   Undecided [3]
Disagree [2]   Strongly disagree [1]

27. EDUCATION IS OF NO HELP IN GETTING A JOB TODAY.
Strongly agree [5]   Agree [4]   Undecided [3]
Disagree [2]   Strongly disagree [1]

28. THERE IS REALLY NO POINT IN LIVING.
Strongly agree [5]   Agree [4]   Undecided [3]
Disagree [2]   Strongly disagree [1]

29. MOST PEOPLE JUST PRETEND THAT THEY LIKE YOU.
Strongly agree [5]   Agree [4]   Undecided [3]
Disagree [2]   Strongly disagree [1]

30. THE FUTURE IS TOO UNCERTAIN FOR A PERSON TO PLAN ON MARRYING.
Strongly agree [5]   Agree [4]   Undecided [3]
Disagree [2]   Strongly disagree [1]

31. LIFE IS JUST A SERIES OF DISAPPOINTMENTS.
Strongly agree [5]   Agree [4]   Undecided [3]
Disagree [2]   Strongly disagree [1]

GA   Ma   Mu   Ma + Mu = Total Morale Score

DIRECTIONS

READ EACH ITEM CAREFULLY AND UNDERLINE QUICKLY THE PHRASE THAT BEST EXPRESSES YOUR FEELING ABOUT THE STATEMENT. WORK RAPIDLY. BE SURE TO ANSWER EVERY ITEM.

1. THE FUTURE IS TOO UNCERTAIN FOR A PERSON TO PLAN ON MARRYING.
   Strongly agree ^{5} Agree ^{4} Undecided ^{3} Disagree ^{2}
   Strongly disagree ^{1} **(M)**

2. AFTER BEING CAUGHT IN A MISTAKE, IT IS HARD TO DO GOOD WORK FOR A WHILE.
   Strongly agree ^{5} Agree ^{4} Undecided ^{3} Disagree ^{2}
   Strongly disagree ^{1} **(I)**

3. HOME IS THE MOST PLEASANT PLACE IN THE WORLD.
   Strongly agree ^{1} Agree ^{2} Undecided ^{3} Disagree ^{4}
   Strongly disagree ^{5} **(F)**

4. THE LAW PROTECTS PROPERTY RIGHTS AT THE EX-PENSE OF HUMAN RIGHTS.
   Strongly agree ^{5} Agree ^{4} Undecided ^{3} Disagree ^{2}
   Strongly disagree ^{1} **(L)**

5. THE GOVERNMENT SHOULD TAKE OVER ALL LARGE INDUSTRIES.
   Strongly agree ^{5} Agree ^{4} Undecided ^{3} Disagree ^{2}
   Strongly disagree ^{1} **(EC)**

6. A MAN CAN LEARN MORE BY WORKING FOUR YEARS THAN BY GOING TO HIGH SCHOOL.
   Strongly agree ^{5} Agree ^{4} Undecided ^{3} Disagree ^{2}
   Strongly disagree ^{1} **(E)**

* Containing the Scales of General Adjustment, Morale, Inferiority, Family, Law, Conservatism, and Education. For scoring, see E. A. Rundquist and R. F. Sletto, as cited, p. 385. Add numbers given by response. Norms are shown above. Items marked *M* are in Morale Scale; *I* items are in Inferiority Scale; *F* items, Family Scale; *L* items, Law Scale; *EC,* Economic Conservatism Scale; *E,* Education Scale.

7. IT IS DIFFICULT TO THINK CLEARLY THESE DAYS.
Strongly agree [5]   Agree [4]   Undecided [3]   Disagree [2]
Strongly disagree [1]   **(M)**

8. IT IS EASY TO EXPRESS ONE'S IDEAS.
Strongly agree [1]   Agree [2]   Undecided [3]   Disagree [4]
Strongly disagree [5]   **(I)**

9 PARENTS EXPECT TOO MUCH FROM THEIR CHILDREN.
Strongly agree [5]   Agree [4]   Undecided [3]   Disagree [2]
Strongly disagree [1]   **(F)**

10. A PERSON SHOULD OBEY ONLY THOSE LAWS THAT
SEEM REASONABLE.
Strongly agree [5]   Agree [4]   Undecided [3]   Disagree [2]
Strongly disagree [1]   **(L)**

11. LABOR SHOULD OBEY ONLY THOSE LAWS THAT SEEM
REASONABLE.
Strongly agree [5]   Agree [4]   Undecided [3]   Disagree [2]
Strongly disagree [1]   **(EC)**

12. THE MORE EDUCATION A MAN HAS THE BETTER HE
IS ABLE TO ENJOY LIFE.
Strongly agree [1]   Agree [2]   Undecided [3]   Disagree [4]
Strongly disagree [5]   **(E)**

13. THE FUTURE LOOKS VERY BLACK.
Strongly agree [5]   Agree [4]   Undecided [3]   Disagree [2]
Strongly disagree [1]   **(M)**

14. IT IS DIFFICULT TO SAY THE RIGHT THING AT THE
RIGHT TIME.
Strongly agree [5]   Agree [4]   Undecided [3]   Disagree [2]
Strongly disagree [1]   **(I)**

15. ONE OUGHT TO DISCUSS IMPORTANT PLANS WITH
MEMBERS OF HIS FAMILY.
Strongly agree [1]   Agree [2]   Undecided [3]   Disagree [4]
Strongly disagree [5]   **(F)**

16. IT IS ALL RIGHT TO EVADE THE LAW IF YOU DO NOT
ACTUALLY VIOLATE IT.
Strongly agree [5]   Agree [4]   Undecided [3]   Disagree [2]
Strongly disagree [1]   **(L)**

17. LEGISLATURES ARE TOO READY TO PASS LAWS TO
CURB BUSINESS FREEDOM.
Strongly agree [1]   Agree [2]   Undecided [3]   Disagree [4]
Strongly disagree [5]   **(EC)**

18. EDUCATION HELPS A PERSON TO USE HIS LEISURE TIME TO BETTER ADVANTAGE.
Strongly agree [1]   Agree [2]   Undecided [3]   Disagree [4]
Strongly disagree [5]   (E)

19. LIFE IS JUST ONE WORRY AFTER ANOTHER.
Strongly agree [5]   Agree [4]   Undecided [3]   Disagree [2]
Strongly disagree [1]   (M)

20. ONE CAN USUALLY KEEP COOL IN IMPORTANT SITUATIONS.
Strongly agree [1]   Agree [2]   Undecided [3]   Disagree [4]
Strongly disagree [5]   (I)

21. IN PLANS FOR THE FUTURE, PARENTS SHOULD BE GIVEN FIRST CONSIDERATION.
Strongly agree [1]   Agree [2]   Undecided [3]   Disagree [4]
Strongly disagree [5]   (F)

22. THE SENTENCES OF JUDGES IN COURTS ARE DETERMINED BY THEIR PREJUDICES.
Strongly agree [5]   Agree [4]   Undecided [3]   Disagree [2]
Strongly disagree [1]   (L)

23. FOR MEN TO DO THEIR BEST, THERE MUST BE THE POSSIBILITY OF UNLIMITED PROFIT.
Strongly agree [1]   Agree [2]   Undecided [3]   Disagree [4]
Strongly disagree [5]   (EC)

24. A GOOD EDUCATION IS A GREAT COMFORT TO A MAN OUT OF WORK.
Strongly agree [1]   Agree [2]   Undecided [3]   Disagree [4]
Strongly disagree [5]   (E)

25. MOST PEOPLE CAN BE TRUSTED.
Strongly agree [1]   Agree [2]   Undecided [3]   Disagree [4]
Strongly disagree [5]   (M)

26. IT IS EASY TO GET ONE'S OWN WAY IN MOST SITUATIONS.
Strongly agree [1]   Agree [2]   Undecided [3]   Disagree [4]
Strongly disagree [5]   (I)

27. A MAN SHOULD BE WILLING TO SACRIFICE EVERYTHING FOR HIS FAMILY.
Strongly agree [1]   Agree [2]   Undecided [3]   Disagree [4]
Strongly disagree [5]   (F)

28. ON THE WHOLE, JUDGES ARE HONEST.
Strongly agree [1]   Agree [2]   Undecided [3]   Disagree [4]
Strongly disagree [5]   (L)

29. POVERTY IS CHIEFLY A RESULT OF INJUSTICE IN THE DISTRIBUTION OF WEALTH.
Strongly agree [5]   Agree [4]   Undecided [3]   Disagree [2]
Strongly disagree [1]   **(EC)**

30. ONLY SUBJECTS LIKE READING, WRITING, AND ARITH-METIC SHOULD BE TAUGHT AT PUBLIC EXPENSE.
Strongly agree [5]   Agree [4]   Undecided [3]   Disagree [2]
Strongly disagree [1]   **(E)**

31. TIMES ARE GETTING BETTER.
Strongly agree [1]   Agree [2]   Undecided [3]   Disagree [4]
Strongly disagree [5]   **(M)**

32. IT IS EASY TO HAVE A GOOD TIME AT A PARTY.
Strongly agree [1]   Agree [2]   Undecided [3]   Disagree [4]
Strongly disagree [5]   **(I)**

33. PARENTS TOO OFTEN EXPECT THEIR GROWN-UP CHILDREN TO OBEY THEM.
Strongly agree [5]   Agree [4]   Undecided [3]   Disagree [2]
Strongly disagree [1]   **(F)**

34. JURIES SELDOM UNDERSTAND A CASE WELL ENOUGH TO MAKE A REALLY JUST DECISION.
Strongly agree [5]   Agree [4]   Undecided [3]   Disagree [2]
Strongly disagree [1]   **(L)**

35. THE GOVERNMENT SHOULD NOT ATTEMPT TO LIMIT PROFITS.
Strongly agree [1]   Agree [2]   Undecided [3]   Disagree [4]
Strongly disagree [5]   **(EC)**

36. EDUCATION IS OF NO HELP IN GETTING A JOB TODAY.
Strongly agree [5]   Agree [4]   Undecided [3]   Disagree [2]
Strongly disagree [1]   **(E)**

37. IT DOES NOT TAKE LONG TO GET OVER FEELING GLOOMY.
Strongly agree [1]   Agree [2]   Undecided [3]   Disagree [4]
Strongly disagree [5]   **(M)**

38. MEETING NEW PEOPLE IS USUALLY EMBARRASSING.
Strongly agree [5]   Agree [4]   Undecided [3]   Disagree [2]
Strongly disagree [1]   **(I)**

39. ONE CANNOT FIND AS MUCH UNDERSTANDING AT HOME AS ELSEWHERE.
Strongly agree [5]   Agree [4]   Undecided [3]   Disagree [2]
Strongly disagree [1]   **(F)**

40. ON THE WHOLE, POLICEMEN ARE HONEST.
    Strongly agree [1]   Agree [2]   Undecided [3]   Disagree [4]
    Strongly disagree [5]   **(L)**

41. THE MORE A MAN LEARNS ABOUT OUR ECONOMIC
    SYSTEM, THE LESS WILLING HE IS TO SEE CHANGES
    MADE.
    Strongly agree [1]   Agree [2]   Undecided [3]   Disagree [4]
    Strongly disagree [5]   **(EC)**

42. MOST YOUNG PEOPLE ARE GETTING TOO MUCH
    EDUCATION.
    Strongly agree [5]   Agree [4]   Undecided [3]   Disagree [2]
    Strongly disagree [1]   **(E)**

43. THE DAY IS NOT LONG ENOUGH TO DO ONE'S WORK
    WELL AND HAVE ANY TIME FOR FUN.
    Strongly agree [5]   Agree [4]   Undecided [3]   Disagree [2]
    Strongly disagree [1]   **(M)**

44. IT IS EASY TO KEEP UP ONE'S COURAGE.
    Strongly agree [1]   Agree [2]   Undecided [3]   Disagree [4]
    Strongly disagree [5]   **(I)**

45. ONE OWES HIS GREATEST OBLIGATION TO HIS FAMILY.
    Strongly agree [1]   Agree [2]   Undecided [3]   Disagree [4]
    Strongly disagree [5]   **(F)**

46. A MAN SHOULD OBEY THE LAWS NO MATTER HOW
    MUCH THEY INTERFERE WITH HIS PERSONAL AM-
    BITIONS.
    Strongly agree [1]   Agree [2]   Undecided [3]   Disagree [4]
    Strongly disagree [5]   **(L)**

47. THE GOVERNMENT OUGHT TO GUARANTEE A LIVING
    TO THOSE WHO CANNOT FIND WORK.
    Strongly agree [5]   Agree [4]   Undecided [3]   Disagree [2]
    Strongly disagree [1]   **(EC)**

48. A HIGH SCHOOL EDUCATION IS WORTH ALL THE TIME
    AND EFFORT IT REQUIRES.
    Strongly agree [1]   Agree [2]   Undecided [3]   Disagree [4]
    Strongly disagree [5]   **(E)**

49. NO ONE CARES MUCH WHAT HAPPENS TO YOU.
    Strongly agree [5]   Agree [4]   Undecided [3]   Disagree [2]
    Strongly disagree [1]   **(M)**

50. IT IS EASY TO IGNORE CRITICISM.
    Strongly agree [1]   Agree [2]   Undecided [3]   Disagree [4]
    Strongly disagree [5]   **(I)**

51. IT IS HARD TO KEEP A PLEASANT DISPOSITION AT HOME.
Strongly agree [5]   Agree [4]   Undecided [3]   Disagree [2]
Strongly disagree [1]   **(F)**

52. COURT DECISIONS ARE ALMOST ALWAYS JUST.
Strongly agree [1]   Agree [2]   Undecided [3]   Disagree [4]
Strongly disagree [5]   **(L)**

53. LARGE INCOMES SHOULD BE TAXED MUCH MORE THAN THEY ARE NOW.
Strongly agree [5]   Agree [4]   Undecided [3]   Disagree [2]
Strongly disagree [1]   **(EC)**

54. OUR SCHOOLS ENCOURAGE AN INDIVIDUAL TO THINK FOR HIMELF.
Strongly agree [1]   Agree [2]   Undecided [3]   Disagree [4]
Strongly disagree [5]   **(E)**

55. ANY MAN WITH ABILITY AND WILLINGNESS TO WORK HARD HAS A GOOD CHANCE OF BEING SUCCESSFUL.
Strongly agree [1]   Agree [2]   Undecided [3]   Disagree [4]
Strongly disagree [5]   **(M)**

56. IT IS EASY TO ACT NATURALLY IN A GROUP.
Strongly agree [1]   Agree [2]   Undecided [3]   Disagree [4]
Strongly disagree [5]   **(I)**

57. PEOPLE IN THE FAMILY CAN BE TRUSTED COMPLETELY.
Strongly agree [1]   Agree [2]   Undecided [3]   Disagree [4]
Strongly disagree [5]   **(F)**

58. IN THE COURTS A POOR MAN WILL RECEIVE AS FAIR TREATMENT AS A MILLIONAIRE.
Strongly agree [1]   Agree [2]   Undecided [3]   Disagree [4]
Strongly disagree [5]   **(L)**

59. MEN WOULD NOT DO THEIR BEST, IF GOVERNMENT OWNED ALL INDUSTRY.
Strongly agree [1]   Agree [2]   Undecided [3]   Disagree [4]
Strongly disagree [5]   **(EC)**

60. THERE ARE TOO MANY FADS AND FRILLS IN MODERN EDUCATION.
Strongly agree [5]   Agree [4]   Undecided [3]   Disagree [2]
Strongly disagree [1]   **(E)**

61. IT IS GREAT TO BE LIVING IN THESE EXCITING TIMES.
Strongly agree [1]   Agree [2]   Undecided [3]   Disagree [4]
Strongly disagree [5]   **(M)**

62. IT IS HARD TO BRING ONESELF TO CONFIDE IN OTHERS.
Strongly agree [1]   Agree [2]   Undecided [3]   Disagree [4]
Strongly disagree [5]   **(I)**

63. ONE BECOMES NERVOUS AT HOME.
Strongly agree [5]   Agree [4]   Undecided [3]   Disagree [2]
Strongly disagree [1]   **(F)**

64. PERSONAL CIRCUMSTANCES SHOULD NEVER BE CON-SIDERED AN EXCUSE FOR LAWBREAKING.
Strongly agree [1]   Agree [2]   Undecided [3]   Disagree [4]
Strongly disagree [5]   **(L)**

65. MOST GREAT FORTUNES ARE MADE HONESTLY.
Strongly agree [1]   Agree [2]   Undecided [3]   Disagree [4]
Strongly disagree [5]   **(EC)**

66. EDUCATION ONLY MAKES A PERSON DISCONTENTED.
Strongly agree [5]   Agree [4]   Undecided [3]   Disagree [2]
Strongly disagree [1]   **(E)**

67. THESE DAYS ONE IS INCLINED TO GIVE UP HOPE OF AMOUNTING TO SOMETHING.
Strongly agree [5]   Agree [4]   Undecided [3]   Disagree [2]
Strongly disagree [1]   **(M)**

68. IT IS HARD TO DO YOUR BEST WHEN PEOPLE ARE WATCHING YOU.
Strongly agree [5]   Agree [4]   Undecided [3]   Disagree [2]
Strongly disagree [1]   **(I)**

69. THE JOYS OF FAMILY LIFE ARE MUCH OVERRATED.
Strongly agree [5]   Agree [4]   Undecided [3]   Disagree [2]
Strongly disagree [1]   **(F)**

70. A MAN SHOULD TELL THE TRUTH IN COURT, REGARD-LESS OF CONSEQUENCES.
Strongly agree [1]   Agree [2]   Undecided [3]   Disagree [4]
Strongly disagree [5]   **(L)**

71. PRIVATE OWNERSHIP OF PROPERTY IS NECESSARY FOR ECONOMIC PROGRESS.
Strongly agree [1]   Agree [2]   Undecided [3]   Disagree [4]
Strongly disagree [5]   **(EC)**

72. SCHOOL TRAINING IS OF LITTLE HELP IN MEETING THE PROBLEMS OF REAL LIFE.
Strongly agree [5]   Agree [4]   Undecided [3]   Disagree [2]
Strongly disagree [1]   **(E)**

73. THERE IS LITTLE CHANCE FOR ADVANCEMENT IN INDUSTRY AND BUSINESS UNLESS A MAN HAS UNFAIR PULL.
Strongly agree [5]   Agree [4]   Undecided [3]   Disagree [2]
Strongly disagree [1]   **(M)**

74. IT IS EASY TO GET ALONG WITH PEOPLE.
Strongly agree [1]   Agree [2]   Undecided [3]   Disagree [4]
Strongly disagree [5]   **(I)**

75. ONE'S PARENTS USUALLY TREAT HIM FAIRLY AND SENSIBLY.
Strongly agree [1]   Agree [2]   Undecided [3]   Disagree [4]
Strongly disagree [5]   **(F)**

76. A PERSON WHO REPORTS MINOR LAW VIOLATIONS IS ONLY A TROUBLEMAKER.
Strongly agree [5]   Agree [4]   Undecided [3]   Disagree [2]
Strongly disagree [1]   **(L)**

77. WITHOUT SWEEPING CHANGES IN OUR ECONOMIC SYSTEM, LITTLE PROGRESS CAN BE MADE IN THE SOLUTION OF SOCIAL PROBLEMS.
Strongly agree [5]   Agree [4]   Undecided [3]   Disagree [2]
Strongly disagree [1]   **(EC)**

78. EDUCATION TENDS TO MAKE AN INDIVIDUAL LESS CONCEITED.
Strongly agree [1]   Agree [2]   Undecided [3]   Disagree [4]
Strongly disagree [5]   **(E)**

79. THE YOUNG MAN OF TODAY CAN EXPECT MUCH OF THE FUTURE.
Strongly agree [1]   Agree [2]   Undecided [3]   Disagree [4]
Strongly disagree [5]   **(M)**

80. IT IS EASY TO FEEL AS THOUGH YOU HAD A WORLD OF SELF-CONFIDENCE.
Strongly agree [1]   Agree [2]   Undecided [3]   Disagree [4]
Strongly disagree [5]   **(I)**

81. ONE SHOULD CONFIDE MORE FULLY IN MEMBERS OF HIS FAMILY.
Strongly agree [1]   Agree [2]   Undecided [3]   Disagree [4]
Strongly disagree [5]   **(F)**

82. A PERSON IS JUSTIFIED IN GIVING FALSE TESTIMONY TO PROTECT A FRIEND ON TRIAL.
Strongly agree [5]   Agree [4]   Undecided [3]   Disagree [2]
Strongly disagree [1]   **(L)**

83. ON THE WHOLE, OUR ECONOMIC SYSTEM IS JUST AND WISE.
Strongly agree [1]   Agree [2]   Undecided [3]   Disagree [4]
Strongly disagree [5]   **(EC)**

84. SOLUTION OF THE WORLD'S PROBLEMS WILL COME THROUGH EDUCATION.
Strongly agree [1]   Agree [2]   Undecided [3]   Disagree [4]
Strongly disagree [5]   **(E)**

85. THIS GENERATION WILL PROBABLY NEVER SEE SUCH HARD TIMES AGAIN.
Strongly agree [1]   Agree [2]   Undecided [3]   Disagree [4]
Strongly disagree [5]   **(M)**

86. MOST PEOPLE JUST PRETEND THAT THEY LIKE YOU.
Strongly agree [5]   Agree [4]   Undecided [3]   Disagree [2]
Strongly disagree [1]   **(I)**

87. ONE FEELS MOST CONTENTED AT HOME.
Strongly agree [1]   Agree [2]   Undecided [3]   Disagree [4]
Strongly disagree [5]   **(F)**

88. A HUNGRY MAN HAS A RIGHT TO STEAL.
Strongly agree [5]   Agree [4]   Undecided [3]   Disagree [2]
Strongly disagree [1]   **(L)**

89. LABOR DOES NOT GET ITS FAIR SHARE OF WHAT IT PRODUCES.
Strongly agree [5]   Agree [4]   Undecided [3]   Disagree [2]
Strongly disagree [1]   **(EC)**

90. HIGH SCHOOL COURSES ARE TOO IMPRACTICAL.
Strongly agree [5]   Agree [4]   Undecided [3]   Disagree [2]
Strongly disagree [1]   **(E)**

91. REAL FRIENDS ARE AS EASY TO FIND AS EVER.
Strongly agree [1]   Agree [2]   Undecided [3]   Disagree [4]
Strongly disagree [5]   **(M)**

92. SO MANY PEOPLE DO THINGS WELL THAT IT IS EASY TO BECOME DISCOURAGED.
Strongly agree [5]   Agree [4]   Undecided [3]   Disagree [2]
Strongly disagree [1]   **(I)**

93. FAMILY TIES ARE STRENGTHENED WHEN TIMES ARE HARD.
Strongly agree [1]   Agree [2]   Undecided [3]   Disagree [4]
Strongly disagree [5]   **(F)**

94. ALL LAWS SHOULD BE STRICTLY OBEYED BECAUSE THEY *ARE* LAWS.
Strongly agree [1]   Agree [2]   Undecided [3]   Disagree [4]
Strongly disagree [5]   **(L)**

95. WHEN A RICH MAN DIES, MOST OF HIS PROPERTY SHOULD GO TO THE STATE.
Strongly agree [5]   Agree [4]   Undecided [3]   Disagree [2]
Strongly disagree [1]   **(EC)**

96. A MAN IS FOOLISH TO KEEP ON GOING TO SCHOOL IF HE CAN GET A JOB.
Strongly agree [5]   Agree [4]   Undecided [3]   Disagree [2]
Strongly disagree [1]   **(E)**

97. LIFE IS JUST A SERIES OF DISAPPOINTMENTS.
Strongly agree [5]   Agree [4]   Undecided [3]   Disagree [2]
Strongly disagree [1]   **(M)**

98. IT IS HARD NOT TO BE SELF-CONSCIOUS.
Strongly agree [5]   Agree [4]   Undecided [3]   Disagree [2]
Strongly disagree [1]   **(I)**

99. PARENTS ARE INCLINED TO BE TOO OLD-FASHIONED IN THEIR IDEAS.
Strongly agree [5]   Agree [4]   Undecided [3]   Disagree [2]
Strongly disagree [1]   **(F)**

100. LAWS ARE SO OFTEN MADE FOR THE BENEFIT OF SMALL SELFISH GROUPS THAT A MAN CANNOT RESPECT THE LAW.
Strongly agree [5]   Agree [4]   Undecided [3]   Disagree [2]
Strongly disagree [1]   **(L)**

101. IF OUR ECONOMIC SYSTEM WERE JUST, THERE WOULD BE MUCH LESS CRIME.
Strongly agree [5]   Agree [4]   Undecided [3]   Disagree [2]
Strongly disagree [1]   **(EC)**

102. SAVINGS SPENT ON EDUCATION ARE WISELY INVESTED.
Strongly agree [1]   Agree [2]   Undecided [3]   Disagree [4]
Strongly disagree [5]   **(E)**

103. ONE SELDOM WORRIES SO MUCH AS TO BECOME VERY MISERABLE.
Strongly agree [1]   Agree [2]   Undecided [3]   Disagree [4]
Strongly disagree [5]   **(M)**

104. IT IS NO TRICK TO BE THE LIFE OF THE PARTY.
Strongly agree [1]   Agree [2]   Undecided [3]   Disagree [4]
Strongly disagree [5]   **(I)**

105. MEMBERS OF THE FAMILY ARE TOO CURIOUS ABOUT ONE'S PERSONAL AFFAIRS.
Strongly agree [5]   Agree [4]   Undecided [3]   Disagree [2]
Strongly disagree [1]   **(F)**

106. ALMOST ANYTHING CAN BE FIXED UP IN THE COURTS IF YOU HAVE ENOUGH MONEY.
Strongly agree [5]   Agree [4]   Undecided [3]   Disagree [2]
Strongly disagree [1]   **(L)**

107. THE INCOMES OF MOST PEOPLE ARE A FAIR MEASURE OF THEIR CONTRIBUTION TO HUMAN WELFARE.
Strongly agree [1]   Agree [2]   Undecided [3]   Disagree [4]
Strongly disagree [5]   **(EC)**

108. AN EDUCATED MAN CAN ADVANCE MORE RAPIDLY IN BUSINESS AND INDUSTRY.
Strongly agree [1]   Agree [2]   Undecided [3]   Disagree [4]
Strongly disagree [5]   **(E)**

109. A MAN DOES NOT HAVE TO PRETEND HE IS SMARTER THAN HE REALLY IS TO "GET BY."
Strongly agree [1]   Agree [2]   Undecided [3]   Disagree [4]
Strongly disagree [5]   **(M)**

110. IT IS EASY TO KEEP PEOPLE FROM TAKING ADVANTAGE OF YOU.
Strongly agree [1]   Agree [2]   Undecided [3]   Disagree [4]
Strongly disagree [5]   **(I)**

111. PARENTS KEEP FAITH IN THEIR CHILDREN EVEN THOUGH THEY CANNOT FIND WORK.
Strongly agree [1]   Agree [2]   Undecided [3]   Disagree [4]
Strongly disagree [5]   **(F)**

112. IT IS DIFFICULT TO BREAK THE LAW AND KEEP ONE'S SELF RESPECT.
Strongly agree [1]   Agree [2]   Undecided [3]   Disagree [4]
Strongly disagree [5]   **(L)**

113. A MAN SHOULD STRIKE IN ORDER TO SECURE GREATER RETURNS TO LABOR.
Strongly agree ^{5} Agree ^{4} Undecided ^{3} Disagree ^{2}
Strongly disagree ^{1} **(EC)**

114. PARENTS SHOULD NOT BE COMPELLED TO SEND THEIR CHILDREN TO SCHOOL.
Strongly agree ^{5} Agree ^{4} Undecided ^{3} Disagree ^{2}
Strongly disagree ^{1} **(E)**

115. SUCCESS IS MORE DEPENDENT ON LUCK THAN ON REAL ABILITY.
Strongly agree ^{5} Agree ^{4} Undecided ^{3} Disagree ^{2}
Strongly disagree ^{1} **(M)**

116. MOST PEOPLE ARE TOO CRITICAL OF ONE'S BEHAVIOR.
Strongly agree ^{5} Agree ^{4} Undecided ^{3} Disagree ^{2}
Strongly disagree ^{1} **(I)**

117. PARENTS ARE TOO PARTICULAR ABOUT THE KIND OF COMPANY ONE KEEPS.
Strongly agree ^{5} Agree ^{4} Undecided ^{3} Disagree ^{2}
Strongly disagree ^{1} **(F)**

118. ON THE WHOLE, LAWYERS ARE HONEST.
Strongly agree ^{1} Agree ^{2} Undecided ^{3} Disagree ^{4}
Strongly disagree ^{5} **(L)**

119. A MAN SHOULD BE ALLOWED TO KEEP AS LARGE AN INCOME AS HE CAN GET.
Strongly agree ^{1} Agree ^{2} Undecided ^{3} Disagree ^{4}
Strongly disagree ^{5} **(EC)**

120. EDUCATION IS MORE VALUABLE THAN MOST PEOPLE THINK.
Strongly agree ^{1} Agree ^{2} Undecided ^{3} Disagree ^{4}
Strongly disagree ^{5} **(E)**

121. A PERSON CAN PLAN HIS FUTURE SO THAT EVERYTHING WILL COME OUT ALL RIGHT IN THE LONG RUN.
Strongly agree ^{1} Agree ^{2} Undecided ^{3} Disagree ^{4}
Strongly disagree ^{5} **(M)**

122. FEAR OF SOCIAL BLUNDERS KEEPS ONE FROM HAVING A GOOD TIME AT A PARTY.
Strongly agree ^{5} Agree ^{4} Undecided ^{3} Disagree ^{2}
Strongly disagree ^{1} **(I)**

123. OBLIGATIONS TO ONE'S FAMILY ARE A GREAT HANDI-
CAP TO A YOUNG MAN TODAY.
Strongly agree⁵ Agree⁴ Undecided³ Disagree²
Strongly disagree¹ **(F)**

124. VIOLATORS OF THE LAW ARE NEARLY ALWAYS DE-
TECTED AND PUNISHED.
Strongly agree¹ Agree² Undecided³ Disagree⁴
Strongly disagree⁵ **(L)**

125. MONEY SHOULD BE TAKEN FROM THE RICH AND
GIVEN TO THE POOR DURING HARD TIMES.
Strongly agree⁵ Agree⁴ Undecided³ Disagree²
Strongly disagree¹ **(EC)**

126. A HIGH SCHOOL EDUCATION MAKES A MAN A BETTER
CITIZEN.
Strongly agree¹ Agree² Undecided³ Disagree⁴
Strongly disagree⁵ **(E)**

127. THERE IS REALLY NO POINT IN LIVING.
Strongly agree⁵ Agree⁴ Undecided³ Disagree²
Strongly disagree¹ **(M)**

128. IT IS EASY TO LOSE CONFIDENCE IN ONESELF.
Strongly agree⁵ Agree⁴ Undecided³ Disagree²
Strongly disagree¹ **(I)**

129. SO FAR AS IDEAS ARE CONCERNED, PARENTS AND
CHILDREN LIVE IN DIFFERENT WORLDS.
Strongly agree⁵ Agree⁴ Undecided³ Disagree²
Strongly disagree¹ **(F)**

130. IT IS ALL RIGHT FOR A PERSON TO BREAK THE LAW
IF HE DOESN'T GET CAUGHT.
Strongly agree⁵ Agree⁴ Undecided³ Disagree²
Strongly disagree¹ **(L)**

131. OUR ECONOMIC SYSTEM IS CRITICIZED TOO MUCH.
Strongly agree¹ Agree² Undecided³ Disagree⁴
Strongly disagree⁵ **(EC)**

132. PUBLIC MONEY SPENT ON EDUCATION FOR THE PAST
FEW YEARS COULD HAVE BEEN USED MORE WISELY
FOR OTHER PURPOSES.
Strongly agree⁵ Agree⁴ Undecided³ Disagree²
Strongly disagree¹ **(E)**

INDEX: THE SCIENCE RESEARCH ASSOCIATES EMPLOYEE INVENTORY

VARIABLE MEASURED: The SRA Employee Inventory provides a measure of employee attitudes toward the work environment. It is a diagnostic instrument identifying attitudinal levels for individuals and groups in such areas as job demands, working conditions, pay, employee benefits, friendliness and cooperation of fellow employees, supervisor-employee interpersonal relations, confidence in management, technical competence of supervision, effectiveness of administration, adequacy of communication, security of job and work relations, status and recognition, identification with the company, opportunity for growth and advancement, and finally reactions to the inventory itself.

DESCRIPTION: The inventory is not just an opinion survey. It is a kind of "morale audit" for work organizations that provides standard scores in each category based upon more than one million employees in a wide variety of business firms. Practical uses include assessing the general level of morale in an organization, locating the problem departments in the organization, determining satisfactions and dissatisfactions among employees, evaluating supervisory and executive training needs, and providing material for supervisory training programs.

WHERE PUBLISHED:
Science Research Associates, Inc.
57 West Grand Avenue
Chicago, Illinois
Copyright, 1952, by the Industrial Relations Center of the University of Chicago. All rights reserved.
Authors of the inventory include Robert K. Burns, L. L. Thurstone, David G. Moore, and Melony E. Baehr.

RELIABILITY: Both individual and group reliability have been determined by the test-retest method with an interval of one week between the test administrations. A sample of 134 employees shows a product moment correlation of .89. Group reliabilities range from .96 to .99 with reliability greater for groups of 50 or more employees.

VALIDITY: Good correspondence was found to exist between the inventory results and the considered judgments of experienced observers. In three of the companies surveyed, validity was established by conducting nondirective interviews among a cross-section of the employees.

STANDARD SCORES: Well standardized scores are available for comparative analysis of attitude levels in similar business firms and within similar departments.

Form A

SRA EMPLOYEE INVENTORY

Instructions

Purpose of the Inventory

Your company would like to know what you think about your job, your pay, your boss, and the company in general. This Inventory is designed to help you tell us your ideas and opinions quickly and easily without signing your name. This booklet contains a number of statements. All you have to do is to mark a cross by each statement to show how you feel. It is easy to do and you can be completely frank in your answers.

How to fill in the Inventory

Read each statement carefully and decide how you feel about it. You will agree with some statements, and you will disagree with others. You may be undecided about some. To help you express your opinion, three possible answers have been placed beside each statement:

	AGREE	?	DISAGREE
I would rather work in a large city than in a small town.	☐	☐	☐

Choose the answer most like your own opinion and mark a cross in the box under it.

For example:

This person feels he wants to work in a large city:

	AGREE	?	DISAGREE
I would rather work in a large city than in a small town.	☒	☐	☐

This person wants to work in a small town:

	AGREE	?	DISAGREE
I would rather work in a large city than in a small town.	☐	☐	☒

This person can't decide between a large city and a small town:

	AGREE	?	DISAGREE
I would rather work in a large city than in a small town.	☐	☒	☐

This is not a test

There are no "right" answers and no "wrong" answers. It is your own, honest opinion that we want.

Work rapidly but answer all statements

Do *not* spend too much time on any one statement. If you cannot decide about a statement, mark the "?" box, and go on to the next statement. If you make a mistake, erase your mark, or fill in the box completely. Then mark a cross in the correct box.

General information

Do *not* sign your name on the booklet. Be *sure* to fill in the blanks for general information on page 2 and page 4 of this booklet. This information will be used only to make the results more meaningful. It will not be used to identify you in any way.

When you have finished

When you have finished filling out the questionnaire, check to see that you have marked every statement. Then turn to page 2 where you will find the space to write your comments. In this space we would like you to write anything about your job or the company that is important to you. If something is irritating or trying for you, please comment on it. If something is pleasing or satisfying, please comment on that also. Or if you have a suggestion to help your job or the company, write that also.

	AGREE	?	DISAGREE
1. The hours of work here are O.K..............................	☐	☐	☐
2. Management does everything possible to prevent accidents in our work..........	☐	☐	☐
3. Management is doing its best to give us good working conditions............	☐	☐	☐
4. In my opinion, the pay here is lower than in other companies............	☐	☐	☐
5. They should do a better job of handling pay matters here........	☐	☐	☐
6. I understand what the company benefit program provides for employees............	☐	☐	☐
7. The people I work with help each other out when someone falls behind or gets in a tight spot............	☐	☐	☐
8. My boss is too interested in his own success to care about the needs of employees............	☐	☐	☐
9. My boss is always breathing down our necks; he watches us too closely............	☐	☐	☐
10. My boss gives us credit and praise for work well done.........	☐	☐	☐
11. Management here does everything it can to see that employees get a fair break on the job..................	☐	☐	☐
12. If I have a complaint to make, I feel free to talk to someone up-the-line..................	☐	☐	☐
13. My boss sees that employees are properly trained for their jobs..................	☐	☐	☐
14. My boss see that we have the things we need to do our jobs..................	☐	☐	☐
15. Management here is really trying to build the organization and make it successful..................	☐	☐	☐
16. Management here sees to it that there is cooperation between departments..................	☐	☐	☐
17. Management tells employees about company plans and developments..................	☐	☐	☐
18. They encourage us to make suggestions for improvements here..................	☐	☐	☐
19. I am often bothered by sudden speedups or unexpected slack periods in my work..................	☐	☐	☐
20. Changes are made here with little regard for the welfare of employees..................	☐	☐	☐
21. Compared with other employees, we get very little attention from management..................	☐	☐	☐
22. Sometimes I feel that my job counts for very little in this organization..................	☐	☐	☐

176

	AGREE	?	DISAGREE
3. The longer you work for this company the more you feel you belong..	☐	☐	☐
4. I have a great deal of interest in this company and its future..	☐	☐	☐
5. I have little opportunity to use my abilities in this organization...	☐	☐	☐
6. There are plenty of good jobs here for those who want to get ahead..	☐	☐	☐
7. I often feel worn out and tired on my job.....................	☐	☐	☐
8. They expect too much work from us around here..............	☐	☐	☐
9. Poor working conditions keep me from doing my best in my work..	☐	☐	☐
0. For my kind of job, the working conditions are O.K...........	☐	☐	☐
1. I'm paid fairly compared with other employees................	☐	☐	☐
2. Compared with other companies, employee benefits here are good..	☐	☐	☐
3. A few of the people I work with think they run the place......:	☐	☐	☐
4. The people I work with get along well together................	☐	☐	☐
5. My boss has always been fair in his dealings with me...........	☐	☐	☐
6. My boss gets employees to work together as a team...........	☐	☐	☐
7. I have confidence in the fairness and honesty of management..	☐	☐	☐
8. Management here is really interested in the welfare of employees..	☐	☐	☐
9. Most of the higher-ups are friendly toward employees..........	☐	☐	☐
0. My boss keeps putting things off; he just lets things ride........	☐	☐	☐
1. My boss lets us know exactly what is expected of us............	☐	☐	☐
2. Management fails to give clear-cut orders and instructions..	☐	☐	☐
3. I know how my job fits in with other work in this organization..	☐	☐	☐
4. Management keeps us in the dark about things we ought to know..	☐	☐	☐

45. Long service really means something in this organization........ AGREE ☐ ? ☐ DISAGREE ☐

46. You can get fired around here without much cause............. AGREE ☐ ? ☐ DISAGRE ☐

47. I can be sure of my job as long as I do good work............. AGREE ☐ ? ☐ DISAGRE ☐

48. I have plenty of freedom on the job to use my own judgment... AGREE ☐ ? ☐ DISAGRE ☐

49. Everybody in this organization tries to boss us around........... AGREE ☐ ? ☐ DISAGRE ☐

50. I really feel part of this organization......................... AGREE ☐ ? ☐ DISAGRE ☐

51. The people who get promotions around here usually deserve them... AGREE ☐ ? ☐ DISAGRE ☐

52. I can learn a great deal on my present job.................... AGREE ☐ ? ☐ DISAGRE ☐

53. My job is often dull and monotonous........................ AGREE ☐ ? ☐ DISAGRE ☐

54. There is too much pressure on my job....................... AGREE ☐ ? ☐ DISAGRE ☐

55. Some of the working conditions here are annoying............. AGREE ☐ ? ☐ DISAGRE ☐

56. I have the right equipment to do my work.................... AGREE ☐ ? ☐ DISAGRE ☐

57. My pay is enough to live on comfortably..................... AGREE ☐ ? ☐ DISAGRE ☐

58. I'm satisfied with the way employee benefits are handled here.. AGREE ☐ ? ☐ DISAGRE ☐

59. The company's employee benefit program is O.K............... AGREE ☐ ? ☐ DISAGRE ☐

60. The people I work with are very friendly..................... AGREE ☐ ? ☐ DISAGRE ☐

61. My boss really tries to get our ideas about things............. AGREE ☐ ? ☐ DISAGRE ☐

62. My boss ought to be friendlier toward employees.............. AGREE ☐ ? ☐ DISAGRE ☐

63. My boss lives up to his promises............................ AGREE ☐ ? ☐ DISAGRE ☐

64. Management here has a very good personnel policy............. AGREE ☐ ? ☐ DISAGRE ☐

65. Management ignores our suggestions and complaints........... AGREE ☐ ? ☐ DISAGRE ☐

66. My boss knows very little about his job...................... AGREE ☐ ? ☐ DISAGRE ☐

178

	AGREE	?	DISAGREE
67. My boss has the work well organized........................	☐	☐	☐
68. This company operates efficiently and smoothly................	☐	☐	☐
69. Management really knows its job............................	☐	☐	☐
70. They have a poor way of handling employee complaints here...	☐	☐	☐
71. You can say what you think around here......................	☐	☐	☐
72. You always know where you stand with this company..........	☐	☐	☐
73. When layoffs are necessary, they are handled fairly............	☐	☐	☐
74. I am very much underpaid for the work that I do.............	☐	☐	☐
75. I'm really doing something worthwhile in my job..............	☐	☐	☐
76. I'm proud to work for this company.........................	☐	☐	☐
77. Filling in this Inventory is a good way to let management know what employees think.....................	☐	☐	☐
78. I think some good may come out of filling in an Inventory like this one.....................................	☐	☐	☐

	AGREE ? DISAGREE		AGREE ? DISAGREE		AGREE ? DISAGREE
79.	☐ ☐ ☐	86.	☐ ☐ ☐	93.	☐ ☐ ☐
80.	☐ ☐ ☐	87.	☐ ☐ ☐	94.	☐ ☐ ☐
81.	☐ ☐ ☐	88.	☐ ☐ ☐	95.	☐ ☐ ☐
82.	☐ ☐ ☐	89.	☐ ☐ ☐	96.	☐ ☐ ☐
83.	☐ ☐ ☐	90.	☐ ☐ ☐	97.	☐ ☐ ☐
84.	☐ ☐ ☐	91.	☐ ☐ ☐	98.	☐ ☐ ☐
85.	☐ ☐ ☐	92.	☐ ☐ ☐	99.	☐ ☐ ☐

General information

1	2	3
4	5	6

Please write your comments here

General information

I	2	3
4	5	6

UTILITY: Inexpensive, easily interpreted, quickly scored, and permits use in all kinds of work organizations. Comparative analysis is facilitated by available standard scores.

RESEARCH APPLICATIONS: David G. Moore and Robert K. Burns, "How Good is Good Morale?" *Factory*, February, 1956, pp. 130-36.

The *SRA Employee Inventory* was prepared by the Employee Attitude Research Group of the Industrial Relations Center, University of Chicago. This group has members from both the University and industry. Thus, both the theoretical and practical aspects are well represented in all development work. Further details are given in the *Manual*.

The *SRA Employee Inventory* is published by SCIENCE RESEARCH AS-SOCIATES, Inc., 57 W. Grand Avenue, Chicago 10, Illinois. It is Copyrighted, 1951, by the Industrial Relations Center of the University of Chicago.

Please use number 7-1591 when reordering this booklet.

INDEX: MORSE INDEXES OF EMPLOYEE SATISFACTION

VARIABLE MEASURED: The degree of satisfaction that individuals obtain from the various roles they play in an organization; specifically (1) satisfaction with doing the actual content of the work, (2) satisfaction with being in the work group, (3) satisfaction with working in the company, (4) satisfaction with pay and job status.

DESCRIPTION: These are indexes of employee satisfaction, each of which contains four items developed through a combined logical and empirical method. The items were initially selected from an employee interview on the basis of the definitions of each area of employee satisfaction. Intercorrelations were then computed among all items that logically appeared to belong in each area. Items that showed very low correlations were removed. The items making up each index were not differentially weighed, but were added with unit weights to give a single measure of each type of employee satisfaction. The four indexes are called *intrinsic job satisfaction, company involvement, financial and job status satisfaction*, and *pride in group performance*. Each index has four items that are answered on a five-point scale ranging from strong like to strong dislike. This gives a range of scores from 4-20 on each index.

WHERE PUBLISHED: Nancy C. Morse, *Satisfactions in the White Collar Job*, Ann Arbor: University of Michigan, *Institute for Social Research*, 1953.

RELIABILITY: No split half or test-retest reliabilities are reported. Internal consistency of the scales is attested by the average intercorrelations of items:

Intrinsic job satisfaction	$r = .50$
Company involvement	$r = .45$
Financial and job status satisfaction	$r = .52$
Pride in group performance	$r = .39$

VALIDITY: The intrinsic job satisfaction, company involvement, and financial job status indexes, both from the intercorrelations of the total index scores and from the item analysis, appear to be significantly interrelated (intercorrelations ranging from $r = .35$ to $r = .43$). These three areas can be used to represent a general morale factor. This factor predicts the individual's desire to stay in the company rather than his productivity.

Pride in group performance (and its subitems) is, with few exceptions, not significantly related to the items of the other indexes or to the indexes themselves. It must be treated as an independent factor.

This index was related to the amount of voluntary help given by members to one another, friendliness in interpersonal relations, and the absence of antiproductivity group norms. It was also correlated with supervisor's identification with employees.

STANDARD SCORES:

		Range	*N*
Intrinsic Job Satisfaction	High Group	04-07	(177)
	Medium Group	08-11	(222)
	Low Group	12-20	(181)
Financial and Job Status			
Satisfaction	High Group	04-08	(160)
	Medium Group	09-12	(227)
	Low Group	13-20	(248)
Company Involvement	High Group	04-08	(250)
	Medium Group	09-12	(255)
	Low Group	13-20	(165)
Pride in Group Performance	High Group	04-08	(227)
	Medium Group	09-10	(264)
	Low Group	11-20	(251)

UTILITY: The indexes consist of easily administered questionnaire items. The time required is about 10 minutes for the administration of all four indexes.

RESEARCH APPLICATIONS: Morse reports relationships between the indexes and various supervisory practices, working conditions, and various background factors such as sex, age, length of service, and education. See *Satisfactions in the White Collar Job,* as cited in the aforementioned.

Company Involvement Index

1. "How do you like working here?"
   code: Five-point scale ranging from strong like, complete satisfaction to strong dislike.
2. "Would you advise a friend to come to work for the Company?"
   code: Three-point scale including: yes, pro-con, and no.
3. An overall coder rating of the employee's feelings about the fairness of the company, based on answers to questions throughout the interview.
   code: Three-point scale including: feels company fair and generous, feels company fair but very exacting, feels company unfair.
4. An overall coder rating of the employee's degree of identification with the company based on answers to questions throughout the interview.
   code: Three-point scale including: strong identification, some identification, and no identification.

Financial and Job Status Index

1. "How well satisfied are you with your salary?"
   code: Five-point scale ranging from very well satisfied to very dissatisfied.
2. "How satisfied are you with your chances of getting more pay?"
   code: Five-point scale ranging from very satisfied to very dissatisfied.
3. "How about your own case, how satisfied are you with the way things have been working out for you?" (This question was preceded by two questions on "getting ahead here at the Company" and was answered in that context.)
   code: Five-point scale ranging from very satisfied to very dissatisfied.
4. Coder overall rating of degree of frustration evidenced by respondent in advancing in his job or in his main vocational objectives. Answers to questions throughout the interview were used to measure the degree to which employee felt his vocational desires were blocked.
   code: Five-point scale ranging from strong frustration to high adjustment, no frustration.

Intrinsic Job Satisfaction Index

1. "How well do you like the sort of work you are doing?"
   code: Five-point scale varying from strong like to strong dislike.
2. "Does your job give you a chance to do the things you feel you do best?"
   code: Five-point scale varying from yes (strong) to no (strong).
3. "Do you get any feeling of accomplishment from the work you are doing?"
   code: Five-point scale varying from strong sense of task completion to no sense of task completion.
4. "How do you feel about your work, does it rate as an important job with you?"
   code: Five-point scale varying from very important to of no importance.

Pride-in-Group-Performance Index

1. "How well do you think your section compares with other sections in the Company in getting a job done?"
   code: Five-point scale ranging from very good, one of best in company, to very poor, one of worst in company.
2. Answers to the section comparison question were also coded on the degree of emotional identification with the section that employee showed. (The use of "we" as opposed to "it" or "they" was one of the indications to the coder of identification.)
   code: Three-point scale: strong identification, mild identification, indifference or lack of identification.
3. "How well do you think your division compares with other divisions in the Company in getting a job done?"
   code: Five-point scale ranging from very good, one of best in company, to very poor, one of worst in company.
4. Answers to the division comparison question were also coded on degree of emotional identification with the division the employee showed.
   code: Three-point scale: strong identification, mild identification, indifference or lack of identification.

INDEX: GUTTMAN SCALES OF MILITARY BASE MORALE

VARIABLE MEASURED: Satisfaction with Air Force, Satisfaction with Air Site, Satisfaction with the Job, Personal Commitment to Aircraft Control and Warning Mission.

WHERE PUBLISHED: Delbert C. Miller and Nahum Z. Medalia, "Efficiency, Leadership, and Morale in Small Military Organizations," *The Sociological Review*, July, 1953, 3: 93-107.

RELIABILITY: Scalability shown by reproducibility coefficients.

Satisfaction with Air Force	$R = .93$
Satisfaction with the Air Site	$R = .90$
Satisfaction with the Job	$R = .90$
Personal Commitment to AC&W Mission	$R = .94$

VALIDITY: Correlation between ratings made by outside military inspectors of site morale and satisfaction with Air Site scale in 50 squadrons show Spearman Rank Correlation of $r_s = .52$.

UTILITY: Scales are short and unidimensional. They may be easily converted to use in other organizations by substituting appropriate unit names. However, as in all Guttman Scales reproducibility varies with respondent samples and must be recomputed.

RESEARCH APPLICATION: Glenn C. McCann, *Morale and Human Relations Problems in AC & W Sites*, Air Force Personnel and Training Research Center Technical Memorandum CRL-TM-56-5, April, 1956.

Nahum Z. Medalia, "Unit Size and Leadership Perception," *Sociometry*, February, 1954, 17: 64-67.

————, "Authoritarianism, Leader Acceptance, and Group Cohesion," *Journal of Abnormal and Social Psychology*, September, 1955, 51: 207-13.

————, and Delbert C. Miller, "Human Relations Leadership and the Association of Morals and the Effectiveness of Work Groups," *Social Forces*, May, 1955, 33: 348-52.

Delbert C. Miller and N. Z. Medalia, "Efficiency, Leadership, and Morale in Small Military Organizations," *The Sociological Review*, July, 1955, 3(1): 93-107.

Delbert C. Miller, Nahum Z. Medalia, Glen C. McCann, and Others, "Morale and Human Relations Leadership as Factors in Organizational Effectiveness," in R. V. Bowers, *Studies in Organizational Effectiveness*, Washington, D.C.: Air Force Office of Scientific Research, 1962.

MORALE SCALES FOR MILITARY ORGANIZATIONS

Satisfaction with Air Force (All items answered by Strongly Agree, Agree, Undecided, Disagree, Strongly Disagree.)

1. I have a poor opinion of the Air Force most of the time.
2. Most of the time the Air Force is not run very well.
3. I am usually dissatisfied with the Air Force.
4. The Air Force is better than any of the other Services.
5. If I remain in military service I would prefer to stay in the Air Force.

Satisfaction with the Air Site

1. In general this Air Site is run very well.
2. This Air Site is the best in the whole Division.
3. I am usually dissatisfied with this Air Site.
4. I would rather be stationed at this Air Site than any I know about.
5. I would like to stay at this Air Site.

Satisfaction with the Job

1. I would be more satisfied with some other job in AC&W than I am with my usual job.
2. My Air Force job is usually interesting to me.
3. I believe the Air Force has placed me in a job that suits me very well.
4. I believe my Air Force job is usually worthwhile.
5. If I have a chance, I will change to some other job at this Site.

Personal Commitment to Aircraft Control and Warning Mission

1. Under present world conditions, I would advise many of my civilian friends to get into AC&W if they should ask my advice on joining the service. (*a*) No, I would advise them to stay out of AC&W. (*b*) I would tell them it makes no difference what you join. (*c*) Yes, I would advise them to join AC&W.
2. Under present world conditions, I feel that I can do more for my country as a member of AC&W than as a civilian. (*a*) No, I would be more valuable as a civilian. (*b*) I am undecided about this. (*c*) Yes, I am more valuable in AC&W.
3. Under present world conditions I feel that I can do more for

my country as a member of some other part of the armed services, rather than as a member of AC&W. (*a*) Yes, I could be of more value elsewhere in the armed services. (*b*) It is a toss-up where I could contribute the most. (*c*) No, I am of more value in AC&W.

4. Under present world conditions I feel I can do more for my country as a member of AC&W than some other part of the Air Force. (*a*) No, I would be of more value elsewhere in the Air Force. (*b*) I'm about of equal value any place in the Air Force. (*c*) Yes, I am definitely more valuable in AC&W.

5. If present world conditions continue to be about the same, I would want to continue to be a member of AC&W as long as I remain in military service. (*a*) No, I would want to transfer from AC&W. (*b*) It doesn't matter whether I am in AC&W or not. (*c*) Yes, I would definitely want to remain in AC&W.

6. If the U.S. should enter a third world war and if I should remain in military service, I would want to stay in AC&W. (*a*) No, I prefer to be in some other part of the service. (*b*) It wouldn't make much difference where I serve. (*c*) Yes, I would prefer to remain in AC&W. (All of the aforementioned items are interspersed when they are administered.)

INDEX: BRAYFIELD AND ROTHE'S INDEX OF JOB SATISFACTION

VARIABLE MEASURED: General measure of job satisfaction.

WHERE PUBLISHED: Arthur H. Brayfield and Harold F. Rothe, "An Index of Job Satisfaction," *Journal of Applied Psychology*, October, 1951, 35: 307-11.

CONSTRUCTION: As a working approach for this study it was assumed that job satisfaction could be inferred from the individual's attitude toward his work. This approach dictated the methodology of attitude scaling. The following requirements were formulated as desirable attributes of an attitude scale designed to provide a useful index of job satisfaction: (1) it should give an index of "overall" job satisfaction rather than specific aspects of job satisfaction; (2) it should be applicable to a wide variety of jobs; (3) it should be sensitive to variations in attitude; (4) the items should be of such a nature (interesting, realistic, and varied) that the scale would evoke cooperation from both management and employees; (5) it should yield a reliable index; (6) it should yield a valid index; (7) it should be brief and easily scored.

The construction of this scale was made a class project in Personnel Psychology for members of an Army Specialized Training Program in personnel psychology at the University of Minnesota in the summer and fall of 1943. Seventy-seven men cooperated. Items referring to specific aspects of a job were eliminated since an "overall" attitudinal factor was desired.

The present index contains 18 items with Thurstone scale values ranging from 1.2 to 10.0 with approximately .5 step intervals. The items are not arranged in the order of magnitude of scale values. The Likert scoring system consisting of five categories of agreement-disagreement was applied to each item, and the Thurstone scoring system of five categories is applied to the items. The Thurstone scale value gives the direction of scoring method so that a low total score would represent the dissatisfied end of the scale and a high total score the satisfied end. The items are selected so that the satisfied end of the scale was indicated by *Strongly Agree* and *Agree,* and *Disagree* and *Strongly Disagree* for the other half. The neutral response is *Undecided.* The Likert scoring weights for each item range from 1 to 5, and the range of possible total scores is 18 to 90 with 54 (Undecided) the neutral point.

RELIABILITY: The revised scale (which is the present one) was administered as part of a study of 231 employed female office employees. The blanks were signed along with other tests. One of the investigators personally administered the tests to employees in small groups. The range of job satisfaction scores for this sample was 35-87. The mean score was 63.8 with an S. D. of 9.4. The odd-even product moment reliability coefficient computed for this sample was .77, which was corrected by the Spearman-Brown formula to a reliability coefficient of .87.

VALIDITY: Evidence for the high validity of the blank rests upon the nature of the items, the method of construction, and its differentiating power when applied to two groups that could reasonably be assumed to differ in job satisfaction. The nature of the individual items is partial, although not crucial, evidence for the validity of the scale. This is an appeal to "face" validity. Additional evidence is furnished by the method of construction. The attitude variable of job satisfaction is inferred from verbal reactions to a job expressed along a favorable-unfavorable continuum.

The job satisfaction blank was administered to 91 adult night school students in classes in Personnel Psychology at the University of Minnesota during 1945 and 1946. The range of job satisfaction scores for this sample was 29-89. The mean score was 70.4 with an S. D. of 13.2. The assumption was made that those persons employed in occupations appropriate to their expressed interest should, on the average, be more satisfied with their jobs than those members of the class employed in occupations inappropriate to their expressed interest in personnel work. The 91 persons accordingly were divided into two groups (Personnel and Nonpersonnel) with respect to their employment in a position identified by payroll title as a personnel function. The mean of the Personnel group was 76.9 with an S. D. of 8.6 as compared to a mean of 65.4 with an S. D. of 14.02 for the Nonpersonnel group. This difference of 11.5 points is significant at the 1 per cent level; the difference between the variances also is significant at the 1 per cent level. It might also be mentioned that scores on this index correlated .92 with scores on the Hoppock job satisfaction scale.

RESEARCH APPLICATIONS: Brayfield, Arthur H., Wells, Richard V., and Strate, Marvin W., "Interrelationships Among Measures of Job Satisfaction and General Satisfaction," *Journal of Applied Psychology,* August, 1957, 41: 201-5.

AN INDEX OF JOB SATISFACTION * †

Some jobs are more interesting and satisfying than others. We want to know how people feel about different jobs. This blank contains 18 statements about jobs. You are to cross out the phrase below each statement that has best described how you feel about your present job. There are no right or wrong answers. We should like your honest opinion on each one of the statements. Work out the sample item numbered (o).

o. There are some conditions concerning my job that could be improved.
Strongly agree, agree, undecided, disagree, strongly disagree.

1. My job is like a hobby to me.
Strongly agree, agree, undecided, disagree, strongly disagree.

2. My job is usually interesting enough to keep me from getting bored.
Strongly agree, agree, undecided, disagree, strongly disagree.

3. It seems that my friends are more interested in their jobs.
Strongly agree, agree, undecided, disagree, strongly disagree.

4. I consider my job rather unpleasant.
Strongly agree, agree, undecided, disagree, strongly disagree.

5. I enjoy my work more than my leisure time.
Strongly agree, agree, undecided, disagree, strongly disagree.

6. I am often bored with my job.
Strongly agree, agree, undecided, disagree, strongly disagree.

7. I feel fairly well satisfied with my job.
Strongly agree, agree, undecided, disagree, strongly disagree.

8. Most of the time I have to force myself to go to work.
Strongly agree, agree, undecided, disagree, strongly disagree.

9. I am satisfied with my job for the time being.
Strongly agree, agree, undecided, disagree, strongly disagree.

10. I feel that my job is no more interesting than others I could get. Strongly agree, agree, undecided, disagree, strongly disagree.

11. I definitely dislike my work. Strongly agree, agree, undecided, disagree, strongly disagree.

12. I feel that I am happier in my work than most other people. Strongly agree, agree, undecided, disagree, strongly disagree.

13. Most days I am enthusiastic about my work. Strongly agree, agree, undecided, disagree, strongly disagree.

14. Each day of work seems like it will never end. Strongly agree, agree, undecided, disagree, strongly disagree.

15. I like my job better than the average worker does. Strongly agree, agree, undecided, disagree, strongly disagree.

16. My job is pretty uninteresting. Strongly agree, agree, undecided, disagree, strongly disagree.

17. I find real enjoyment in my work. Strongly agree, agree, undecided, disagree, strongly disagree.

18. I am disappointed that I ever took this job. Strongly agree, agree, undecided, disagree, strongly disagree.

* Arthur H. Brayfield and Harold F. Rothe, *Journal of Applied Psychology*, October, 1951, 35(5): 307-11.

† This blank containing 18 items with Thurstone scale values ranging from 1.2 to 10.0 with approximately .5 step intervals is not arranged in order of magnitude of scale values. The Likert scoring system of five categories is applied to each item. Thurstone scale values give the direction of scoring method. Likert scoring weights range for each item 1 to 5. The range of possible total scores became 18 to 90 with the undecided or neutral point at 54.

SECTION D

Community

Measures of community variables are scarce. One of the first attempts to secure measures of the "goodness" of a city was made by E. L. Thorndike. His research monograph, *Our City* (New York: Harcourt, Brace, 1939), provided the first careful attempt to evaluate the quality of American cities. Ratings of 310 American cities over 300,000 population were made. In his *144 Smaller Cities*, Thorndike applied his "goodness" rating to cities between 20,000 and 30,000 population. The method requires the gathering of statistics on factors not too easily obtained. Paul B. Gillen in his *The Distribution of Occupations as a City Yardstick* (New York: Columbia University Press, 1951) presents a shorter technique based on the occupational distribution of the city. These indexes are recommended if a comparative rating of cities is desired.

The scales chosen for this section are chosen for more diagnostic research within a given community. Bosworth's *Community Attitude Scale* is designed to assess the degree of progressive attitude evidenced by members of a community. Fessler's *Community Solidarity Index* purports to measure community member solidarity. This scale is useful in determining relationships between community progress and solidarity. The *Community Rating Schedule* is a useful rating device in ascertaining the different views of such groups as business men, labor leaders, ministers, teachers, welfare workers, etc. *The Scorecard for Community Services Activity* can be used to assess participation in the community services activity of the community. The relationship of community member progressiveness and community service activity might be fruitfully explored. Each scale opens possibilities of studying the relation of such background factors as occupation, social class, education, age, sex, and marital status upon community participation and progress.

INDEX: COMMUNITY ATTITUDE SCALE

VARIABLE MEASURED: The degree of progressive attitude evidenced on such areas of community life as (1) general community improvement, (2) living conditions, (3) business and industry, (4) health and recreation, (5) education, (6) religion, (7) youth programs, (8) utilities, and (9) communications.

DESCRIPTION: A cross section of a wide range of groups in various communities defined the meaning of progress by submitting a number of statements that they designated as progressive and unprogressive. These statements provided 364 items that were placed on a five point Likert-type format. A representative panel of leaders independently designated each item as progressive or unprogressive. Various tests showed that 60 items were most discriminating. These 60 items were compiled into three subscales with 20 items each. These scales are identified as Community Integration, Community Services, and Civic Responsibilities.

WHERE PUBLISHED: A Ph.D. dissertation by Claud A. Bosworth, submitted to the University of Michigan, 1954.

RELIABILITY: 60 item scale, $r = .56$.

VALIDITY: Total mean scores discriminated significantly between a progressive and an unprogressive group at the .025 level. It was also found that those citizens who positively endorsed the scale items designed to measure attitudes toward other phases of community progress also voted for the sewer extension plan.

UTILITY: The scale is easily administered either in an interview or by questionnaire. Approximate time required is 20 minutes.

COMMUNITY ATTITUDE SCALE

Claud A. Bosworth

(Community Services Subscale)

	St. Agree	Agree	?	Disagree	St. Dis.

1. The school should stick to the 3 R's and forget about most of the other courses being offered today.

2. Most communities are good enough as they are without starting any new community improvement programs.

3. Every community should encourage more music and lecture programs.

4. This used to be a better community to live in.

5. Long term progress is more important than immediate benefits.

6. We have too many organizations for doing good in the community.

7. The home and the church should have all the responsibility for preparing young people for marriage and parenthood.

8. The responsibility for older people should be confined to themselves and their families instead of the community.

9. Communities have too many youth programs.

10. Schools are good enough as they are in most communities.

11. Too much time is usually spent on the planning phases of community projects.

12. Adult education should be an essential part of the local school program.

13. Only the doctors should have the responsibility for the health program in the community.

14. Mental illness is not a responsibility of the whole community.

15. A modern community should have the services of social agencies.

COMMUNITY ATTITUDE SCALE—(Continued)

	St. Agree	Agree	?	Disagree	St. Dis.
(Community Services Subscale)					
16. The spiritual needs of the citizens are adequately met by the churches.	—	—	—	—	—
17. In order to grow, a community must provide additional recreation facilities.	—	—	—	—	—
18. In general, church members are better citizens.	—	—	—	—	—
19. The social needs of the citizens are the responsibility of themselves and their families and not of the community.	—	—	—	—	—
20. Churches should be expanded and located in accordance with population growth.	—	—	—	—	—
(Community Integration Subscale)					
21. No community improvement program should be carried on that is injurious to a business.	—	—	—	—	—
22. Industrial development should include the interest in assisting local industry.	—	—	—	—	—
23. The first and major responsibility of each citizen should be to earn dollars for his own pocket.	—	—	—	—	—
24. More industry in town lowers the living standards.	—	—	—	—	—
25. The responsibility of citizens who are not actively participating in a community improvement program is to criticize those who are active.	—	—	—	—	—
26. What is good for the community is good for me.	—	—	—	—	—
27. Each one should handle his own business as he pleases and let the other businessmen handle theirs as they please.	—	—	—	—	—
28. A strong Chamber of Commerce is beneficial to any community.	—	—	—	—	—
29. Leaders of the Chamber of Commerce are against the welfare of the majority of the citizens in the community.	—	—	—	—	—

COMMUNITY ATTITUDE SCALE—(Continued)

(Community Integration Subscale)

	St. Agree	Agree	?	Disagree	St. Dis.

30. A community would get along better if each one would mind his own business and others take care of theirs.

31. Members of any community organization should be expected to attend only those meetings that affect him personally.

32. Each of us can make real progress only when the group as a whole makes progress.

33. The person who pays no attention to the complaints of the persons working for him is a poor citizen.

34. It would be better if we would have the farmer look after his own business and we look after ours.

35. All unions are full of Communists.

36. The good citizens encourage the widespread circulation of all news including that which may be unfavorable to them and their organizations.

37. The good citizen should help minority groups with their problems.

38. The farmer has too prominent a place in our society.

39. A citizen should join only those organizations that will promote his own interests.

40. Everyone is out for himself at the expense of everyone else.

(Civic Responsibilities Subscale)

41. Busy people should not have the responsibility for civic programs.

42. The main responsibility for keeping the community clean is up to the city officials.

43. Community improvements are fine if they don't increase taxes.

COMMUNITY ATTITUDE SCALE—(Continued)

(Civic Responsibilities Subscale)

	St. Agree	Agree	?	Disagree	St. Dis.

44. The younger element have too much to say about our community affairs.

45. A progressive community must provide adequate parking facilities.

46. Government officials should get public sentiment before acting on major municipal projects.

47. A good citizen should be willing to assume leadership in a civic improvement organization.

48. Progress can best be accomplished by having only a few people involved.

49. Community improvement should be the concern of only a few leaders in the community.

50. A community would be better if less people would spend time on community improvement projects.

51. Only those who have the most time should assume the responsibility for civic programs.

52. Living conditions in a community should be improved.

53. A good citizen should sign petitions for community improvement.

54. Improving slum areas is a waste of money.

55. The police force should be especially strict with outsiders.

56. The paved streets and roads in most communities are good enough.

57. The sewage system of a community must be expanded as it grows even though it is necessary to increase taxes.

58. Some people just want to live in slum areas.

59. The main problem we face is high taxes.

60. Modern methods and equipment should be provided for all phases of city government.

INDEX: COMMUNITY SOLIDARITY INDEX

VARIABLE MEASURED: Amount of consensus among members of primary rural communities (250-2,000 pop.).

DESCRIPTION: Eight major areas of community behavior are examined:

1. community spirit
2. interpersonal relations
3. family responsibility toward the community
4. schools
5. churches
6. economic behavior
7. local government
8. tension areas

These eight areas are covered in a series of 40 statements that are rated by the respondent on a five-item scale according to his judgment of how the statements apply to his community. The items range from "very true" to "definitely untrue" with scores ranging from 5 for the "very true" response to 1 for the "definitely untrue" response. The standard deviation of the scores of all the schedules for the community is taken as a measure of the degree of consensus and, therefore, of solidarity in the community. The smaller the S, the greater the solidarity is assumed to be. The mean of the total score is considered to be an index of the members' opinion of the quality of the community. For comparison with other communities an octagonal profile may be used.

WHERE PUBLISHED: Donald R. Fessler, "The Development of a Scale for Measuring Community Solidarity," *Rural Sociology*, 1952, 17: 144-52.

RELIABILITY: Split-half r was described as being high but not given.

VALIDITY: Face validity.

UTILITY: This index measures an important community variable. When relationships are examined between community action programs and community solidarity, this measure may be highly predictive of the success or failure of community efforts.

RESEARCH APPLICATION: None known.

COMMUNITY SOLIDARITY INDEX SCHEDULE

Name _____ Community _____

Occupation _____ Married _____ Single _____

If married, number of children in school, if any _____

boys _____ girls _____, number of children out of school _____.

Number of years resident in community _____. Location of residence:

in town _____ outside of town _____ how far _____ miles?

Think of each of the statements below as relating to the people of this entire community both in town and on neighboring farms. If you think the statement fits this community very well, after the statement circle *vt* (for very true); if it applies only partially, circle *t* (for true); if you cannot see how it relates one way or another to this particular community, circle *nd* (for not decided); if you think it is not true, circle *u* (for untrue); and if it definitely is not true, circle *du* (for definitely untrue). PLEASE RECORD THE IMPRESSION THAT FIRST OCCURS TO YOU. Do not go back and change your answers.

1. Real friends are hard to find in this community. *vt t nd u du* (2) *

2. Our schools do a poor job of preparing young people for life. *vt t nd u du* (4)

3. Local concerns deal fairly and squarely with everyone. *vt t nd u du* (6)

4. The community is very peaceful and orderly. *vt t nd u du* (8)

5. A lot of people here think they are too nice for you. *vt t nd u du* (1)

6. Families in this community keep their children under control. *vt t nd u du* (3)

7. The different churches here cooperate well with one another. *vt t nd u du* (5)

* The number in parentheses indicates the area to which the statement belongs.

8. Some people here "get by with murder" while others take the rap for any little misdeed. *vt t nd u du* (7)

9. Almost everyone is polite and courteous to you. *vt t nd u du* (2)

10. Our schools do a good job of preparing students for college. *vt t nd u du* (4)

11. Everyone here tries to take advantage of you. *vt t nd u du* (6)

12. People around here show good judgment. *vt t nd u du* (8)

13. People won't work together to get things done for the community. *vt t nd u du* (1)

14. Parents teach their children to respect other people's rights and property. *vt t nd u du* (3)

15. Most of our church people forget the meaning of the word brotherhood when they get out of church. *vt t nd u du* (5)

16. This community lacks real leaders. *vt t nd u du* (7)

17. People give you a bad name if you insist on being different. *vt t nd u du* (2)

18. Our high-school graduates take an active interest in making their community a better place in which to live. *vt t nd u du* (4)

19. A few people here make all the dough. *vt t nd u du* (6)

20. Too many young people get into sex difficulties. *vt t nd u du* (8)

21. The community tries hard to help its young people along. *vt t nd u du* (1)

22. Folks are unconcerned about what their kids do so long as they keep out of trouble. *vt t nd u du* (3)

23. The churches are a constructive factor for better community life. *vt t nd u du* (5)

24. The mayor and councilmen run the town to suit themselves. *vt t nd u du* (7)

25. I feel very much that I belong here. *vt t nd u du* (2)

26. Many young people in the community do not finish high school. *vt t nd u du* (4)

27. The people here are all penny pinchers. *vt t nd u du* (6)

28. You must spend lots of money to be accepted here. *vt t nd u du* (8)

29. The people as a whole mind their own business. *vt t nd u du* (1)

30. Most people get their families to Sunday School or church on Sunday. *vt t nd u du* (3)

31. Every church wants to be the biggest and the most impressive. *vt t nd u du* (5)

32. A few have the town politics well sewed up. *vt t nd u du* (7)

33. Most of the students here learn to read and write well. *vt t nd u du* (4)

34. People are generally critical of others. *vt t nd u du* (2)

35. Local concerns expect their help to live on low wages. *vt t nd u du* (6)

36. You are out of luck here if you happen to be of the wrong nationality. *vt t nd u du* (8)

37. No one seems to care much how the community looks. *vt t nd u du* (1)

38. If their children keep out of the way, parents are satisfied to let them do whatever they want to do. *vt t nd u du* (3)

39. Most of our churchgoers do not practice what they preach. *vt t nd u du* (5)

40. The town council gets very little done. *vt t nd u du* (7)

INDEX: COMMUNITY RATING SCHEDULE

VARIABLE MEASURED: The quality of community life, of "goodness" of the community, is assessed.

DESCRIPTION: Ten institutional areas of community life are rated as good, fair, or poor. The areas selected include education, housing and planning, religion, equality of opportunity, economic development, cultural opportunities, recreation, health and welfare, government, and community organization. Scores range from 0-100.

WHERE PUBLISHED: New York State Citizen's Council, *Adult Leadership*, October, 1952.

RELIABILITY: Not known.

VALIDITY: Rests upon face validity.

STANDARD SCORES:

> Good communities = 90-100
> Fair communities = 70-89
> Poor communities = 0-69

UTILITY: The schedule is easy to administer; the time required is about 10 minutes. Raters often have difficulty in making a general judgment and express qualifications. These should be expected. The special advantage of this index is that it permits analysis of individual raters. Individual raters from business, labor, welfare, education, and religion often differ widely in their assessments of the same community.

RESEARCH APPLICATIONS: No reported studies. However, the index opens possibilities of examining the patterns of new industrial locations with quality of the community. The relationship of leadership to community quality is an important area that should be explored.

COMMUNITY RATING SCHEDULE *

Ask respondent to rate community as good, fair, or poor as judged by similar communities in the United States.

Good Fair Poor

Standard No. 1 Education

Modern education available for every child, youth and adult. Uncrowded, properly equipped schools in good physical conditions. Highly qualified, well paid teachers.

Standard No. 2 Housing and Planning

Every family decently housed. Continuous planning for improvement of residential areas, parks, highways, and other community essentials. Parking, traffic, and transportation problems under control.

Standard No. 3 Religion

Full opportunity for religious expression accorded to every individual—churches strong and well supported.

Standard No. 4 Equality of Opportunity

People of different races, religions, and nationalities have full chance for employment and for taking part in community life. Dangerous tensions kept at minimum by avoidance of discrimination and injustices.

Standard No. 5 Economic Development

Good jobs available. Labor, industry, agriculture, and government work together to insure sound economic growth.

Standard No. 6 Cultural Opportunities

Citizens' lives strengthened by ample occasion to enjoy music, art, and dramatics. A professionally administered library service benefits people of all ages. Newspapers and radio carefully review community affairs.

* Prepared by New York State Citizen's Council; Reprinted in *Adult Leadership,* October, 1952, p. 19.

Continued on page 204.

COMMUNITY RATING SCHEDULE—(Continued)

Good Fair Poor

Standard No. 7 Recreation

Enough supervised playgrounds and facilities for outdoor activities. Full opportunity to take part in arts and crafts, photography, and other hobbies.

Standard No. 8 Health and Welfare

Positive approach to improving health of entire community. Medical care and hospitalization readily available. Provision made for under-privileged children, the aged, and the handi-capped. Families in trouble can secure needed assistance.

Standard No. 9 Government

Capable citizens seek public office. Officials con-cerned above all with community betterment. Controversy stems from honest differences of opinion, not from squabbles over privilege.

Standard No. 10 Community Organization

An organization-community forum, citizen's council, or community federation-representative of entire town, is working for advancement of the whole community. Citizens have oppor-tunity to learn about and take part in local affairs. There is an organized, community-wide discussion program. Specialized organizations give vigorous attention to each important civic need.

	Good ____	10 points for each item ____
Total Score for your Town	Fair ____	5 points for each item ____
	Poor ____	no points
	Total	____

INDEX: SCORECARD FOR COMMUNITY SERVICES ACTIVITY

VARIABLE MEASURED: Individual participation in community services.

DESCRIPTION: The Scorecard is an arbitrary index to assess individual participation in community services. Fifteen possible behavioral items are presented as those that compose bulk of community service activity. Scores of 0-15 may be recorded as each item participation is given a weight of one.

WHERE PUBLISHED: Unpublished.

RELIABILITY: No tests have been made.

VALIDITY: Rests on face validity.

STANDARD SCORES:

    10-15 outstanding community member
    6-9   an average member
    0-5   low participating member

Cutting points were based upon a random sample of 100 adults in a middle class community.

UTILITY: Administration of the Scorecard takes less than four minutes. It provides for both individual and group assessment.

RESEARCH APPLICATIONS: None reported. However, the index opens possibilities of exploring important facets of citizenship including the importance of background factors such as age, sex, education, race, and social class. The relation between community service activity, community solidarity, and community rating is a challenging research endeavor.

SCORECARD FOR COMMUNITY SERVICES ACTIVITY

Constructed by Delbert C. Miller

(* Score one point for each "yes")

FINANCIAL SUPPORT—Did you, in the past year,

_____ Contribute money to a community chest campaign?

_____ Contribute money to a church?

_____ Contribute money for other charitable purposes?

GENERAL ACTIVITY—Did you, in the past year,

_____ Serve on any board responsible for civic programs?

_____ Serve on any committee working to improve civic life?

_____ Assume leadership of any civic action program?

COMMUNITY ISSUES AND PROBLEMS—Did you, in the past year,

_____ Inform yourself about civic issues and problems?

_____ Discuss civic problems frequently with more than one person?

_____ Persuade others to take a particular position?

_____ Get advice from others?

_____ Speak to key leaders about problems?

_____ Visit community organizations or board meetings to inform yourself?

_____ Write letters, or circulate literature, or hold home meetings?

* 10-15 points—An outstanding community member
  6-9 points—An average member
  0-5 points—A low participating member

GROUP ACTION—Did you, in the past year,

_____ Belong to one or more organizations that takes stands on community issues and problems?

_____ Make group visits or invite visits of community officials to your organization?

_____ Total Score

FOR THE ADVANCED STUDENT

1. Consult *Urban Research Methods,* ed. Jack P. Gibbs, Princeton, N.J.: D. Van Nostrand, 1961.
2. Robert C. Angell, "Moral Integration of Cities," *American Journal of Sociology,* July, 1951, Vol. 57, Part 2.
3. Eshref Shevky and Wendell Bell, *Social Area Analysis,* Stanford: Stanford University Press, 1955. Contains indexes of social rank, urbanization, and segregation.
4. Christian T. Jonassen, *The Measurement of Community Dimensions and Elements,* Columbus: Center for Educational Administration, Ohio State University Press, 1959. Cf. his "Functional Unities in Eighty-eight Community Systems," *American Sociological Review,* June, 1961, 26: 399-407.

SECTION E

Social Participation

This section includes *Chapin's Social Participation Scale*. It is a general scale of participation in voluntary organizations of all kinds —professional, civic, and social. It is used when the total participation pattern is an important variable. The *Leisure Participation and Enjoyment Scale* enables the researcher to get a detailed picture of leisure patterns and also to get a score for each respondent on both participation and enjoyment.

Two measures of neighborhood participation are included. *Bernard's Neighboring Practices Schedule* is an instrument for scoring neighboring practices of both husband and wife. *Wallin Women's Neighborliness Scale* is a Guttman-type scale that has exhibited unidimensionality on the samples of respondents that have been tested. It is designed to be answered by women respondents only. If the problem is amenable to the *Wallin Women's Neighborliness Scale* it is recommended because of the Guttman construction. However, the researcher must remember that unidimensionality must be shown for his sample before this character of the scale may be assumed.

The *Citizen Political Action Schedule* is a scorecard for political behavior reported by a community resident. If the respondent reports accurately, the scale can reveal the behavioral acts in the political sphere.

INDEX: CHAPIN'S SOCIAL PARTICIPATION SCALE, 1952 EDITION

VARIABLE MEASURED: Degree of a person's or family's participation in community groups and institutions.

DESCRIPTION: This is a Guttman-type scale with reproducibility coefficients of .92 to .97 for groups of leaders. High scores of 18 and over represent titular leader achievement. The five components are (1) Member, (2) Attendance, (3) Financial contributions, (4) Member of Committees, (5) Offices held. These components measure different dimensions: intensity of participation by Nos. 2, 3, 4, and 5; extensity by No. 1. Also, rejection-acceptance in formal groups is measured by Nos. 1, 4, and 5, for which the intercorrelations are found to be of the order of $r_{14} = .53$ to $.58$; $r_{15} = .36$ to $.40$; $r_{45} = .36$ to $.40$. Social participation is measured by Nos. 2 and 3 with intercorrelations of $r_{23} = .80$ to $.89$. Other intercorrelations among the components have been found to be of the order of $r_{12} = .88$; $r_{13} = .89$; $r_{24} = .60$; $r_{34} = .40$; $r_{35} = .35$; and $r_{45} = .50$ to $.58$.

WHERE PUBLISHED: F. Stuart Chapin: *Experimental Designs in Sociological Research*, New York: Harper, 1955, Appendix B, pp. 275-78.

RELIABILITY: $r = .89$ to $.95$.

VALIDITY:

With Chapin's social status scale scores	$r = .62$ to $.66$
With income class	$r = .52$
With occupational groups	$r = .63$
With years of formal education	$r = .54$
Between husband and wife	$r = .76$

STANDARD SCORES: Mean scores for occupational groups are as follows:

    I. Professional and II. Managerial and Proprietary, 20.
    III. Clerical, 16.
    IV. Skilled, 12.
    V. Semiskilled, 8.
    VI. Unskilled, 4.

UTILITY: One sheet is used for entries on each group affiliation of subject recorded in five entries under five columns by the visitor in reply to questions answered by the subject. It takes 10 to 15 minutes to fill in the subject's answers.

    The scale may also be self-administered.

RESEARCH APPLICATIONS: Note use in F. S. Chapin, "The Effects of Slum Clearance on Family and Community Relationships in Minneapolis in 1935-1936," *American Journal of Sociology*, March, 1938, pp. 744-63.

F. S. Chapin, "Social Participation and Social Intelligence," *American Sociological Review*, April, 1939, 4: 157-66.

Walter T. Martin, "A Consideration of Differences in the Extent and Location of the Formal Associational Activities of Rural-Urban Fringe Residents," *American Sociological Review*, December, 1952, 17: 687-94.

G. A. Lundberg and Margaret Lansing, "The Sociography of Some Community Relations," *American Sociological Review*, June, 1937, 2: 318-28.

SOCIAL PARTICIPATION SCALE

Address _____   Case No. _____

Husband

Age _____ Education _____ Race or Nationality _____

Occupation _____ Income _____

Name of Organization	1. Member *	2. Attendance	3. Financial Contributions	4. Member of Committees (Not Name)	5. Offices Held
1.					
2.					
3.					
4.					
5.					
6.					
7.					
8.					
9.					
10.					
Totals					

Wife

Age ——— Education ——— Race or Nationality ———
Occupation ——— Income ———

Name of Organization	1. Member *	2. Attendance	3. Financial Contributions	4. Member of Committees (Not Name)	5. Offices Held
1.					
2.					
3.					
4.					
5.					
6.					
7.					
8.					
9.					
10.					
Totals					

Date ——— Investigator ———

* Enter *L* if purely local group; enter *N* if a local unit of a state or national organization.
Distribution of total scores from a representative sample of an urban population, a *J*-curve; skewed to higher scores of 100 and over; mode at 0 to 11 points.

211

SOCIAL PARTICIPATION SCALE, 1952 EDITION *

F. Stuart Chapin, University of Minnesota

DIRECTIONS

1. List by name the organizations with which the husband and wife are affiliated (at the present time) as indicated by the five types of participation No. 1 to No. 5 across the top of the schedule (over).

    It is not necessary to enter the date at which the person became a member of the organization. It is important to enter *L* if the membership is in a purely local group, and to enter *N* if the membership is in a local unit of some state or national organization.

2. An organization means some active and organized grouping, usually but not necessarily in the community or neighborhood of residence, such as club, lodge, business or political or professional or religious organization, labor union, etc.; subgroups of a church or other institution are to be included separately *provided they are organized* as more or less independent entities.

3. Record under attendance the mere fact of attendance or nonattendance without regard to the number of meetings attended (corrections for the number attended *have not* been found to influence the final score sufficiently to justify such labor).

4. Record under contributions the mere fact of financial contributions or absence of contributions, and *not the amount* (corrections for amount of contributions *have not* been found to influence the final score sufficiently to justify such labor).

5. Previous memberships, committee work, offices held, etc., should *not be* counted or recorded or used in computing the final score.

6. Final score is computed by counting each membership as 1, each attended as 2, each contributed to as 3, each committee membership as 4, and each office held as 5. If both parents are living regularly in the home, add their total scores and divide the sum by two. The result is the mean social participation score of the family. In case only one parent lives in the home, as widow, widower, etc., the sum of that one person's participations is the score for the family (unless it is desired to obtain scores on children also).

---

* University of Minnesota Press, Minneapolis. Copyright 1938 by the University of Minnesota.

INDEX: LEISURE PARTICIPATION AND ENJOYMENT

VARIABLE MEASURED: The customary use of and degree of enjoyment of leisure time.

DESCRIPTION: The scale includes 47 items that are activities in which one might be expected to participate. Each item is ranked on two five-point scales. Leisure participation is scaled according to frequency of participation (1. Never, 2. Rarely, 3. Occasionally, 4. Fairly Often, 5. Frequently), and leisure enjoyment is scaled according to likes (1. Dislike very much, 2. Dislike, 3. Indifferent, 4. Like, 5. Like very much). The appropriate degree on each scale is circled for each item. No ranking on the like-dislike scale is given for those items in which the individual never participates.

WHERE PUBLISHED: C. R. Pace, *They Went to College*, Minneapolis: University of Minnesota Press, 1941. Copyright 1941 by the University of Minnesota.

RELIABILITY: Not known.

VALIDITY:
Leisure participation

with Income	$r = .019$
with Sociocivic activities scale	$r = .40$
with Cultural status	$r = .039$

STANDARD SCORES: A summary of responses to the questionnaire on the Minnesota study is included on pages 142-45 of the Pace book.

	1924-25		1928-29	
	Grads.	Non-grads.	Grads.	Non-grads.
Median leisure participation for men	125.00	123.24	132.29	131.72
Median leisure enjoyment for men	169.83	167.53	171.67	170.65
Median leisure participation for women	139.80	137.90	137.50	133.97
Median leisure enjoyment for women	177.73	178.75	180.38	176.87

UTILITY: This scale is easily administered and may be self-administered. It is equally easy to score. It takes little time to administer.
Both leisure participation and leisure enjoyment scores are derived
and can be compared.

RESEARCH APPLICATIONS: Comparative study of 951 graduates
and nongraduates of the University of Minnesota (C. R. Pace, *They
Went to College*).

YOUR LEISURE-TIME ACTIVITIES

The use of leisure time is supposed to be an increasingly important
social problem. We want to know how people usually spend their leisure
time. Here is a list of activities. On the left side of the page put a circle
around the number that tells how often you do these things now, using
the key at the top of the column. On the right side of the page put a
circle around the number that tells how well you like these things, using
the key at the top of the column. If you never do the activity mentioned,
circle number one in the left column to indicate no participation, and
circle no number on the right side of the page. Try not to skip any item.

How Often Do You Do These Things	How Well Do You Like These Things
1. Never	1. Dislike very much
2. Rarely	2. Dislike
3. Occasionally	3. Indifferent
4. Fairly often	4. Like
5. Frequently	5. Like very much

1 2 3 4 5	1. Amateur dramatics	1 2 3 4 5
1 2 3 4 5	2. Amusement parks and halls	1 2 3 4 5
1 2 3 4 5	3. Art work (individual)	1 2 3 4 5
1 2 3 4 5	4. Attending large social functions (balls, benefit bridge, etc.)	1 2 3 4 5
1 2 3 4 5	5. Attending small social entertainments (dinner parties, etc.)	1 2 3 4 5
1 2 3 4 5	6. Book reading for pleasure	1 2 3 4 5
1 2 3 4 5	7. Conventions	1 2 3 4 5
1 2 3 4 5	8. Conversation with family	1 2 3 4 5
1 2 3 4 5	9. Card playing	1 2 3 4 5
1 2 3 4 5	10. Church and related organizations	1 2 3 4 5
1 2 3 4 5	11. Dancing	1 2 3 4 5
1 2 3 4 5	12. Dates	1 2 3 4 5

How Often Do You Do		How Well Do You Like
These Things		These Things
1. Never		1. Dislike very much
2. Rarely		2. Dislike
3. Occasionally		3. Indifferent
4. Fairly often		4. Like
5. Frequently		5. Like very much

1 2 3 4 5	13. Entertaining at home	1 2 3 4 5
1 2 3 4 5	14. Fairs, exhibitions, etc.	1 2 3 4 5
1 2 3 4 5	15. Informal contacts with friends	1 2 3 4 5
1 2 3 4 5	16. Informal discussions, e.g., "bull sessions"	1 2 3 4 5
1 2 3 4 5	17. Indoor team recreation or sports—basketball, volleyball	1 2 3 4 5
1 2 3 4 5	18. Indoor individual recreation or sports—bowling, gym, pool, billiards, handball	1 2 3 4 5
1 2 3 4 5	19. Knitting, sewing, crocheting, etc.	1 2 3 4 5
1 2 3 4 5	20. Lectures (not class)	1 2 3 4 5
1 2 3 4 5	21. Listening to radio or TV	1 2 3 4 5
1 2 3 4 5	22. Literary writing—poetry, essays, stories, etc.	1 2 3 4 5
1 2 3 4 5	23. Magazine reading (for pleasure)	1 2 3 4 5
1 2 3 4 5	24. Movies	1 2 3 4 5
1 2 3 4 5	25. Newspaper reading	1 2 3 4 5
1 2 3 4 5	26. Odd jobs at home	1 2 3 4 5
1 2 3 4 5	27. Organizations or club meetings as a member	1 2 3 4 5
1 2 3 4 5	28. Organizations or club meetings as a leader (as for younger groups)	1 2 3 4 5
1 2 3 4 5	29. Outdoor individual sports—golf, riding, skating, hiking, tennis	1 2 3 4 5
1 2 3 4 5	30. Outdoor team sports—hockey, baseball, etc.	1 2 3 4 5
1 2 3 4 5	31. Picnics	1 2 3 4 5
1 2 3 4 5	32. Playing musical instrument or singing	1 2 3 4 5
1 2 3 4 5	33. Shopping	1 2 3 4 5
1 2 3 4 5	34. Sitting and thinking	1 2 3 4 5
1 2 3 4 5	35. Spectator of sports	1 2 3 4 5
1 2 3 4 5	36. Symphony or concerts	1 2 3 4 5
1 2 3 4 5	37. Telephone visiting	1 2 3 4 5
1 2 3 4 5	38. Theater attendance	1 2 3 4 5
1 2 3 4 5	39. Traveling or touring	1 2 3 4 5
1 2 3 4 5	40. Using public library	1 2 3 4 5

Continued on page 216.

How Often Do You Do These Things	How Well Do You Like These Things
1. Never	1. Dislike very much
2. Rarely	2. Dislike
3. Occasionally	3. Indifferent
4. Fairly often	4. Like
5. Frequently	5. Like very much

1 2 3 4 5 41. Visiting museums, art galleries, etc. 1 2 3 4 5

1 2 3 4 5 42. Volunteer work—social service, etc. 1 2 3 4 5

1 2 3 4 5 43. Writing personal letters 1 2 3 4 5

1 2 3 4 5 44. Special hobbies—stamps, photography, shop work, gardening, and others not included above 1 2 3 4 5

1 2 3 4 5 45. Fishing or hunting 1 2 3 4 5

1 2 3 4 5 46. Camping 1 2 3 4 5

1 2 3 4 5 47. Developing and printing pictures 1 2 3 4 5

INDEX: BERNARD'S NEIGHBORING PRACTICES SCHEDULE

VARIABLE MEASURED: The relative amount of neighboring by different kinds of people in different parts of the city.

DESCRIPTION: The scale consists of a number of questions that can be answered either by "Yes" or "No" or by other simple one-word phrases. Some questions pertain directly to neighborhood practices, while others have to do with matters that might be associated with neighboring or its absence.

WHERE PUBLISHED: Some of the questions and a description are published in Stuart A. Queen and Lester F. Thomas, *The City*, New York: McGraw-Hill, 1939, pp. 308-10. The original is an unpublished Ph.D. dissertation by Jessie S. Bernard called "An Instrument for the Measurement of Neighborhood with Experimental Application."

RELIABILITY: Not known.

VALIDITY: Negative correlations of neighborhood scores with mobility, median rentals, and multiple dwellings were found. Positive correlations of neighboring with single dwellings, home ownership, and percentage married were found.

UTILITY: The schedule is easily administered and could be self-administered, though the interviewer should be there to answer any possible questions. The questions and answers are simple and easily understood.

RESEARCH APPLICATIONS: Dr. Bernard's standardization was done in various parts of metropolitan St. Louis (p. 310).

NEIGHBORING PRACTICES SCHEDULE

1. About how many of the people who live in your neighborhood would you recognize by sight if you saw them in a large crowd?
   Answer: None Few Some Many Most All

2. About how often do you chat or "visit with" your neighbors?
   Answer: Never Rarely Sometimes Often

3. Do you and your neighbors exchange things, such as books, magazines, patterns, recipes, jellies, jams, preserves, suggestions, tools, dishes, seeds, plant clippings, or any other similar things?
   Answer: Never Rarely Sometimes Often

4. Do you and your neighbors exchange favors or services, such as receiving parcels, telephone messages, or other similar favors?
   Answer: Never Rarely Sometimes Often

5. Do you and your neighbors ever go to the movies together?
   Answer: Never Rarely Sometimes Often

6. Do you and your neighbors ever go shopping together?
   Answer: Never Rarely Sometimes Often

7. Do your neighbors ever talk over their problems with you when they are worried, or ask you for advice or help?
   Answer: Never Rarely Sometimes Often

8. Do you and your neighbors ever take care of each other's children when the other one is sick or busy?
   Answer: Never Rarely Sometimes Often

9. Do you and your neighbors ever have picnics or outings or parties together?
   Answer: Never Rarely Sometimes Often

10. Is the church you usually attend in your present neighborhood?
    Answer: Yes No Do not attend church usually

11. Do you belong to a church club, such as a Ladies' Aid, or sewing club, or a mothers' club, or a church men's club of any kind *in your neighborhood?*
    Answer: Yes No

12. Do you belong to a school club, such as a Parent-Teacher Association, or a mothers' club, or some other school organization in your neighborhood?
Answer: Yes No

13. Do you belong to any social club or group, such as a bridge club, gymnasium class, dancing club, sewing club, or any similar organization in your neighborhood?
Answer: Yes No

14. Do you belong to a local improvement association (or Farmers' Grange, if you live in the country)?
Answer: Yes No

15. Do your best friends live in your present neighborhood?
Answer: None Few Some Many

16. Would you rather live in some other neighborhood?
Answer: Yes No Do not know

17. Are your neighbors of the same nationality as you?
Answer: None Few Some Many Most All Do not know

18. How many years have you lived in your present neighborhood?
_____

19. Do you own your home?
No Yes (This includes mortgaged homes)

INDEX: A GUTTMAN SCALE FOR MEASURING WOMEN'S NEIGHBORLINESS

VARIABLE MEASURED: The neighborliness of women under sixty years.

DESCRIPTION: This instrument is a unidimensional Guttman scale consisting of twelve items. The scale items can be simply scored for any sample by counting each *GN* (greater neighborliness) answer as 1 and each *LN* (lesser neighborliness) as 0. The possible range of scores is 13 to 0.

WHERE PUBLISHED: Paul Wallin, "A Guttman Scale for Measuring Women's Neighborliness," *The American Journal of Sociology,* 1953, 59: 243-46. Copyright 1953 by the University of Chicago.

RELIABILITY: The coefficient of reproducibility of the scale from two samples of women was .920 and .924.

VALIDITY: Face validity.

UTILITY: A short, easy-to-administer scale that may be used for investigating factors accounting for individual differences in neighborliness. The scale also can be used for testing hypotheses as to intracommunity and intercommunity difference in neighborliness.

RESEARCH APPLICATIONS: Sylva F. Fava, "Suburbanism as a Way of Life," *American Sociological Review,* 1956, 21: 34-37.
Scott Greer, "Urbanism Reconsidered: A Comparative Study of Local Areas in a Metropolis," *American Sociological Review,* 1956, 21: 19-25.
Alex S. Edelstein and Otto N. Larsen, "The Weekly Press's Contribution to a Sense of Urban Community," *Journalism Quarterly,* Autumn, 1960, pp. 489-98.
Otto N. Larsen and Alex S. Edelstein, "Communication, Consensus and the Community Involvement of Urban Husbands and Wives," *Acta Sociologia,* Copenhagen, 1960, 5: 15-30.

A GUTTMAN SCALE FOR MEASURING WOMEN'S NEIGHBORLINESS

Paul Wallin

1. How many of your best friends who live in your neighborhood did you get to know since you or they moved into the neighborhood? Two or more (GN); one or none (LN).
2. Do you and any of your neighbors go to movies, picnics, or other things like that together? Often or sometimes (GN); rarely or never (LN).
3. Do you and your neighbors entertain one another? Often or sometimes (GN); rarely or never (LN).
4. If you were holding a party or tea for an out-of-town visitor, how many of your neighbors would you invite? Two or more (GN); one or none (LN).
5. How many of your neighbors have ever talked to you about their problems when they were worried or asked you for advice or help? One or more (GN); none (LN).
6. How many of your neighbors' homes have you ever been in? Four or more (GN); three or less (LN).
7. Do you and your neighbors exchange or borrow things from one another such as books, magazines, dishes, tools, recipes, preserves, or garden vegetables? Often, sometimes, or rarely (GN); none (LN).
8. About how many of the people in your neighborhood would you recognize by sight if you saw them in a large crowd? About half or more (GN); a few or none (LN).
9. With how many of your neighbors do you have a friendly talk fairly frequently? Two or more (GN); one or none (LN).
10. About how many of the people in your neighborhood do you say "Hello" or "Good morning" to when you meet on the street? Six or more (GN); five or less (LN).
11. How many of the names of the families in your neighborhood do you know? Four or more (2); one to three (1); none (0).*
12. How often do you have a talk with any of your neighbors? Often or sometimes (GN); rarely or never (LN).

* Responses to this question ended as a trichotomy in the scale. They can be scored as shown in the parentheses following the response categories.

INDEX: CITIZEN POLITICAL ACTION SCHEDULE

VARIABLE MEASURED: Individual participation in citizen political action.

DESCRIPTION: This is an arbitrary index to assess individual participation in community services. Twelve possible behavioral items are presented as those that compose bulk of citizen political activity. Scores of 0-12 may be recorded as each item participation is given a weight of one.

WHERE PUBLISHED: League of Women Voters of Pennsylvania, Publication No. 101, Philadelphia, Pa.

RELIABILITY: No tests have been made.

VALIDITY: Face validity.

STANDARD SCORES:

> 10-12 an outstanding citizen!
> 6-9 an average citizen.
> 0-5 a citizen?

UTILITY: May be administered in less than four minutes. It provides a measure suitable for both individual and group assessment.

RESEARCH APPLICATION: None reported. However, index opens possibilities of exploring important facets of political behavior including the importance of background factors of age, sex, education, race, and social class. The relationships between citizen political action and community quality and solidarity are challenging research problems.

SCORE CARD FOR CITIZEN POLITICAL ACTION

*Published by the League of Women Voters of Pennsylvania,
Publication No. 101*

(* Score one point for each "yes")

VOTING—Did you vote

—Once in the last four years? ____

—Two to five times? ____

—Six or more times? ____

PUBLIC ISSUES—Do you

—Inform yourself from more than one source on public issues? ____

—Discuss public issues frequently with more than one person? ____

INDIVIDUAL ACTION ON PUBLIC ISSUES—Did you

—Write or talk to your Congressman or any other public official —local, state or national—to express your views once in the past year? ____

—Two or more times? ____

GROUP ACTION ON PUBLIC ISSUES—Do you

—Belong to one or more organizations that take stands on public issues? ____

PRIMARY ELECTION ACTIVITY— Did you

—Discuss the qualifications needed for the offices on the ballot? ____

—Work for the nomination of a candidate before the primary election once in the last four years? ____

GENERAL OR MUNICIPAL ELECTION ACTIVITY—Did you

—Work for the election of a candidate once in the last four years? ____

FINANCIAL SUPPORT—Did you

—Contribute money to a party or candidate once in the last four years? ____

TOTAL SCORE ____

* 10-12 points—An outstanding citizen!
6-9 points—An average citizen.
5-0 points—a citizen?

223

SECTION F

Leadership in the Work Organization

This section contains two leadership scales that may be widely used in work organizations. The first scale, the *Leadership Opinion Questionnaire,* is designed to find answers to the question, "What *should you* as a supervisor do?" The second scale, the *Supervisory Behavior Description,* is designed to find answers to the question, "What does *your own supervisor* actually do?" Note that these two scales make it possible to get measures of two levels of leadership in an organization. The relation of a supervisor to his immediate superior has been shown to be a very important one. The use of both questionnaires makes it possible to secure a comparison between the two levels. However, each scale may be used for the specific purpose for which it was designed. Use the *Leadership Opinion Questionnaire* whenever a measure of a leader's personal orientation is desired. Use the *Supervisory Behavior Description* when it is desirable to get the perceptions of a supervisor by those who report to him. This scale can be given to employees or any group of supervisors or managers. These two scales have been subjected to repeated refinement and may be considered highly reliable and valid in terms of present progress in scale construction.

The *Work Patterns Profile* is an analysis form, which permits a description of work activity patterns. This schedule has its greatest worth as a diagnostic instrument. The relation of the work patterns profile to the leadership orientation of initiation and consideration offer interesting research problems.

Many measures of organizational analyses might be included. Space prevents their addition, but the following measures are annotated for the consideration of the organizational researcher:

1. Executive Position Description

This description contains 191 items to determine the basic characteristics of executive positions in business and industry. Part I covers Position Activities; Part II, Position Responsibilities; Part III, Position Demands and Restrictions; Part IV, Position Characteristics. See John K. Hemphill, *Dimensions of Executive Positions,* Ohio State University, Columbus: Bureau of Business Research, 1960.

2. Responsibility, Authority, and Delegation Scales

These scales were designed to measure different degrees of perceived responsibility, authority, and delegation as exhibited by individuals who occupy administrative or supervisory positions. See Ralph M. Stogdill and Carroll L. Shartle, *Methods in the Study of Administrative Leadership,* Columbus: Ohio State University Bureau of Business Research, 1955, pp. 33-43.

3. Multirelational Sociometric Survey

This survey measures interpersonal variables surrounding work activities. Five dimensions are included: the prescribed, the perceived, the actual, the desired, and the rejected. See Robert Tannenbaum, Irving W. Weschler, and Fred Massarik, *Leadership and Organization: A Behavioral Science Approach,* New York: McGraw-Hill, 1961, pp. 346-70.

4. A Method for the Analysis of the Structure of Complex Organizations

This is an application of sociometric analysis based on work contracts. The method enables the researcher to depict the organization coordination structure as established through the activities of liaison persons and the existence of the contacts between groups. See Robert S. Weiss and Eugene Jacobson, "A Method for the Analysis of the Structure of Complex Organizations," *American Sociological Review,* December, 1955, 20: 661-68. Cf. with Ralph M. Stogdill and Carroll L. Shartle, *Methods in the Study of Administrative Leadership,* Columbus: Ohio State University Bureau of Business Research, 1955, pp. 18-32.

INDEX: LEADERSHIP OPINION QUESTIONNAIRE

VARIABLE MEASURED: The questionnaire measures leader's orientation around two major factors, *Structure* and *Consideration*.

Structure (S): Reflects the extent to which an individual is likely to define and structure his own role and those of his subordinates toward goal attainment. A high score on this dimension characterizes individuals who play a more active role in directing group activities through planning, communicating information, scheduling, trying out new ideas, etc.

Consideration (C): Reflects the extent to which an individual is likely to have job relationships characterized by mutual trust, respect for subordinate's ideas, and consideration of their feelings. A high score is indicative of a climate of good rapport and two-way communication. A low score indicates the superior is likely to be more impersonal in his relations with group members.

DESCRIPTION: This is a forty item questionnaire divided into the two factors, *Structure* and *Consideration*. Each factor is tested by 20 items. The items are presented with a five point continuum with scoring weights of zero to four depending on item's orientation to total dimension.

WHERE PUBLISHED: Copyright 1960, Science Research Associates, Inc., Chicago, Illinois. Scale is sold as Leadership Opinion Questionnaire by Edwin A. Fleishman. It was first presented to social scientists in Ralph M. Stogdill and Alvin E. Coons (eds.), *Leader Behavior: Its Description and Measurement,* Columbus: Ohio State University Bureau of Business Research, 1957, pp. 120-33.

RELIABILITY: Test-retest coefficients *for 31 foremen* after a 3 month interval show

$r = .80$ on Consideration,

$r = .74$ on Initiating Structure;

for 24 Air Force NCO's

$r = .77$ on Consideration,

$r = .67$ on Initiating Structure.

Split half reliability estimates for the Consideration and Initiating Structure were found to be .69 and .73, respectively.

VALIDITY: Validity was evaluated through correlations with independent leadership measures, such as merit rating by supervisors, peer ratings, forced choice performance reports by management, and leaderless group situation tests. Relatively low validities were found for the particular criteria employed, although a few statistically significant correlations were found. Correlations with other measures revealed that scores on the *Leadership Opinion Questionnaire* were independent of the "intelligence" of the supervisor, an advantage not achieved by other available leadership attitude questionnaires.

The Questionnaire scores have been found to be sensitive for discriminating reliability between leadership attitudes in different situations as well as for evaluating the effects of leadership training.

Science Research Associates have compiled evidence for validity from recent studies in many different organizational settings. It has been used in a test battery to ascertain effectiveness of sales supervisors. It has been administered to foremen in a large wholesale pharmaceutical company, to first line supervisors in a large petrochemical refinery, to department managers in a large shoe manufacturing company, and to bank managers. In all instances, significant correlations between the Questionnaire and proficiency have been shown. The Leadership Opinion Questionnaire has also shown that leadership patterns are directly related to organizational stress and effectiveness in three hospitals.

STANDARDIZED SCORES (Published in Edwin A. Fleishman, "The Measurement of Leadership Attitudes in Industry," *Journal of Applied Psychology*, June, 1953, p. 156.)

Dimension	Level in Organization	Mean	S.D.
Consideration	Superintendents ($N = 13$)	52.6	8.1
	General Foremen ($N = 30$)	53.2	7.1
	Foremen ($N = 122$)	53.9	7.2
	Workers ($N = 394$)	57.0	5.5
Structure	Superintendents ($N = 13$)	55.5	5.7
	General Foremen ($N = 30$)	53.6	6.9
	Foremen ($N = 122$)	53.3	7.8
	Workers ($N = 394$)	44.2	3.9

UTILITY: Easily administered and scored. Time of administration, 10-15 minutes.

RESEARCH APPLICATIONS: B. M. Bass, "Leadership Opinions as Forecasters of Supervisory Success," *Journal of Applied Psychology*, 1956, 345-46.

E. A. Fleishman, *Leadership Climate and Supervisory Behavior*, Columbus: Personnel Research Board, Ohio State University, 1951.

————, "The Measurement of Leadership Attitudes in Industry," *Journal of Applied Psychology*, June, 1953, 153-58.

————, "Leadership Climate, Human Relations Training, and Supervisory Behavior," *Personnel Psychology*, 1953, 6: 205-22.

————, E. F. Harris, and H. E. Burtt, *Leadership and Supervision in Industry*, Columbus: Bureau of Educational Research, Ohio State University.

J. K. Hemphill, *Leader Behavior Description*, Columbus: Personnel Research Board, Ohio State University, 1950.

LEADERSHIP OPINION QUESTIONNAIRE *

This questionnaire contains forty items when presented as a complete scale. The items that follow exemplify the type found in the longer questionnaire. They are presented here so that the researcher may evaluate them for his possible use of the complete scale.

Structure

ASSIGN PEOPLE IN THE WORK GROUP TO PARTICULAR TASKS.

1. Always   2. Often   3. Occasionally   4. Seldom   5. Never

STRESS BEING AHEAD OF COMPETING WORK GROUPS.

1. A great deal   2. Fairly much   3. To some degree
4. Comparatively little   5. Not at all

CRITICIZE POOR WORK.

1. Always   2. Often   3. Occasionally   4. Seldom   5. Never

EMPHASIZE MEETING OF DEADLINES.

1. A great deal   2. Fairly much   3. To some degree
4. Comparatively little   5. Not at all

Consideration

PUT SUGGESTIONS MADE BY PEOPLE IN THE WORK GROUP INTO OPERATION.

1. Always   2. Often   3. Occasionally   4. Seldom   5. Never

HELP PEOPLE IN THE WORK GROUP WITH THEIR PERSONAL PROBLEMS.

1. Often   2. Fairly often   3. Occasionally   4. Once in a while
5. Seldom

GET THE APPROVAL OF THE WORK GROUP ON IMPORTANT MATTERS BEFORE GOING AHEAD.

1. Always   2. Often   3. Occasionally   4. Seldom   5. Never

* Reproduced by permission of Science Research Associates, Inc., Chicago, Ill.

INDEX: SUPERVISORY BEHAVIOR DESCRIPTION

VARIABLE MEASURED: Perceptions of subordinates of the leadership behavior demonstrated by their immediate superior. Factor analysis revealed that "Initiating Structure" and "Consideration" items are the most significant factors in distinguishing leadership performance. "Initiating Structure" reflects the extent to which the supervisor facilitates group interaction toward goal attainment; "Consideration" reflects the extent to which the supervisor is considerate of the feelings of those under him. All questions are worded in terms of "What does your own supervisor actually do?"

DESCRIPTION: This is a 48-item questionnaire divided into two independent areas of leadership called "Initiating Structure" and "Consideration." The first area includes 20 items and the second is made up of 28 items. The items were presented with a five-point continuum answer scale that has scoring weights of zero to four depending on the item orientation to the total dimension. Highest possible score was 112 on "Consideration" and 80 for "Initiation."

WHERE PUBLISHED: Edwin A. Fleishman, "A Leader Behavior Description for Industry," in *Leader Behavior: Its Description and Measurement*, Ralph M. Stogdill and Alvin E. Coons (eds.), Columbus: Ohio State University Bureau of Business Research, 1957, pp. 103-19.

RELIABILITY: Test-retest reliability coefficients based on numerous samples range from .46 to .87.

| | | Dimension | |
Sample	Time Between Administration	Consideration *r*	Initiating Structure *r*
Workers describing 18 foremen	11 months	.87	.75
Workers describing 59 foremen	11 months	.58	.46
Workers describing 31 foremen	3 weeks	.56	.53

Split half reliabilities are reported for samples as between .68 to .98.

VALIDITY: The correlation between "Consideration" and "Initiating Structure" was found to be −.02 when based on replies of 122 foremen. The intercorrelation was shown to be −.33 when administered to 394 workers who described the 122 foremen. The correlation between the two scales was shown to be −.05 when administered to 176 Air Force and Army ROTC students who described their superior officers. The independence of the two factors appears to be confirmed.

Correlations have been obtained between descriptions of foreman behavior and independent indexes of accident rates, absenteeism, grievances, and turnover among the foreman's own work groups. In production departments, high scores on the "Consideration" scale were predictive of low ratings of proficiency by the foreman's supervisor, but low absenteeism among the workers. A high score on "Initiating Structure" was predictive of a high proficiency rating, but high absenteeism and labor grievances as well.

Among nonproduction departments, a foreman with a high score on "Consideration" was predictive of low accident rates with a trend toward low absenteeism as well. A high score on "Initiating Structure" was related to high labor turnover in nonproduction departments.

STANDARD SCORES:

MEANS AND STANDARD DEVIATIONS OF
SUPERVISORY BEHAVIOR DESCRIPTION SCORES

	Dimension			
	Consideration		Initiating Structure	
Sample	M	SD	M	SD
Descriptions of 122 foremen	79.8	14.5	41.5	7.6
Descriptions of 31 foremen	71.5	13.2	37.5	6.3
Descriptions of 31 foremen	73.0	12.7	40.7	7.3
Descriptions of 8 Civil Service Supervisors	75.1	17.6	37.3	9.6
Descriptions of 60 General Foremen	82.3	15.5	51.5	8.8

UTILITY: The questionnaire may be administered in a 10-15 minute period. When used in group applications, it is very efficient. By using this questionnaire in conjunction with the Leader Behavior Description, it is possible to get a view of how a supervisor thinks he should lead and compare this view with an assessment by his subordinates of his actual leadership performance.

RESEARCH APPLICATIONS: The best summary of research is found in the monograph cited in the aforementioned. Other references may be found in the publications cited under the Leadership Opinion Questionnaire. Most of the research has been done by E. A. Fleishman in the plants of the International Harvester Company.

TABLE 2

ITEMS SELECTED FOR THE REVISED FORM OF THE
SUPERVISORY BEHAVIOR DESCRIPTION

Item Number	Item *

Consideration: Revised Key

1. He refuses to give in when people disagree with him.
2. He does personal favors for the foremen under him.
3. He expresses appreciation when one of us does a good job.
4. He is easy to understand.
5. He demands more than we can do.
6. He helps his foremen with their personal problems.
7. He criticizes his foremen in front of others.
8. He stands up for his foremen even though it makes him unpopular.
9. He insists that everything be done his way.
10. He sees that a foreman is rewarded for a job well done.
11. He rejects suggestions for changes.
12. He changes the duties of people under him without first talking it over with them.
13. He treats people under him without considering their feelings.
14. He tries to keep the foremen under him in good standing with those in higher authority.
15. He resists changes in ways of doing things.
16. He "rides" the foreman who makes a mistake.
17. He refuses to explain his actions.
18. He acts without consulting his foreman first.
19. He stresses the importance of high morale among those under him.
20. He backs up his foremen in their actions.
21. He is slow to accept new ideas.
22. He treats all his foremen as his equal.
23. He criticizes a specific act rather than a particular individual.
24. He is willing to make changes.
25. He makes those under him feel at ease when talking with him.
26. He is friendly and can be easily approached.
27. He puts suggestions that are made by foremen under him into operation.
28. He gets the approval of his foremen on important matters before going ahead.

* Most items were answered as: 1. always; 2. often; 3. occasionally; 4. seldom; 5. never.

Item	
Number	*Item*

Initiating Structure: Revised Key

1. He encourages overtime work.
2. He tries out his new ideas.
3. He rules with an iron hand.
4. He criticizes poor work.
5. He talks about how much should be done.
6. He encourages slow-working foremen to greater effort.
7. He waits for his foremen to push new ideas before he does.
8. He assigns people under him to particular tasks.
9. He asks for sacrifices from his foremen for the good of the entire department.
10. He insists that his foremen follow standard ways of doing things in every detail.
11. He sees to it that people under him are working up to their limits.
12. He offers new approaches to problems.
13. He insists that he be informed on decisions made by foremen under him.
14. He lets others do their work the way they think best.
15. He stresses being ahead of competing work groups.
16. He "needles" foremen under him for greater effort.
17. He decides in detail what shall be done and how it shall be done.
18. He emphasizes meeting of deadlines.
19. He asks foremen who have slow groups to get more out of their groups.
20. He emphasizes the quantity of work.

INDEX: WORK PATTERNS PROFILE

VARIABLE MEASURED: The roles in the organization as composed of certain activities.

DESCRIPTION: The profile includes fourteen descriptions of leadership functions that have been found within leadership jobs. These include inspection of the organization; investigation and research; planning; preparation of procedures and methods; coordination; evaluation; interpretation of plans and procedures; supervision of technical operations; personnel activities; public relations; professional consultation; negotiations; scheduling, routing, and dispatching; technical and professional operations. By using questionnaire and interview methods, each person studied in the organization indicates the proportion of time spent on each activity.

WHERE PUBLISHED: Ralph M. Stogdill and Carroll L. Shartle, *Methods in the Study of Administrative Leadership*, Columbus: Ohio State University Bureau of Business Research, 1955, pp. 44-53; also Carroll L. Shartle, *Executive Performance and Leadership*, Englewood Cliffs, N.J.: Prentice-Hall, 1956, pp. 81-93.

RELIABILITY: Forms were administered to 32 officers in a Naval District Command Staff. One month later, the forms were administered again to the same officers. Test-retest coefficients are shown for the fourteen major responsibilities.

Inspection	.51
Research	.59
Planning	.49
Preparing Procedures	.55
Coordination	.60
Evaluation	.58
Interpretation	.18
Supervision	.03
Personal Functions	.46
Professional Consultation	.61
Public Relations	.83
Negotiations	.83
Scheduling	.38
Technical and Professional Performance	.59

VALIDITY: In a study of a Naval Air Station, 34 officers kept a log of work performance for a period of three days. Results suggest that there is a fairly high degree of correspondence between logged time and estimated time for objectively observable performances. More subjective, less observable performances, such as planning and reflection are not estimated in terms that correspond highly with time recorded on the log. A number of officers expressed the feeling that their estimates of time spent in planning were more accurate than the log, for the reason that they were not always aware at the moment that what they were doing constituted planning.

STANDARD SCORES: The fourteen activities are plotted in per cent of time spent in the activities. No standard scores have been developed since many roles must first be analyzed.

UTILITY: This instrument will make it possible to compare patterns of performance. Therefore, executive selection may be made more appropriately in relation to the role as defined in the organization.

RESEARCH APPLICATIONS: Ralph M. Stogdill, Carroll L. Shartle, Alvin E. Coons, and William E. Janes, *A Predictive Study of Administrative Work Patterns*, Columbus: Ohio State University Bureau of Business Research, 1956.
Ralph M. Stogdill, Carroll L. Shartle, and Others, *Patterns of Administrative Performance*, Columbus: Ohio State University Bureau of Business Research, 1956, Chapter IV.

WORK PATTERNS PROFILE

The Ohio State University Personnel Research Board

The purpose of this analysis is to determine the relative proportion of your time devoted to major administrative and operative responsibilities, disregarding the methods of accomplishment.

Please consider your entire range of responsibilities from day to day. Attempt to account as accurately as possible for the relative percentage of time devoted to various administrative and technical functions.

Before each item below, please write the approximate percentage of time spent in the responsibility described.

(%)   1. *Inspection of the Organization*—Direct observation and personal inspection of installations, buildings, equipment, facilities, operations, services or personnel—for the purpose of determining conditions and keeping informed.

(%)   2. *Investigation and Research*—Acts involving the accumulation and preparation of information and data. (Usually prepared and presented in the form of written reports.)

(%)   3. *Planning*—Preparing for and making decisions that will affect the aims or future activities of the organization as to volume or quality of business or service. (Including thinking, reflection and reading, as well as consultations and conferences with persons relative to short-term and long-range plans.)

(%)   4. *Preparation of Procedures and Methods*—Acts involving the mapping of procedures and methods for putting new plans into effect, as well as devising new methods for the performance of operations under existing plans.

(%)   5. *Coordination*—Acts and decisions designed to integrate and coordinate the activities of units within the organization or of persons within units, so as to achieve the maximal overall efficiency, economy, and control of operations.

(%)   6. *Evaluation*—Acts involving the consideration and evaluation of reports, correspondence, data, plans, divisions, or performances in relation to the aims, policies, and standards of the organization.

(%)   7. *Interpretation of Plans and Procedures*—Acts involving the interpretation and clarification for assistants and other personnel of directives, regulations, practices, and procedures.

(%)   8. *Supervision of Technical Operations*—Acts involving the direct supervision of personnel in the performance of duties.

(%)   9. *Personnel Activities*—Acts involving the selection, training, evaluation, motivation or disciplining of individuals, as well as acts designed to affect the morale, motivation, loyalty, or harmonious cooperation of personnel.

(%) 10. *Public Relations*—Acts designed to inform outside persons, regarding the program and functions of the organization, to obtain information regarding public sentiment, or to create a favorable attitude toward the organization.

(%) 11. *Professional Consultation*—Giving professional advice and specialized assistance on problems of a specific or technical nature to persons within or outside the organization.

(Other than technical supervision and guidance of own staff personnel.)

(%) 12. *Negotiations*—Purchasing, selling, negotiating contracts or agreements, settling claims, etc.

(%) 13. *Scheduling, Routing, and Dispatching*—Initiating action and determining the time, place, and sequence of operations.

(%) 14. *Technical and Professional Operations*—The performance of duties specific to a specialized profession (e.g., practice of medicine, conducting religious services, classroom teaching, auditing records, operating machines, or equipment).

(100%)   Total time spent in major responsibilities.

SECTION G

Important Attitude Scales

This section includes some attitude scales that may be useful in a wide array of problems. The *Wants and Satisfaction Scale* may be used in a wide variety of comparative analyses. Both scale of living and aspiration for a higher standard of living may be assessed. Such a scale might be useful in research on underdeveloped countries.

The *Chapin Social Insight Scale* is one of the few attempts to measure this very elusive variable. Research has not explored this area, and opportunities for proceeding in this challenging area are suggested by the scale. An adaptation was made at Minnesota for the appraisal of social workers.

The scale for *Union and Management Attitudes* offers an opportunity to open some new research areas in the field of industrial relations.

The Stouffer scales to measure *Perception of the Internal Communist Danger* and the *Toleration of Nonconformists* facilitates important research in the area of civil liberties.

Osgood's *Semantic Differential* represents a scaling idea that has challenged a growing number of researchers. There is evidence that the scales are comparable across different types of subjects and that a whole cluster of attitudes can be predicted for each type. This facility presents some entirely new approaches to attitude research.

Innumerable attitude scales are in existence. Some important sources of other scales are:

G. MURPHY and R. LIKERT, *Public Opinion and the Individual,* New York: Harper & Bros., 1938.

H. H. REMMERS (ed.), *Studies in Attitudes,* Lafayette, Ind.: Purdue University Studies in Higher Education, 26. Bulletin of Purdue University, 1934, Vol. 35, No. 4.

H. H. REMMERS and E. F. SILANCE, "Generalized Attitude Scales," *Journal of Social Psychology,* 5: 298-312.

MATILDA W. RILEY, J. W. RILEY, JR., and JACKSON TOBY, *Sociological Studies in Scale Analysis: Applications, Theory, Procedures,* New Brunswick, N.J.: Rutgers University Press, 1954.

L. L. THURSTONE and E. J. CHAVE, *The Measurement of Attitude, A Psychophysical Method,* Chicago: University of Chicago Press, 1929.

Interest in the measurement of *values* is growing. Some important sources of information on this topic are:

G. W. ALLPORT and P. E. VERNON, "A Test for Personal Values," *Journal of Abnormal and Social Psychology,* 26: 231-48.

ROY E. CARTER, "An Experiment in Value Measurement," *American Sociological Review,* April, 1956, 21: 156-63.

STUART C. DODD, "Ascertaining National Goals: Project Aimscales," *The American Behavioral Scientist,* March, 1961, 4: 11-15.

WILLIAM A. SCOTT, "Empirical Assessment of Values and Ideologies," *American Sociological Review,* June, 1959, 24: 299-310.

L. L. THURSTONE, *The Measurement of Values,* Chicago: University of Chicago Press, 1959.

ARCHIBALD O. HALLER and IRWIN W. MILLER, *The Occupational Aspiration Scale: Theory, Structure, and Correlates,* Technical Bulletin 288, East Lansing: Michigan State University, Agricultural Experiment Station, 1963.

SCALE: WANTS AND SATISFACTION SCALE

VARIABLE MEASURED: The scale attempts to measure wants (synonymous with wishes and interests) and the degree in which they are satisfied.

DESCRIPTION: The 71 items were classed in 11 categories of wants: house and yard, household conveniences, food, clothing, education, health, recreation, participation, work conditions, automobiles, and security. These items were arranged in random order. Each item was checked yes or no in respect to: 1, now have or have available; 2, do not have, but would like to have; 3, would like better quality; 4, would like greater quantity; and a five-point scale for rating the present situation with regard to the item—5, excellent; 6, good; 7, fair; 8, poor; 9, very bad. In scoring, the items are weighted to yield a deprivation score and a dissatisfaction score.

The items were selected on the basis of various consumption studies. Mr. McVoy warns that it is valid probably only for American married couples of relatively low socioeconomic limits.

WHERE PUBLISHED: Edgar C. McVoy, "A Method of Measuring the Satisfaction of Wants," *Sociometry,* February, 1942, 5: 80-88.

RELIABILITY: The deprivation and dissatisfaction scores correlated .90 ± .03.

The weighted scores and the raw scores correlated .97 ± .01.

VALIDITY: Face validity.

STANDARD SCORES: MEAN DISSATISFACTION SCORES

	N	Dissatisfaction Scores (m)	SD
Total group	112	1.63	0.45
Farm	60	1.89	0.35
Village	52	1.30	0.31

UTILITY: The index is not difficult to administer, although the classifications for checking each item are not especially clear on the questionnaire. The index helps in determining a satisfaction ratio by putting possessions over wants.

RESEARCH APPLICATIONS: The index is used in the original study by Edgar C. McVoy. His sample was in Isanti County, Minnesota. He correlated the dissatisfaction score with socioeconomic status, social status, general adjustment, participation, income, number of children at home, age of husband, and wife's years of education.

In the columns of the schedule are spaces for checking, with respect to each item:

    I—now have or have available
    II—do not have, but would like to have
    III—would like better quality
    IV—would like greater quantity

A five-point scale for rating the present situation with regard to the item:

    V—excellent
    VI—good
    VII—fair
    VIII—poor
    IX—very bad

In the schedule, items were mixed at random, in order to avoid danger of a halo effect. In the attempt to get an index of general dissatisfaction on the items covered, several methods of weighting were tried. It was decided at the outset to give all items equal value, although it was obvious that the items do not represent equal units of dissatisfaction.

In scoring the various columns, the following weights were given:

Deprivation score: for each check in column   II—2 points
                                              III—1 point
                                            IV—1 point

Dissatisfaction score: for each check in column   V—0 points
                                            VI—1 point
                                            VII—2 points
                                          VIII—3 points
                                          IX—4 points

When the total Dissatisfaction score is divided by 71, the number of items, the resulting quotient is an index that shows the average dissatisfaction of the subject in terms of the ratings given.

WANTS AND SATISFACTIONS

Edgar C. McVoy

(Use √ for yes; o for no.)

	Have I	Like II	Quality III	Quantity IV	Present Situation					REMARKS: In what way is situation unsatisfactory?
					E V	G VI	F VII	P VIII	VB IX	
Children's schools										
Medical care										
House										
Security of work										
Hired help										
Sewage disposal system										
Vacations										
Travel										
Roof on house										
Parties you attend										
Life insurance										
Family physician										
Oranges										
Paint on house										
Automobile										
Fresh vegetables										
Friends										

Care of mother before and during birth of children								
Radio								
Strenuousness of work								
Books in home								
Electricity								
Outdoor sports								
Savings								
Rest								
Play space in yard								
Old age care prospects								
Lawn								
Hospital								
Screens on house								
Coats								
Newspapers								
Sleep								
Bathroom(s)								
Concerts								
Meat								
Hours of work								
Insurance on house								
Recreation facilities (self)								

243

WANTS AND SATISFACTIONS (Continued)

Edgar C. McVoy

(Use √ for yes; o for no.)

	Have I	Like II	Quality III	Quantity IV	Present Situation					REMARKS: In what way is situation unsatisfactory?
					E V	G VI	F VII	P VIII	VB IX	
Running water										
Community										
Visits to friends										
Room in house										
Way of paying health bills										
Auto insurance										
Monotony of work										
Clothing										
Education (self)										
Public library books										
Washing machine										
Flower garden										
Recreation facilities (children)										
Optical care										
Central heating plant										
Visits from friends										
Children's job prospects										
Magazines										

244

Fruit	Dental care	Education (children)	Hired help in home	Movies	Vacuum cleaner	Refrigerator	Kitchen stove	Food	Living room furniture	Milk and cream	Parties you give	Telephone	Neighborhood

INDEX: SOCIAL INSIGHT SCALE

VARIABLE MEASURED: Degree of social insight by means of verbal response.

DESCRIPTION: Social insight is described as a person's ability to recognize in principle in a given situation (1) the existence and operation of specific substitute responses such as projection, rationalization, regression, sublimation, transference, etc., and (2) the need of some specific stimulus to adjust group conflicts or tensions such as known remarks to relax a dangerous intensity, a suggested compromise to attain temporary agreement, a face-saving remark to avoid embarrassment and to preserve status, or to discover the missing part to complete a thought. The scale was constructed by the selection of examples to illustrate the working hypothesis through problem situations that might be reacted to in several ways. A total of 45 items were constructed from which 25 were selected to appear in the form of a scale.

WHERE PUBLISHED: F. Stuart Chapin, "Preliminary Standardization of a Social Insight Scale," *American Sociological Review*, April, 1942, 7: 214-25. The copyright is now held by Consulting Psychologists Press, Inc., 577 College Ave., Palo Alto, Calif., and permission for reproduction is gratefully acknowledged.

RELIABILITY: In the long form of the *Social Insight Scale,* an odd-even test of the 45 items was made. The correlation gave split half reliability = .60 for 41 cases; r = .41 between the score on Part I and the score on Part II.

VALIDITY: Executives and supervisors of several social agencies were asked to rate (independently and confidentially) the members of their staff who had taken the test and who had more than the average degree of social insight. The biserial r = +.21. Another check of validity was to test 33 persons on social participation and social insight. The Pearsonian r = +.149. Also, 156 social workers in Twin City social agencies were scored on social participation and on social insight. Pearsonian r = +.179. The last test of validity was made by comparing the mean scores of social insight of two different groups with varying degrees of social work training. The two groups used were 68 social workers with graduate training and 46 clerical workers working for the same social work agency. The critical ratio of the difference between the mean scores was 7.23.

STANDARD SCORES: Each item was scored according to its discriminating power. Fourteen items were valued at 1 point per item. Six items were given 2 points for the correct answer and five items received 3 points. This made a total of 41 points possible if all items were answered correctly.

UTILITY: This is an exceedingly different variable to measure. This scale can be administered in approximately 45 minutes.

SOCIAL INSIGHT TEST, PRELIMINARY FORM, 1941

F. Stuart Chapin, University of Minnesota

Directions: Please read carefully:

In each of the following statements, a situation is described followed by four comments that seem to offer alternative explanations. Social insight is the ability to "see into" social situations that involve individual needs to avoid embarrassment or to achieve some satisfaction as an offset to some frustration.

You are asked to consider each statement upon its own merits. Then indicate by crossing out (X) that letter on the *answer sheet* that corresponds to *the one statement* that in your judgment is the most appropriate, intelligent, or logical comment upon it. There are no absolutely right or wrong, true or false, correct or incorrect answers in a mathematical sense. Each problem is a matter for judicial analysis and inference. Judgments made by different persons on the same situation may differ. As a guide, you should ask yourself the question, "Which comment represents the most probable inference or conclusion expressed in terms of the one response that will create the least embarrassment or most satisfaction to the person concerned?"

Part I

1. Joseph Runway occasionally drinks too much. He has a steady job but has never succeeded in all the years of continuous employment in getting the promotion to a better paid assistant managership, which he deeply desires in the firm for which he works. His younger brother had been the "apple of his mother's eye," and now Joseph's wife is very partial to the one son in the family otherwise consisting of three girls. To help Mr. Runway, a friend of the family:
    a. Takes strong measures to deprive him of access to all liquor and strong drink.

    b. Advises that he leave home and "take the cure" to correct his tendency to drink.

    c. Sympathetically hears his story and recognizes the contribution to the security of his family that he has made by steadiness on the job.

    d. Secretly urges Mrs. Runway to take the children and go away, thus to establish a separate residence leading to ultimate divorce.

2. Mr. H. left high school before graduation to take a job as a clerk in a store. Although still a clerk, he has always had steady work and an income sufficient to enable him to marry, buy a home, equip and maintain it in a very comfortable manner, although this has required him to do without many other things (e.g., children, social-recreational activities, etc.). When Mr. H. is with other people in an informal group, his chief topic of conversation is the quality and cost of the various articles he has purchased for his home. The reason for Mr. H.'s chief topic of conversation is:

    a. He has ideals of quality and believes "production should be for use rather than for profit."

    b. He wishes to keep conversation limited to subjects on which he is informed.

    c. By talking about subjects on which he is informed, he diverts conversation from subjects he is ignorant of but that most people are informed about and interested in.

    d. He wishes to appear pleasant, to make conversation, and to avoid giving offense.

3. Mr. Smith, a business man, is strongly opposed to suggestions favoring social planning and control of business by government, because he says, "World conditions have caused our depression" and "Industrial cycles are normal and if the government interferes it will be worse." His opposition to government planning and control probably is the result of:

    a. His belief in individual initiative.

    b. His opposition to any form of socialism.

    c. His own business activities just manage to "keep within" the law.

    d. His experience had shown that private business is more efficient than government.

4. The principal of the school attended by James reported that he showed generally bad behavior in the schoolroom, constant teasing and bullying of younger children, and occasional petty thieving. He was conspicuous in classes for his lack of attention and concentration. He was a pale slim boy, rather tall for his twelve years. Out of school, he played little with boys of his own age and was frequently found bullying and teasing younger children. His father

was a traveling salesman. James's right arm was broken twice when he was seven and eight years old. When he was nine, his left leg was fractured while in rough play with children. His mother discouraged his playing with older boys. He had a real passion for movies that showed western and adventure stories. His reading consisted of two to three books a week, preferably of the boy adventurer type. James's behavior is due to the fact that:

a. He is discontented because he cannot go on trips and see the country with his father.

b. He feels the need to make up for his weak physical condition by gaining mastery and attention of his playmates.

c. He is an incipient criminal of the "moral imbecile" type.

d. He is a moron and can never hope to develop a superior intelligence because his parents have mediocre minds.

5. Martha, an overconscientious girl of 19 years, is given to self-analysis. She is always concerned with what others think about her and the things she has done. Martha finds it difficult to start conversations with strangers and frequently analyzes the motives of others. Another trait that is characteristic of Martha's behavior is:

a. Worrying over possible misfortunes.

b. Frequent craving of excitement.

c. Showing consideration of others' feelings.

d. Preference for reading about something rather than experiencing it.

6. Mr. Jenks when in a restaurant sharply orders the waiters about and is rude and critical about the service he receives. He has not many friends because of his tendency to be bossy and critical toward them. In the office in which he works, he:

a. Agitates for better working conditions.

b. Is ingratiating and subservient to his employer.

c. Is openly critical of the many rules and regulations governing his work.

d. Tries to give orders to his fellow workers that are only supposed to be given by his superior.

7. Mr. A.'s son is in danger of flunking out of medical school because of low grades and apparent lack of interest and ability in medical courses, but Mr. A. insists that his son stay in a medical course and put more effort into his studies. The son however would prefer to take a business course, but Mr. A. persistently blocks all attempts to make this change. Mr. A.'s attitude suggests that:

a. Mr. A. in his youth wanted to become a doctor, but circumstances prevented.

b. Mr. A. believes that the medical profession is better than that of pharmacy.

    c. Mr. A. believes that the income of his son will be more secure as a doctor.

    d. Mr. A. believes that it is "education in character" to force one's self to do a distasteful task.

8. A man bought an expensive automobile after some hesitation because it cost more than he could well afford to pay. However, when a friend later questioned him as to why he bought such an expensive car, he gave several reasons, but the one reason he did *not* give was:

    a. His wife and children needed to get out into the country and he bought a big car so that they could all drive together.

    b. The car would save him money in the long run because it would not need the repairs that an older or cheaper car would.

    c. The friend had bought a car almost as expensive although his income was not much greater.

    d. He expected to receive some money from an estate by the death of a critically ill relative.

9. A boy, aged ten, had temper tantrums and was disobedient to his parents. In school, he refused to follow directions, was a troublemaker, and was often fighting. Both parents were living, and he had one younger sister. He told imaginary stories about his parents' wealth and about all his toys and travels. He interrupted others to talk about himself. Frequently, he reported to teachers that other children were picking on him. In order to overcome these behavior difficulties, this boy should be placed:

    a. In activities with children who are older and more mature than he.

    b. In activities at home and school in which he can more easily and immediately succeed.

    c. In activities at home and school with more responsibility.

    d. In activities with children who will accept him as a leader.

10. Mr. Thomas frequently protests against the irreligious attitudes of others, asserts the religious depravity of persons with religious beliefs conflicting with his own, is ardent in uncovering and crusading against vice and immorality in his community, and is held up by the members of his church as a model and virtuous person. Mr. Thomas' conduct indicates that:

    a. He has been brought up in an extremely religious family.

    b. He is trying to become a leader in his community.

    c. He has impulses to do the things he publicly is fighting against.

    d. He feels he must "save" others.

11. A young man reacted with intense emotion to any indulgence in alcoholic drinks. If any of his friends as much as took a single drink, he went out of his way to denounce them in most emphatic terms. The explanation was:

   a. That his mother had been a leader in the Women's Christian Temperance Union.

   b. That his father had been a drunkard, who had treated his mother brutally and finally deserted her.

   c. He was himself a secret drunkard at late parties.

   d. His ancestors came from strict Puritan stock.

12. A weakly child was overprotected by his parents and other adult relatives, who were the only persons with whom he came into frequent contact. On entering school, he was ignored or rebuffed by his classmates. To this situation, he reacted by:

   a. Avoiding other children and spending his time in daydreaming.

   b. Fighting with and bullying the other children.

   c. Trying to attract attention by competing in games played by the group of children.

   d. Attempting to get other children to accept him by persistently "hanging around" or "tagging along" with them.

13. Mrs. Thompson constantly consulted physicians about her daughter's health at the slightest sign of illness. She bought her expensive clothing and toys. She frequently irritated the child with excessive attention. She complained that the child would not obey her, and at times she punished her severely for slight misbehavior. Mrs. Thompson's reactions toward her daughter probably indicate that:

   a. She was inclined to be a hypochondriac.

   b. She was trying to do for her daughter things which she had been denied as a child.

   c. Because her daughter was the only child, she expected too much of her.

   d. She had resentments toward the child that she was trying to cover up.

14. Mrs. Harvey, age 22, disapproved of smoking, especially by her husband or by women. She also disapproved of card playing and refused to attend many movies because the love scenes were "immorally presented." She is socially isolated, taking part in few activities with other people. She often asserts that people are more lax in moral matters in present times than they were in earlier times. Her attitudes on these matters suggest that:

   a. She was morally superior to her associates.

   b. As a young girl on several occasions she had been severely scolded by her parents for repeating "sex" stories heard from other girls.

   c. As a girl, she had been taught that such activities as card playing, etc., were not approved of by her church.

   d. As a girl, she had been isolated from such activities and therefore had not learned to enjoy them.

15. A boy, 10, dominated his brother, 12, and his sister, 14. When he was opposed in his domineering behavior, he became abusive and destructive. In school, he refused to abide by ordinary routine activities and directions, and he:

    a. Asserted that the teachers were picking on him.

    b. Said he had no interest in any of his schoolwork.

    c. Would not play or take part in competitive games in which he might be defeated.

    d. Was well behaved and did his work only in his manual training class.

16. A boy, age, 15, is complained about by his parents and teachers. He stays out late at night, is irresponsible, uncooperative, apathetic, and inconsiderate. He is unpopular and annoys other children. He has tendencies to lie and steal whenever he can "get away with it." He has little or no interest in school. In the following list of factors, indicate the one that probably would be most closely associated with this boy's misbehavior:

    a. He is lazy.

    b. He is disobedient in school.

    c. He has an introverted personality.

    d. He has an extroverted personality.

Part II

17. In an executive staff meeting, Mr. Goodrich, sales manager and a loyal and respected man, hears for the first time of a new "selling point" recently introduced by a competitor of the firm in the eastern sales area. This information was supplied to the staff conference by Mr. White, the brilliant young production manager. The managing director is presiding over the staff conference as chairman. Should he:

    a. Ask Mr. Goodrich to discuss the point in detail so that the others may profit by his ideas?

    b. Ask Mr. White to elaborate the point in detail and give his views?

    c. Ask Mr. Goodrich to report on the results of his recent and extended trip of inspection of the Far West sales territory?

    d. In the interests of sales efficiency and promotion, require Mr. Goodrich then and there to explain why he did not know of this new point?

18. A Community Fund in a large city is faced with the problem of preserving good working relations among the social agencies that are members of the Fund, to preserve the advantages of a single common campaign of soliciting for financial support, and to promote

the idea of cooperative planning for the community. In this situation, the financial campaign falls short by 10 per cent of the goal needed to keep the agencies operating at the existing rate of efficiency and skilled services. Cuts in the budgets of all agencies are made, but one large and powerful member agency, X, refuses to take its proportionate cut and maintains, through the Chairman of its Board of Directors and through its Executive, that it meets a special need and should not be cut at all, but rather have its budget raised. Which of the following procedures should the Chest adopt in order to preserve its function in the city?

    a. Allow the agency X to withdraw from the Fund and try to raise its budget by a separate financial campaign.

    b. Give the agency X the amount it needs and distribute the cut to other fellow agencies.

    c. Call a conference of the Chairmen of the Boards and the Executives of all other agencies to hear the arguments of the officials of agency X, and try by amicable discussion to reach a mutual understanding.

    d. Reprimand the officials of agency X for lack of consideration of fellow agency needs and threaten to drop it from the Fund unless it conforms.

19. During a conference, the discussion becomes so argumentative and heated that everyone seems to be angry at someone else. Finally, one member who seems to be getting the worst of the argument angrily stalks out. The chairman of the group should then:

    a. Immediately declare the meeting adjourned.

    b. Send someone to ask the departed member to return.

    c. Ask for a vote whether the meeting should be adjourned.

    d. Ignore the departure and continue with the order of business remaining.

20. The manager and his chief associates in a high grade employment agency are considering the problem of recommending James Smith for a position. How much information about Smith should go into the letter of recommendation? Smith became unemployed when the printing company for which he has been working continuously for the past five years closed because its funds were tied up by a bank failure. Smith has the technical qualifications for filling a more important position in any one of three vacant positions in other firms. Assuming that the letter of recommendation should mention the fact that ten years ago Smith had been discharged from another firm for an unexplained cause, which one of the three following firms should he be recommended to?

    a. A firm with an unknown personnel policy.

    b. A firm with an established and respected personnel policy.

    c. A firm whose personnel policy has been questioned on grounds of ethical dealings with employees.

21. A large organization is faced with the need of adapting its policies to changed conditions in the community. In order to supply the Directors of the organization with unbiased facts for the determination of major policies, a research bureau is set up as a special department within the organization. After consideration of the ways and means of making the best use of the new fact-finding function, the Directors decided to establish the research bureau:

    a. With authority immediately to carry out in practice its own recommendations derived from fact-finding.

    b. With responsibility to report its findings directly to the Board of Directors.

    c. With responsibility to report its findings to the chief executive only.

    d. With the stipulation that its findings be reported to a subcommittee of the Board on planning, of which the chief executive is to be a member, but not the chairman.

22. A dispute arose among the employees and officers of a small manufacturing company as to the use of an adjoining parking lot owned by the company. Some held that favoritism was shown in the assignment of the better parking spaces. The procedure for the manager to follow would be:

    a. To ignore a trivial dispute of this sort on the assumption that it would clear up of itself, given time.

    b. To adjudicate the dispute promptly and carefully.

    c. To terminate the parking facilities upon due notice.

    d. To reprimand both parties to the dispute.

23. A committee was appointed by a club to draft a formula that would solve a problem of conflict among the members due to the opposition led by a wealthy Mr. Jones to plans for locating the new clubhouse. The committee met and carefully considered the problem; after discussion, it was decided to:

    a. Appoint Mr. Jones as a member of the committee.

    b. Take a caucus and force a favorable vote.

    c. Delay action until the opposition could be converted.

    d. Expel Mr. Jones from membership in the club.

24. A group of citizens of X assemble to hear a visiting architect describe a new plan for the location and construction of a needed high school building for the town. A main highway cuts through the town. Homes are located in sections on both sides of the highway and some persons who live on one side also own property on the

other side. Should the chairman of the meeting, who was asked by the School Board to obtain a judgment on public opinion:

a. Limit the meeting to the architect's presentation?

b. Summarize the architect's address and give the summary to the School Board?

c. Declare an open discussion of the address, record how the individual votes were cast, and transmit this information to the School Board?

d. Limit comments on the address to neutral persons who live outside the town, thus avoiding undue acrimony?

25. The Directors of a settlement house and those who contributed largely to its support were concerned about reports of radical meetings held in its rooms by residents of the slum neighborhood, some communistic and some fascist. It was decided to hold a meeting with Board members to ask questions of the resident staff of social workers. Some feeling developed on the part of the social workers who felt embarrassed or resentful and on the part of Board members who felt that something was being withheld. The situation grew more and more strained until the tension was suddenly broken by the following remark of a staff member:

a. "A young resident of the house confessed to making inflammatory remarks at a meeting a month ago but was not reappointed at the expiration of her contract because she had a nervous breakdown and had to go to a convalescent home for rest."

b. "The executive of the settlement spotted a notorious labor racketeer two weeks ago attending a meeting and talking too much. Since the man had a police record and this was called to his attention, he dropped out of subsequent meetings."

c. "I remember one man distinctly, who was very radical in his statements at meetings, but he has moved away to another city."

d. "Oh, you know, there was someone around here who talked against the government, but she was a Republican."

SCALE: GUTTMAN-TYPE SCALES FOR UNION AND MANAGEMENT ATTITUDES TOWARD EACH OTHER

VARIABLE: Degree of favorability of management toward the union and the union toward management.

WHERE PUBLISHED: Ross Stagner, W. Ellison Chalmers, and Milton Derber, "Guttman-Type Scales for Union and Management Attitudes toward Each Other," *Journal of Applied Psychology*, October, 1958, 42: (5), 293-300; see also Milton Derber, W. Ellison Chalmers, and Ross Stagner, *The Local Union-Management Relationship*, "Institute of Labor and Industrial Relations," Urbana: Univ. of Illinois, 1960.

DESCRIPTION: Unidimensional scales were established both for management attitudes toward the union and for union attitudes toward management, utilizing Guttman's scalogram analysis and supported by correlational data. An eleven-item scale was devised for the measurement of management attitudes, while the scale measuring union attitudes consists of nine items. The items are of a multiple-choice question nature. The scales have a generalized tendency to measure approval in attitudes and are designed for administration to the top officials of each group.

RELIABILITY:
Guttman "coefficient of reproducibility"—management scale = .915
Guttman "coefficient of reproducibility"—union scale = .902

VALIDITY: Face validity.

UTILITY: This instrument provides a quick estimate of the labor-management social climate.

SCALE FOR MANAGEMENT ATTITUDE TOWARD UNION

1. Are the union officers effective leaders of their organization?
   1. very much
   2. pretty good
   3. mediocre
   4. very poor   (2.5) *

2. Is the union generally reasonable or not in its claims?
   1. very reasonable
   2. reasonable most of the time
   3. frequently unreasonable
   4. extremely unreasonable   (2.5)

3. Does the union interfere seriously with how the company is managed, or does the management have a reasonably free hand in running the plant?
   1. union is no problem
   2. it interferes a little but not seriously
   3. it interferes quite often
   4. it seriously interferes with management   (2.0)

4. Are the union officers interested in the welfare of the rank-and-file workers?
   1. very much so
   2. pretty much
   3. slightly
   4. very little   (2.0)

5. Does the union cooperate with management on production matters or not?
   1. they are extremely cooperative
   2. they will go along but not positively support
   3. they do not interfere seriously but sometimes are obstructionist
   4. they restrict production improvements quite often   (2.5)

6. In general, how do you personally feel about your company's relations with the union?
   1. very satisfied
   2. moderately satisfied
   3. moderately dissatisfied
   4. very dissatisfied   (2.0)

* Numbers in parentheses, such as (2.5), indicate the cutting point between an answer considered favorable and one considered unfavorable.

7. Has the union tended to weaken employee discipline, or has it co-operated with management on disciplinary matters?
   1. cooperative and helpful
   2. sometimes helps but not always
   3. sometimes interferes with discipline
   4. has created some serious disciplinary problems   (2.5)

8. Does the union have too much power in your establishment?
   1. not too much
   2. too much in a few respects
   3. too much in many respects
   4. far too much   (1.5)

9. Does the union have the support of the workers?
   1. most of the workers are strongly behind it
   2. only a few really active people but most workers go along
   3. not too much feeling either way
   4. a lot of the workers are hostile   (1.0)

10. How do you feel about using the union as the main channel of communication to the workers on company policies?
    1. strongly favor
    2. moderately favor
    3. moderately oppose
    4. strongly oppose   (combine with No. 11)

11. Are the *local* union officers skillful bargainers?
    1. very much so
    2. pretty good
    3. mediocre
    4. very poor   (favorable if Nos. 10 and 11 = 3 or less)

SCALE FOR UNION ATTITUDE TOWARD MANAGEMENT

1. Are the top management officials effective executives of the establishment?
   1. very much so
   2. pretty good
   3. mediocre
   4. very poor   (2.0)

2. What is the top management attitude toward the union?
   1. strongly favorable
   2. moderately favorable
   3. moderately unfavorable
   4. strongly unfavorable   (2.0)

3. Does the company try to live up to its agreements?
   1. always
   2. usually
   3. frequently does not
   4. rarely   (2.0)

4. Does the company abuse its power in this establishment?
   1. rarely
   2. occasionally
   3. frequently
   4. very often   (1.5)

5. In general, how do you personally feel about your union's relations with the company?
   1. very satisfied
   2. moderately satisfied
   3. moderately dissatisfied
   4. very dissatisfied   (2.0)

6. Has the management shown any understanding of your problems as a union officer?
   1. very understanding
   2. understands the union situation pretty well
   3. understanding of union problems is limited
   4. little or no understanding of union problems   (2.0)

7. Has the management tried to undermine the union position through direct dealings with the workers, or has it been careful to safeguard the union position in such contacts?
   1. is always careful not to hurt union
   2. is usually careful not to hurt union
   3. occasionally tries to weaken union
   4. frequently tries to weaken union   (2.0)

8. Is the top management generally reasonable or not when it comes to discussing union claims?
   1. very reasonable
   2. reasonable most of the time
   3. frequently unreasonable
   4. extremely unreasonable   (1.5)

9. Are the top management officials interested in the welfare of the workers?
   1. very much so
   2. pretty much
   3. slightly
   4. very little   (1.5)

INDEX: PERCEPTION OF INTERNAL COMMUNIST DANGER

VARIABLE MEASURED: The images in the minds of Americans about the internal Communist threat.

DESCRIPTION: This is a Guttman-type scale consisting of 9 items grouped into six categories. Each group consists of one question with one or two other items if there is any yes answer to the original question. For example, group 5 question is "Do you think there are any Communists teaching in American public schools, or not?" If any yes answer is given, then the following question was asked: "How much danger is there that these Communists in public schools can hurt the country—a great danger, some danger, not much danger, or no danger."

WHERE PUBLISHED: Samuel A. Stouffer, *Communism, Conformity and Civil Liberties,* Garden City, New York: Doubleday & Co., 1955, pp. 266-69.

RELIABILITY: The coefficient of reproducibility is .94.

VALIDITY: None is given.

STANDARD SCORES: Subjects are classified in certain groups when they answer at least one in the group.
See relatively great internal Communist threat—Groups 5 and 4.
In-between—Groups 2 and 3.
See relatively little internal Communist threat—Groups 1 and 0.

UTILITY: The scale deals with a difficult-to-measure variable. It is not difficult to administer or score and gives an objective measure.

RESEARCH APPLICATIONS: This scale was used in a report on the reactions of Americans to the danger of the Communist conspiracy outside and inside the country and to the danger of those who in thwarting the conspiracy would sacrifice some of the very liberties that the enemy would destroy (*Communism, Conformity and Civil Liberties* by Samuel A. Stouffer).

SCALE OF PERCEPTION ON THE INTERNAL
COMMUNIST DANGER *

This scale yields the same number of rank groups as the scale of tolerance and is based on the same cumulative principle to provide a test of internal consistency.

The way individual items are cross-tabulated to provide each of the rank groups is somewhat different, however:

GROUP 5. Those in the group seeing greatest danger are scored + on the following questions:
Do you think there are any Communists teaching in American public schools, or not?

IF ANY YES ANSWER: How much danger is there that these Communists in public schools can hurt the country—a great danger, some danger, not much danger, or no danger?

> + Great
> — Some
> — Not much
> — None
> — Don't know

GROUP 4. Do not qualify for Group 5, but answer is scored + on the following question:
Do you think there might be any Communists within the American Government now, or not?

IF ANY YES ANSWER: How much danger is there that these Communists within the Government can hurt the country—a great danger, some danger, not much danger, or no danger?

> + Great
> — Some
> — Not much
> — None
> — Don't know

* From *Communism, Conformity and Civil Liberties* by Samuel A. Stouffer. Copyright 1955 by Samuel A. Stouffer. Reprinted by permission of Doubleday & Co., Inc.

GROUP 3. Do not qualify for Groups 5 and 4, but answer is scored +
on the following question:

How great a danger do you feel that American Communists are to
this country at the present time—a very great danger, a great danger,
some danger, hardly any danger, or no danger?

> \+ A very great danger
> \+ A great danger
> − Some danger
> − Hardly any danger
> − No danger
> − Don't know

GROUP 2. Do not qualify for Groups 5, 4, and 3, but answer is scored
\+ on the following questions:

Do you think there are any Communists teaching in American colleges
and universities now, or not?

IF YES: If you had to guess, how many would you think—just a
few, or hundreds, or thousands?

> Yes, a few
> Yes, hundreds
> Yes, thousands
> Yes, don't know how many
> − No, don't think there are any
> \+ Don't know if there are any

OF, IF ANY YES ANSWER: How much danger is there that the
Communists in colleges and universities can hurt the country—a great
danger, some danger, not much danger, or no danger?

> \+ Great
> \+ Some
> − Not much
> − None
> \+ Don't know

GROUP 1. Do not qualify for Groups 5, 4, 3, and 2, but answer is
scored + on the following questions:

Do you think there are any Communists working in key defense plants
now, or not?

IF YES: If you had to guess, how many would you think—just a few, or hundreds, or thousands?

>   Yes, a few
>   Yes, hundreds
>   Yes, thousands
>   Yes, don't know how many
> — No, don't think there are any
> + Don't know if there are any

OR, IF ANY YES ANSWER: How much danger is there that these Communists in defense plants can hurt the country—a great danger, some danger, not much danger, or no danger?

> + Great
> + Some
> — Not much
> — None
> + Don't know

GROUP o.   Do not give answer scored + in any of the aforementioned groups.

An additional requirement is that those in Group 5 be scored + on all items below Group 5; that those in Group 4 be scored + on all items below Group 4, etc.

INDEX: WILLINGNESS TO TOLERATE NONCONFORMISTS

VARIABLE MEASURED: The degree to which individuals respect the civil rights of radicals and other nonconformists, even though they may suspect or disapprove their opinions.

DESCRIPTION: This Guttman-type scale includes 15 items grouped into 5 subtests of 3 items each. Each item is answered as a positive-negative dichotomy, with a possible choice of "Don't know." These are scored + or −. The items are so chosen that a person "tolerant" on a subtest in which few other people would be tolerant is also very likely to be so in a subtest on which many other people would be "tolerant."

WHERE PUBLISHED: Samuel A. Stouffer, *Communism, Conformity and Civil Liberties*, Garden City, N.Y.: Doubleday & Co., Inc., 1915, pp. 262-66.

RELIABILITY: The degree of consistency measured by a coefficient of reproducibility is .96.

VALIDITY: None given.

STANDARD SCORES: Subjects are classified in certain groups when they answer 2 or 3 questions in the group positively.
"Relatively more tolerant"—Groups 5 and 4.
"In-between"—Groups 3 and 2.
"Relatively less tolerant"—Groups 1 and 0.

UTILITY: The scale deals with a difficult-to-measure variable. It is not difficult to administer or score and gives an objective measure.

RESEARCH APPLICATIONS: This scale was used in a report on the reactions of Americans to the danger of the Communist conspiracy outside and inside the country and to the danger of those who in thwarting the conspiracy would sacrifice some of the very liberties that the enemy would destroy. (*Communism, Conformity and Civil Liberties*, Samuel A. Stouffer.)

WILLINGNESS TO TOLERATE NONCONFORMISTS *

This scale is based on 15 items from the questionnaire. There are five sets of three items each. Each set of three items may be thought

* From *Communism, Conformity and Civil Liberties* by Samuel A. Stouffer. Copyright 1955 by Samuel A. Stouffer. Reprinted by permission of Doubleday & Co., Inc.

of as a subtest. The questions are so chosen that a person who is "tolerant" on a subtest in which few other people would be tolerant is also very likely to be so in a subtest on which many other people would be "tolerant."

From our five groups of three questions each we can rank people in six groups. Those in Group 5 tend to be tolerant on all five subtests, those in Group 4 in all except the hardest to be tolerant on, etc. The last group, Group o, would be tolerant on none.

To accomplish this, we dichotomized the answer to each item. This was not done arbitrarily, but on the basis of analysis of how each answer category related to a provisional total score. The rank groups are defined as follows:

GROUP 5. The most tolerant of all. Make + answers to at least two out of three of these items:
Now, I should like to ask you some questions about a man who admits he is a Communist.
Suppose this admitted Communist wants to make a speech in your community. Should he be allowed to speak, or not?

> \+ Yes
> — No
> — Don't know

Suppose he wrote a book that is in your public library. Somebody in your community suggests the book should be removed from the library. Would you favor removing it, or not?

> — Favor
> \+ Not favor
> — Don't know

Suppose this admitted Communist is a radio singer. Should he be fired, or not?

> — Should be fired
> \+ Not be fired
> — Don't know

GROUP 4. The next most tolerant. Fail to qualify in Group 5 but make + answers to at least two out of three of the following:
Should an admitted Communist be put in jail, or not?

> — Yes
> \+ No
> — Don't know

There are always some people whose ideas are considered bad or dangerous by other people. For instance, somebody who is against all churches and religion.

If such a person wanted to make a speech in your city (town, community) against churches and religion, should he be allowed to speak, or not?

+ Yes
− No
− Don't know

If some people in your community suggested that a book he wrote against churches and religion should be taken out of your public library, would you favor removing this book or not?

− Yes
+ No
− Don't know

GROUP 3. Fail to qualify in Groups 5 or 4, but make + answers to at least two out of three of the following:

Now suppose the radio program he (an admitted Communist) is on advertises a brand of soap. Somebody in your community suggests you stop buying that soap. Would you stop, or not?

− Would stop
+ Would not stop
− Don't know

Or consider a person who favored government ownership of all the railroads and all big industries.

If this person wanted to make a speech in your community favoring government ownership of all the railroads and big industries, should he be allowed to speak, or not?

+ Yes
− No
− Don't know

If some people in your community suggested that a book he wrote favoring government ownership should be taken out of your public library, would you favor removing the book, or not?

− Yes
+ No
− Don't know

GROUP 2. Fail to qualify in Groups 5, 4, or 3, but make + answers to at least two out of three of the following:

Now I would like you to think of another person. A man whose loyalty has been questioned before a Congressional committee, but who swears under oath he has never been a Communist.

Suppose he is teaching in a college or university. Should he be fired, or not?

- − Yes
- + No
- − Don't know

Should he be allowed to make a speech in your community, or not?

- + Yes
- − No
- − Don't know

Suppose this man is a high school teacher. Should he be fired, or not?

- − Yes
- + No
- − Don't know

GROUP 1. The next to least tolerant group. Fail to qualify in Groups 5, 4, 3, 2, but make + answers to two out of three of the following (with respect to a man whose loyalty has been questioned but who swears he is not a Communist).

Suppose he has been working in a defense plant. Should he be fired, or not?

- − Yes
- + No
- + Don't know

Suppose he is a clerk in a store. Should he be fired, or not?

- − Yes
- + No
- + Don't know

Suppose he wrote a book that is in your public library. Somebody in your community suggests the book should be removed from the library. Would you favor removing it, or not?

- − Favor
- + Not favor
- + Don't know

GROUP 0. The least tolerant group. Fail to qualify in any of the afore-mentioned groups.

INDEX: SEMANTIC DIFFERENTIAL

VARIABLE MEASURED: Meaning of an object to an individual.

DESCRIPTION: The subject is asked to rate a given concept (e.g., "Negro," "Republican," "wife," "me as I would like to be," "me as I am") on a series of seven-point, bipolar rating scales. Any concept, whether it is a political issue, a person, an institution, or a work of art, can be rated. The seven-point scales include such bipolar scales as the following: (A) fair–unfair, clean–dirty, good–bad, valuable–worthless; (B) large–small, strong–weak, heavy–light; (C) active–passive, fast–slow, hot–cold. The rating is made according to the respondent's perception of the relatedness or association of the adjective to the word concept. Osgood and his colleagues have inferred that the three subgroups (A), (B), and (C) measure the following three dimensions of attitude:

A—the individual's *evaluation* of the object or concept being rated, corresponding to the favorable–unfavorable dimension of more traditional attitude scales.

B—the individual's perception of the *potency* or power of the object or concept.

C—his perception of the *activity* of the object or concept.

The authors suggest that the measuring instrument is not grossly affected by the nature of the object being measured or by the type of persons using the scale. If this proves to be true, the semantic differential would be a solution to many of the problems of attitude measurement. Evidence submitted by Osgood, Suci, and Tannenbaum indicates different types of subjects use the scales in similar ways—thus Taft Republicans, Eisenhower Republicans, and Stevenson Democrats use the same underlying dimensions in their reactions.

WHERE PUBLISHED: Charles E. Osgood, George J. Suci, and Percy H. Tannenbaum, *The Measurement of Meaning,* Urbana: University of Illinois Press, 1957.

RELIABILITY: As given by authors:

(meaning in general) test-retest $r = .85$
(attitudes) test-retest $r = .91$

VALIDITY:

Thurstone scale	$r = .74$ to $.82$
Guttman scale	$r = .78$
Bogardus Social Distance Scale (three factors)	$r = .72$ to $.80$

See Raymond G. Smith, "Validation of a Semantic Differential," *Speech Monographs,* March, 1963, 30: 50-55.

UTILITY: A 100-item test can be administered in about ten to fifteen minutes. A 400-item test takes about one hour. The semantic differential may be adapted through choice of concepts and scales to the study of numerous phenomena. It may be useful in constructing and analyzing sociometric scales.

RESEARCH APPLICATIONS: Various researches are cited in the original publication. See also:

Proceedings of The Fourteenth Conference of American Association For Public Opinion Research, "The Semantic Differential: Its Use And Abuse," abstracted in *The Public Opinion Quarterly,* Fall, 1959, 23: 435-38.

Roy E. Carter, Jr., "Newspaper 'Gatekeepers' and the Source of News," *Public Opinion Quarterly,* Summer, 1958, 22: 133-44.

Jum C. Nunnally and Howard M. Bobren, "Attitude Change With False Information," *Public Opinion Quarterly,* Summer, 1959, 23: 260-66.

Reuben Mehling, "A Simple Test for Measuring Intensity of Attitudes," *Public Opinion Quarterly,* Winter, 1959-60, 23: 576-78.

———, "Attitude Changing Effect of News and Photo Combinations," *Journalism Quarterly,* 1959, 36: 189-98.

Jean S. Kerrick, "News Pictures, Captions and the Point of Resolution," *Journalism Quarterly,* 1959, 36: 183-88.

Raymond G. Smith, "Development of a Semantic Differential for Use with Speech Related Concepts," *Speech Monographs,* November, 1959, 26: 263-72.

———, "A Semantic Differential for Theatre Concepts," *Speech Monographs,* March, 1961, 28: 1-8.

Jenkins, Group differences in perception (of reverberation) Am. Jl. for Jan 66, p. 412 - 429.

TYPICAL INSTRUCTIONS

The purpose of this study is to measure the *meanings* of certain things to various people by having them judge against a series of descriptive scales. In taking this test, please make your judgments on the basis of what these things mean to *you*. On each page of this booklet you will find a different concept to be judged and beneath it a set of scales. You are to rate the concept on each of these scales in order.

Here is how you are to use these scales:

If you feel that the concept at the top of the page is *very closely related* to one end of the scale, you should place your check mark as follows:

fair __X__:____:____:____:____:____:____ unfair

or

fair ____:____:____:____:____:____:__X__ unfair

If you feel that the concept is *quite closely related* to one or the other end of the scale (but not extremely), you should place your check mark as follows:

strong ____:__X__:____:____:____:____:____ weak

or

strong ____:____:____:____:____:__X__:____ weak

If the concept seems *only slightly related* to one side as opposed to the other side (but is not really neutral), then you should check as follows:

active ____:____:__X__:____:____:____:____ passive

or

active ____:____:____:____:__X__:____:____ passive

The direction toward which you check, of course, depends upon which of the two ends of the scale seem most characteristic of the thing you're judging.

If you consider the concept to be *neutral* on the scale, both sides of the scale *equally associated* with the concept, or if the scale is *completely irrelevant*, unrelated to the concept, then you should place your check mark in the middle space:

safe ____:____:____:__X_:____:____:____ dangerous

IMPORTANT:

(1) Place your check marks *in the middle of spaces,* not on the boundaries:

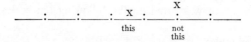

(2) Be sure you check every scale for every concept— *do not omit any.*

(3) Never put more than one check mark on a single scale.

Sometimes you may feel as though you've had the same item before on the test. This will not be the case, *so do not look back and forth* through the items. Do not try to remember how you checked similar items earlier in the test. *Make each item a separate and independent judgment.* Work at a fairly high speed through this test. Do not worry or puzzle over individual items. It is your first impressions, the immediate "feelings" about the items, that we want. On the other hand, please do not be careless, because we want your true impressions.

A SAMPLE OF A SEMANTIC DIFFERENTIAL SCALE *

Fifteen concepts:

Love; Child; My Doctor; Me; My Job; Mental Sickness; My Mother; Peace of Mind; Fraud; My Spouse; Self-control; Hatred; My Father; Confusion; Sex;
Each concept was rated on the following ten scales:

valuable ___:___:___:___:___:___:___ worthless

clean ___:___:___:___:___:___:___ dirty

tasty ___:___:___:___:___:___:___ distasteful

large ___:___:___:___:___:___:___ small

strong ___:___:___:___:___:___:___ weak

deep ___:___:___:___:___:___:___ shallow

fast ___:___:___:___:___:___:___ slow

active ___:___:___:___:___:___:___ passive

hot ___:___:___:___:___:___:___ cold

tense ___:___:___:___:___:___:___ relaxed

---

* This sample Semantic Differential was used in a study reported by Charles E. Osgood and Zella Luria, "A Blind Analysis of a Case of Multiple Personality Using the Semantic Differential," *Journal of Abnormal and Social Psychology,* 1954, 49: 579-91.

SECTION H

Family and Marriage

The *Marriage-Prediction Schedule* and the *Marriage-Adjustment Schedule* are products of intensive research efforts led by Ernest W. Burgess and his associates and aided by many social researchers who have been seeking factors associated with success or failure in marriage.

The *Marriage-Prediction Schedule* is used in assessing the probabilities of engaged couples to be able to establish happy marital adjustment if they should marry.

The *Marriage-Adjustment Schedule* is for married couples. It can be used as a diagnostic instrument to help the marriage counselor detect the social areas where difficulties exist. The researcher may use it to assess new relationships such as the role of parent-child relations and marital adjustment.

INDEX: MARRIAGE-PREDICTION SCHEDULE AND MARRIAGE-ADJUSTMENT SCHEDULE

VARIABLE MEASURED: The marital prediction schedule predicts the statistical probabilities of success in marriage; the marriage adjustment schedule is predictive of adjustment in marriage.

DESCRIPTION: The marital adjustment schedule was the first schedule developed. Five hundred and twenty-six Illinois couples who had been married one to six years were studied. Marital adjustment was defined as (1) Agreement between husband and wife upon matters that might be made critical issues; (2) Common interests and joint activities; (3) Frequent overt demonstrations of affection and mutual confidence; (4) Few complaints; (5) Few reports of feeling lonely, miserable, irritable, etc. Items classified under these five headings serve as indicators of marital adjustment. Each of the items shows a measurable relationship to the ratings given by the couples to their expressed happiness rating of their marriage. For the development of

273

the marital adjustment schedule see E. W. Burgess and Leonard S. Cottrell, *Predicting Success or Failure in Marriage,* Prentice-Hall, 1939. Cf. Nathan Hurvitz, "The Measurement of Marital Strain," *American Journal of Sociology,* May, 1960, 65: 610-15.

The marital prediction schedule was developed by seeking items predictive of marriage adjustment among 1,000 engaged couples. Selected background items significantly associated with marital adjustment were combined into an expectancy table for premarital prediction of success in marriage. For the development of the marital prediction schedule see Ernest W. Burgess and Paul Wallin, *Engagement and Marriage,* J. B. Lippincott, 1953.

WHERE PUBLISHED: Ernest W. Burgess and Harvey J. Locke, *The Family,* 2nd ed.; New York: American Book Co., 1960, pp. 693-716. (Contains the refined version of the schedules based upon approximately 25 years of research.)

RELIABILITY: Husband-wife adjustment scores correlated with $r = .88$. ($N = 526$ couples)

VALIDITY:

Happiness ratings and adjustment scores correlated .92. ($n = 526$ couples)

Second sample of 63 cases showed correlation between happiness ratings and adjustment scores of .95.

Correlation between happiness ratings and absence of marital disorganization, divorce, separation, and contemplation of divorce or separation. $r = .89$.

Harvey Locke computed Burgess-Cottrell Adjustment scores for divorced men, divorced women, happily married men, and happily married women. Correlations between scores attained in this way and scores from the 29 questions in his test were respectively, .83, .87, .85, and .88.

Burgess and Wallin gave an adjustment test to 1,000 engaged couples, and then, three years after marriage, gave a marital adjustment test to as many couples as could be contacted. Correlation between adjustment scores of engaged couples was .57; three years after marriage, marital adjustment scores of 505 husbands and wives correlated .41. See Lewis M. Terman and Paul Wallin, "The Validity of Marriage Prediction and Marital Adjustment Tests," *American Sociological Review,* August, 1949, 14: 497-504; Harvey J. Locke and Robert G. Williamson, "Marriage Adjustment: A Factor Analysis Study," *American Sociological Review,* October, 1958, 23: 562-69.

Scoring the Marriage-Prediction and Marriage-Adjustment Schedules

The narrow columns at the right side of each page of the *Marriage-Prediction Schedule* and the *Marriage-Adjustment Schedule* are provided for scoring the replies to the questions. The score values assigned are arbitrary in the sense that usually each gradation in reply differs by one point. Although arbitrary, the score values are in general conformity with the findings of the studies in this field, particularly those of E. W. Burgess and L. S. Cottrell, *Predicting Success or Failure in Marriage;* L. M. Terman and Others, *Psychological Factors in Marital Happiness;* E. W. Burgess and Paul Wallin, *Engagement and Marriage;* and Harvey J. Locke, *Predicting Adjustment in Marriage: A Comparison of a Divorced and a Happily Married Group.*

The two-digit numbers after each subdivision of the questions provide the code for scoring the replies. The score value of each response is obtained simply by adding together the two digits in the number that is a subscript under the last letter of the final word of the response that has been checked. For example, if you have checked a response numbered 42, your score for that item is $4 + 2 = 6$. To obtain your total score, follow these steps:

1. For each item, enter in Column 1 at the right-hand side of each page the two-digit number that appears as a subscript under the last letter of the final word of the answers to each question. An example is: What is your present state of health? chronic ill-health (13)____; temporary ill-health (23)____; average health (15)____; healthy (25)____; very healthy (17)____. If your answer to this question is "average health," then write 15 in Column 1.

   In Part Two of the Marriage-Prediction Schedule, put only the score of your fiancé(e) in the blank on the right-hand margin.

2. Enter in Column 2 the sum of the two digits appearing in Column 1 for each item. For each part of the questionnaire, compute the total of the values appearing in Column 2, and enter that figure in the space provided at the end of that section.

3. In scoring Part Two of the Marriage-Adjustment Schedule, multiply the total number of check marks in each of the four columns as follows:

Column A by 6	Column C by 4
Column B by 5	Column D by 6

Add together the four figures obtained in the four columns. This sum equals your total score for Part Two.

4. Enter the total score for each part in the spaces provided at the end of the questionnaire. Your total score on the inventory equals the sum of the total scores of the separate parts and is your marriage-adjustment score.

STANDARD SCORES

A. Marriage-Prediction Schedule

High scores on the Marriage-Prediction Schedule, those above 630, are favorable for marital adjustment, as indicated by research findings that approximately 75 per cent of persons with these scores in the engagement period are well adjusted in their marriages. Low scores, or those below 567, are much less favorable for happiness in marriage, as shown by the probability that only 25 per cent of persons with these scores will be well adjusted in married life. Scores between 567 and 630 indicate that there is about a 50 per cent chance for marital success and about a 50 per cent chance for marital failure.

The prediction score of a person and his corresponding matrimonial-risk-group assignment should be interpreted with extreme caution. The following points should be kept in mind:

1. The prediction does not apply directly to the individual. It states the statistical probabilities of marital success for a group of persons of which the individual is one. If he belongs to the lower risk group, in which 75 per cent of the marriages turn out unhappily, there is no way of telling by this statistical prediction whether he falls in the 25 per cent of the marriages with varying degrees of happiness or in the 75 per cent of unhappy unions.

2. The prediction is for an individual's general matrimonial risk irrespective of the particular person to whom he is engaged. The individual's specific matrimonial risk for marriage to a given person is much more valuable but also more complicated, and therefore not suited for self-scoring.

3. In the majority of cases the specific matrimonial risk of a couple may be roughly estimated from the two general matrimonial-risk groups to which the two persons are assigned. An average of the two scores will generally be close to what may be expected from a specific matrimonial-risk-group assignment.

4. With the aforementioned reservations in mind, a low prediction score should not be taken as indicating lack of suitability for marriage. It should, however, be helpful to the person in stimulating him to secure adequate preparation for marriage, to be more careful in the selection of a marriage partner, and to give attention to the solving of any difficulties in the relation before, rather than after, the marriage.

B. *Marriage-Adjustment Schedule*

In evaluating the total score secured on the Marriage-Adjustment Schedule, see the following table:

MARRIAGE-ADJUSTMENT SCORES AS INDICATIVE OF
ADJUSTMENT IN MARRIAGE

Marital-Adjustment Scores	Adjustment in Marriage
720 and over	Extremely well adjusted
700 to 719	Decidedly well adjusted
680 to 699	Fairly adjusted
660 to 679	Somewhat adjusted
640 to 659	Indifferently adjusted
620 to 639	Somewhat unadjusted
600 to 619	Unadjusted
580 to 599	Decidedly unadjusted
579 and under	Extremely unadjusted

UTILITY: Each form may be filled out in approximately 30 minutes. The measure may be used for both research and counseling purposes. Short marital-adjustment and prediction tests are now available. It is claimed that "with the short tests, measurement or prediction can be accomplished with approximately the same accuracy in a few minutes as ordinarily would require an hour or more with the longer ones." Harvey J. Locke and Karl M. Wallace, "Short Marital-Adjustment and Prediction Tests: Their Reliability and Validity," *Marriage and Family Living*, August, 1959, 21: 251-55.

RESEARCH APPLICATIONS: Charles Bowerman, "Adjustment in Marriage, Overall and Specifications," *Sociology and Social Research*, March-April, 1957, 257-63.

Charles King, "The Burgess-Cottrell Method of Measuring Marital Adjustment Applied to a Non-White Southern Urban Population," *Marriage and Family Living*, November, 1952, 280-85.

Harvey J. Locke, *Predicting Adjustment in Marriage: A Comparison of a Divorced and a Happily Married Group*, New York: Henry Holt, 1951.

E. W. Burgess and Paul Wallin, "Predicting Adjustment in Marriage from Adjustment in Engagement," *American Journal of Sociology*, 1944, 49: 324-30.

Georg Karlsson, *Adaptability and Communication in Marriage: A Swedish Predictive Study of Marital Satisfaction*, Uppsala, Sweden: Almquist and Wiksells, 1951.

Harvey J. Locke and Georg Karlsson, "Marital Adjustment and Prediction in Sweden and the United States," *American Sociological Review,* February, 1952, 17: 10-17.

Harvey J. Locke and Muriel Mackeprang, "Marital Adjustment and the Employed Wife," *American Journal of Sociology,* 1949, 54: 536-38.

Harvey J. Locke and William J. Klausner, "Marital Adjustment of Divorced Persons in Subsequent Marriages, *Sociology and Social Research,* 1948, 33: 97-101.

Gerald J. Schnepp, "Do Religious Factors Have Predictive Value," *Marriage and Family Living,* 1952, 14: 301-4.

Robert F. Winch, "Personality Characteristics of Engaged and Married Couples," *American Journal of Sociology,* 1941, 46: 686-97.

SCHEDULES FOR THE PREDICTION AND MEASUREMENT OF MARRIAGE ADJUSTMENT

I. Marriage-Prediction Schedule *

Please Read Carefully Before and After Filling Out Schedule.

This schedule is prepared for persons who are seriously considering marriage. Although designed for couples who are engaged or who have a private understanding to be married, it can also be filled out by other persons who would like to know their probability of success in marriage. The value of the findings of the schedule depends upon your frankness in answering the questions.

The following points should be kept in mind in filling out the schedule:

1. Be sure to answer every question.
2. Do not leave a blank to mean a "no" answer.
3. The word "fiancé(e)" will be used to refer to the person to whom you are engaged or are considering as a possible marriage partner.
4. Do not confer with your fiancé(e) on any of these questions.

* Reproduced by permission of Ernest W. Burgess, Leonard S. Cottrell, Paul Wallin, and Harvey J. Locke.

Part One

1. What is your present state of health? chronic ill-health (13)____; temporary ill-health (23)____; average health (15)____; healthy (25)____; very healthy (17)____

2. Give your present marital status: single (35)____; widowed (43) ____; separated (41)____; divorced (31)____

3. Total number of years of schooling completed at present time:
   Grades (22)   High School (32)   College (15) ·
   1__2__3__4__5__6__7__8__; 1__2__3__4; 1__2__3__4__; graduate of college (25); number of years beyond college in graduate work or professional training (35)____

4. Work record: regularly employed (17)____; worked only during vacations and/or only part time while in school (34)____; none because in school or at home (24)____; always employed but continually changing jobs (32)____; irregularly employed (13)____

5. Are you a church member? yes (16)____; no (23)____
   Your activity in church: never attend (40)____; attend less than once a month (23)____; once or twice a month (33)____; three times a month (16)____; four times a month (26)____

6. At what age did you stop attending Sunday school or other religious school for children and young people? never attended (31)____; before 10 years old (23)____; 11-18 years (42)____; 19 and over (16)____; still attending (35)____

7. How many organizations do you belong to or attend regularly, such as church club, athletic club, social club, luncheon club (like the Rotary, Kiwanis, Lions), fraternal order, college fraternity, college sorority, civic organization, music society, patriotic organization, Y.W.C.A., Y.M.C.A., C.Y.O., Y.M.H.A.? none (22)____; one (32)____; two (15)____; three or more (25)____

8. What do you consider to have been the economic status of your parents during your adolescence? well-to-do (34)____; wealthy (43)____; comfortable (15)____; meager (32)____; poor (40)____

9. What do you consider to be the social status of your parents in their own community? one of the leading families (26)____; upper class (16)____; upper-middle class (42)____; middle class (32)____; lower-middle class (40)____; lower class (21)____; no status as they are dead (33)____

10. Marital status of your parents: married (both living) (24)____; separated (41)____; divorced (31)____; both dead (15)____; one dead (specify which one) (33)____

11. Your appraisal of the happiness of your parents' marriage; very happy (36)____; happy (16)____; average (24)____; unhappy (41)____; very unhappy (31)____

12. Indicate your attitudes toward your parents on the following scales:

(1) Your attitude toward your father when you were a child; very strong attachment (35)_____; considerable attachment (25)_____; mild attachment (41)_____; mild hostility (13) _____; considerable hostility (30)_____; very strong hostility (21)_____

(2) Your present attitude toward your father: very strong attachment (44)_____; considerable attachment (16)_____; mild attachment (23)_____; mild hostility (22)_____; considerable hostility (12)_____; very strong hostility (21) _____; no attitude as he is dead (24)_____

(3) Your attitude toward your mother when you were a child: very strong attachment (26)_____; considerable attachment (34)_____; mild attachment (14)_____mild hostility (31)_____; considerable hostility (30)_____; very strong hostility (12)_____

(4) Your present attitude toward your mother: very strong attachment (17)_____; considerable attachment (43)_____; mild attachment (32)_____; mild hostility (13)_____; considerable hostility (21)_____; very strong hostility (30) _____; no attitude as she is dead (15)_____

13. Rate your parents' appraisal of the happiness of their marriage. Write *M* for mother's rating; *F* for father's rating; extraordinarily happy (27)_____; decidedly happy (25)_____; happy (41) _____; somewhat happy (30)_____; average (30)_____; somewhat unhappy (12)_____; unhappy (21)_____; decidedly unhappy (30)_____; extremely unhappy (12)_____

14. Outside your family and kin, how many separated and divorced people do you know personally? none (26)_____; one (43) _____; two (23)_____; three (40)_____; four (30)_____; five (12)_____; six or more (21)_____

15. How do you rate your first information about sex? wholesome (16)_____; unwholesome (23)_____
Where did you get your first information about sex? from parent (35)_____; from wholesome reading (16)_____; brother (41) _____; sister (41)_____; other relative (41)_____; other adult or teacher (24)_____; other children (31)_____; from pernicious reading (12)_____; other (specify) (15)_____

Do you consider your present knowledge of sex adequate for marriage? yes (34)_____; no (14)_____; doubtful (42)_____

16. Do you smoke? not at all (26)_____; rarely (15)_____; occasionally (32)_____; often (22)_____

17. Do you drink? not at all (35)_____; rarely (42)_____; occasionally (33)_____; often (31)_____

Rate the following personality traits of yourself, your fiancé(e), your father, your mother. Write *F* for father, *M* for mother, *S* for fiancé(e), and *Y* for yourself. If either of your parents is dead, rate as remembered. Be sure to rate your father, your mother, your fiancé(e), and yourself on each trait.

Trait	Very much so	Con- siderably	Some- what	A little	Not at all	1	2
Willingly takes responsibility	26	16	6	23	13		
Dominating	13	23	33	16	44		
Irritable	40	14	24	25	17		
Punctual	35	25	15	14	13		
Moody	22	41	51	43	35		
Angers easily	40	50	60	34	26		
Ambitious	13	23	33	25	44		
Jealous	31	41	15	16	26		
Sympathetic	17	16	24	32	4		
Easygoing	44	43	42	14	22		
Stubborn	22	14	24	25	17		
Sense of duty	26	25	15	41	31		
Sense of humor	35	34	24	23	22		
Easily hurt	31	23	51	52	35		
Self-confident	44	16	15	14	13		
Selfish	22	23	33	43	44		
Nervous	22	23	24	25	35		
Likes belonging to organizations	26	16	33	41	13		
Impractical	40	14	6	34	17		
Easily depressed	13	5	42	16	26		
Easily excited	31	32	24	7	44		
					T		

Part Three

1. What is the attitude of your closest friend or friends to your fiancé(e)? approve highly (25)____; approve with qualification (15)____; are resigned (32)____; disapprove mildly (13) ____; disapprove seriously (31)____

2. How many of your present men and women friends are also friends of your fiancé(e)? all (17)____; most of them (25) ____; a few (23)____; none (13)____

3. How would you rate the physical appearance of your fiancé(e)? very good looking (35)____; good looking (25)____; fairly good looking (41)____; plain looking (22)____; very plain looking (31)____

4. Do you think your fiancé(e) is spending a disproportionate amount of present income on any of the following (check only one)? clothes (or other personal ornamentation) (13)____; recreation (41)____; hobbies (22)____; food (24)____; rent (33)____; education (16)____; do not think so (35)____

5. With how many of the opposite sex, other than your fiancé(e), have you gone steadily? none (25)____; one (42)____; two (24)____; three or more (15)____

6. Defining friends as something more than mere acquaintances but not necessarily as always having been boon companions, give an estimate of the number of your men friends before going steadily with your fiancé(e): none (31)____; few (14)____; several (24)____; many (34)____; (in round numbers, how many? ____)

7. Estimate the number of your women friends before going steadily with your fiancé(e): none (4)____; few (32)____; several (33)____; many (16)____; (in round numbers, how many? ____)

8. Have you ever been engaged before (or had any previous informal understanding that you were to be married)? never (35)____; once (42)____; twice (14)____; three or more times (31)____

9. Give the attitude of your father and mother toward your marriage: both approve (26)____; both disapprove (31)____; one disapproves: (your father (22)____, your mother (31) ____)

10. What is your attitude toward your future father-in-law? like him very much (25)____; like him considerably (15)____; like him mildly (32)____; mild dislike (40)____; considerable dislike (12)____; very strong dislike (30)____; no attitude, as he is dead (42)____
    mother-in-law: like her very much (34)____; like her considerably (24)____; like her mildly (41)____; mild dislike (22) ____; considerable dislike (21)____; very strong dislike (12) ____; no attitude, as she is dead (24)____

283

11. How long have you been keeping company with your fiancé(e)? less than 3 months (13)_____; 3 to 5 months (32)_____; 6 to 11 months (24)_____; 12 to 17 months (25)_____; 18 to 23 months (35)_____; 24 to 35 months (17)_____; 36 months or more (44)_____

12. How many months will elapse between your engagement (or time at which you both had a definite understanding that you were to be married) and the date selected for your marriage? less than 3 months (40)_____; 3 to 5 months (14)_____; 6 to 11 months (33)_____; 12 to 17 months (25)_____; 18 to 23 months (35)_____; 24 or more months (44)_____

Part Four

1. Do you and your fiancé(e) engage in interests and activities together? all of them (43)_____; most of them (15)_____; some of them (23)_____; a few of them (31)_____; none of them (22)_____

2. Is there any interest vital to you in which your fiancé(e) does not engage? yes (31)__; no (43)_____

3. Do you confide in your fiancé(e)? about everything (36)_____; about most things (16)_____; about some things (23)_____; about a few things (22)_____; about nothing (30)_____

4. Does your fiancé(e) confide in you? about everything (27) _____; about most things (25)_____; about some things (41) _____; about a few things (31)_____; about nothing (12)_____

5. What is the frequency of demonstrations of affection you show your fiancé(e) (kissing, embracing, etc.)? occupies practically all of the time you are alone together (18)_____; very frequent (26)_____; occasional (14)_____; rare (31)_____; almost never (12)_____

6. Who generally takes the initiative in the demonstration of affection? mutual (26)_____; you (23)_____; your fiancé(e) (41) _____

7. Are you satisfied with the amount of demonstration of affection? yes (35)_____; (no: desire less (30)_____; desire more (12) _____)

8. Is your fiancé(e) satisfied with the amount of demonstration of affection? yes (44)_____; (no: desires less (3)_____; desires more (30)_____)

9. In leisure-time activities: we both prefer to stay at home (26) _____; we both prefer to be "on the go" (14)_____; one prefers to stay at home and the other to be "on the go" (40)_____

10. State the present approximate agreement or disagreement with your fiancé(e) on the following items. Please place a check in the proper column opposite every item.

I	2
T	

284

Check one column for each item below	Always agree (35)	Almost always agree (16)	Occasionally disagree (42)	Frequently disagree (14)	Almost always disagree (22)	Always disagree (30)	Never discussed (15)	1	2
Money matters									
Matters of recreation									
Religious matters									
Demonstrations of affection									
Friends									
Table manners									
Matters of conventionality									
Philosophy of life									
Ways of dealing with your families									
Arrangements for your marriage									
Dates with one another									

11. When disagreements arise between you and your fiancé(e) they usually result in: agreement by mutual give and take (53)____; your giving in (16)____; your fiancé(e) giving in (30)____; neither giving in (21)____

12. Do you ever wish you had not become engaged? never (44)____; once (14)____; occasionally (13)____; frequently (40)____

13. Have you ever contemplated breaking your engagement? never (35)____; once (41)____; occasionally (31)____; frequently (40)____

14. Has your steady relationship with your fiancé(e) ever been broken off temporarily? never (61)____; once (23)____; twice (40)____; three or more times (13)____

15. How confident are you that your marriage will be a happy one? very confident (25)____; confident (33)____; a little uncertain (14)____; very uncertain (40)____

T

Part Five

1. Where do you plan to be married? at church (35)___; at home (16)___; elsewhere (32)___

2. By whom do you plan to be married? minister, priest, or rabbi (16)___; other person (14)___

3. Where do you plan to live after marriage? private house (26) ___; small apartment building (52)___; large apartment building (15)___; apartment hotel (41)___; hotel (22)___; rooming house (30)___

4. Have bought a home (44)___; plan to buy a home (25)___; plan to rent a home (14)___

5. Population of city or town where you plan to live: open country (27)___; 2,500 or under (35)___; 2,500 to 10,000 (16) ___; 10,000 to 50,000 (42)___; 50,000 to 100,000 (32)___; 100,000 to 500,000 (4)___; over 500,000 (30)___; suburb (17)___

6. After marriage where do you plan to live? in own home (53) ___; with your parents (13)___; with parents-in-law (30) ___; with other relatives (21)___; with relatives-in-law (3)___; with other persons (12)___

7. What is your attitude toward having children? desire children very much (25)___; mildly desire them (41)___; mild objection to them (31)___; object very much to having them (13)___

8. How many children would you like to have? four or more (17) ___; three (52)___; two (33)___; one (41)___ none (13)___

9. What is your fiancé(e)'s attitude toward having children? desires children very much (43)___; mildly desires them (14) ___; mild objection to them (40)___; objects very much to having them (31)___

	T	

Part I___, Part II___, Part III___, Part IV___, Part V___, Total___

II. Marriage-Adjustment Schedule *

To Be Filled Out by Married Persons

This schedule may be filled out by either the husband or the wife. Frank and sincere replies are of the highest importance if the findings are to be of value to the person filling it out or for research purposes. There are no right or wrong answers.

The following points are to be kept in mind in filling out the schedule:

1. Be sure to answer all questions.
2. Do not leave any blanks, as is sometimes done, to signify a "no" reply.
3. The word spouse is used to refer to your husband or wife.
4. Do not confer with your spouse in answering these questions or show your answers to your spouse.

Your Present Marital Status

1. Are you now (check): married____? divorced____? separated ____? widowed____?
2. If divorced or separated, how long have you been separated? months____

   (If you are divorced or separated, answer the questions as of the time of your separation.)

---

* Reproduced by permission of Ernest W. Burgess, Leonard S. Cottrell, Paul Wallin, and Harvey J. Locke.

Part One

1. Present occupation of husband (be as specific as possible)____
   _____ If unemployed, check here____
   How satisfied are you, on the whole, with present occupation of
   husband? If unemployed, answer this question about his usual
   occupation: extremely satisfied (26)____; very much satisfied
   (34)____; satisfied (14)____; somewhat satisfied (40)____;
   somewhat dissatisfied (3)____; dissatisfied (21)____; very
   much dissatisfied (30)____; extremely dissatisfied (12)____

2. To what extent were you in love with your spouse before marriage? "head over heels" (17)____; very much (25)____;
   somewhat (32)____; a little (22)____; not at all (13)____

3. To what extent was your spouse in love with you before your
   marriage? "head over heels" (26)____; very much (43)____;
   somewhat (23)____; a little (40)____; not at all (22)____

4. How much conflict (arguments, etc.) was there between you
   before your marriage? none at all (35)____; a little (43)____;
   some (5)____; considerable (31)____; very much (13)____

5. To what extent do you think you knew your spouse's faults and
   weak points before your marriage? not at all (44)____; a little
   (52)____; somewhat (32)____; considerably (40)____; very
   much (4)____

6. To what extent do you think your spouse knew your faults and
   weaknesses before your marriage? not at all (17)____; a little
   (43)____; somewhat (41)____; considerably (22)____; very
   much (13)____

7. What is your attitude toward your father-in-law? like him very
   much (61)____; considerably (15)____; somewhat (50)____;
   a little (4)____; dislike him a little (30)____; dislike him
   somewhat (12)____; dislike him considerably (3)____; dislike
   him very much (21)____; no attitude, as he is dead (24)____

8. What is your attitude toward your mother-in-law? like her very
   much (25)____; like her considerably (42)____; like her somewhat (32)____; like her a little (22)____; dislike her a little
   (12)____; dislike her somewhat (30)____; dislike her considerably (3)____; dislike her very much (21)____; no attitude, as she is dead (51)____

9. What is your attitude to having children? desire children very
   much (16)____; desire children a good deal (62)____; desire
   children somewhat (33)____; desire children a little (5)____;
   desire no children (31)____

10. If children have been born to you, what effect have they had on
    your happiness? added to it very much (27)____; added to it
    considerably (61)____; added to it somewhat (14)____;
    added to it a little (40)____; have had no effect (30)____;
    have decreased it a little (12)____; have decreased it somewhat
    (21)____; have decreased it considerably (3)____; have de-
    creased it very much (30)____; no children (24)____

288

I	2

11. In leisure-time activities: we both prefer to stay at home (26) _____; we both prefer to be "on the go" (41)_____; one prefers to be "on the go" and the other to stay at home (22)_____

12. Do you and your spouse engage in outside interests together? all of them (44)_____; most of them (51)_____; some of them (14)_____; a few of them (40)_____; none of them (22)_____

13. Do you kiss your spouse? every day (62)_____; almost every day (70)_____; quite frequently (24)_____; occasionally (32) _____; rarely (13)_____; almost never (40)_____

14. Do you confide in your spouse? about everything (17)_____; about most things (52)_____; about some things (5)_____; about a few things (13)_____; about nothing (40)_____

15. Does your spouse confide in you? about everything (26)_____; about most things (52); about some things (41)_____; about a few things (4)_____; about nothing (31)_____

16. Are you satisfied with the amount of demonstration of affection in your marriage? yes (25)_____; no: (desire less (22)_____; desire more (13)_____)

17. Is your spouse satisfied with the amount of demonstration of affection? yes (16)_____; no: (desires less (40)_____; desires more (31)_____)

18. How frequently do you "humor" your spouse? frequently (4) _____; occasionally (32)_____; rarely (51)_____; never (16) _____

19. Has your spouse ever failed to tell you the truth? often (22) _____; a few times (14)_____; once (33)_____; never (25)_____

20. If until now your marriage has been at all unhappy, how confident are you that it will work out all right in the future? very confident (32)_____; confident (13)_____; somewhat uncertain (21)_____; very uncertain (30)_____; marriage has not been at all unhappy (15)_____

21. Everything considered, how happy has your marriage been for you? extraordinarily happy (45)_____; decidedly happy (16) _____; happy (50)_____; somewhat happy (13)_____; average (31)_____; somewhat unhappy (3)_____; unhappy (12)_____; decidedly unhappy (30)_____; extremely unhappy (21)_____

22. If your marriage is now at all unhappy, how long has it been so (in months)? less than 3 (23)_____; 3 to 11 (31)_____; 12 or more (12)_____; marriage has not been at all unhappy (33) _____

23. Everything considered, how happy has your marriage been for your spouse? extraordinarily happy (36)_____; decidedly happy (43)_____; happy (32)_____; somewhat happy (4)_____; average (21)_____; somewhat unhappy (30)_____; unhappy (12) _____; decidedly unhappy (3)_____; extremely unhappy (21) _____

	1	2

24. Indicate your approximate agreement or disagreement with your spouse on the following things. Do this for each item by putting a check in the column that shows extent of your agreement or disagreement.

Check one column for each item below	Always agree (35)	Almost always agree (16)	Occasionally disagree (42)	Frequently disagree (23)	Almost always disagree (22)	Always disagree (12)		
Handling family finances								
Matters of recreation								
Religious matters								
Demonstration of affection								
Friends								
Table manners								
Matters of conventionality								
Philosophy of life								
Ways of dealing with your families								
Wife's working								
Intimate relations								
Caring for the baby								
Sharing of household tasks								
Politics								

25. When disagreements arise between you and your spouse they usually result in: agreement by mutual give and take (44)_____; your giving in (52)_____; your spouse giving in (33)_____; neither giving in (40)_____

26. Have you ever considered either separating from or divorcing your spouse? have never considered it (26)_____; not seriously (61)_____; somewhat seriously (40)_____; seriously (22)_____

27. How many serious quarrels or arguments have you had with your spouse in the past twelve months; none (27)_____; one (42)_____; two (32)_____; three (13)_____; four or more (30)_____

28. Indicate to what extent you are in love with your spouse by placing a check in one square on the boxed line below, which ranges from extraordinarily in love to somewhat in love:

Extraor-dinarily in love	A	B	C	D	E	F	G	H	I	J	Somewhat in love
	36	17	25	43	15	33	23	41	40	13	

Indicate by a cross in the above scale the extent to which you think your spouse is in love with you.

29. How does your present love for your spouse compare with your love before marriage? very much stronger (27)_____; considerably stronger (52)_____; somewhat stronger (24)_____; a little stronger (14)_____; a little weaker (30)_____; somewhat weaker (12)_____; considerably weaker (3)_____; very much weaker (21)_____

30. If you had your life to live over, what do you think you would do? marry the same person: (certainly (35)_____; possibly (41)_____;) marry a different person (22)_____; not marry at all (31)_____

31. If your spouse could do it over again, do you think your spouse would marry you? (certainly (44)_____; possibly (50)_____); marry a different person (13)_____; not marry at all (40)_____

32. How satisfied, on the whole, are you with your marriage; entirely satisfied (18)_____; very much satisfied (52)_____; satisfied (23)_____; somewhat satisfied (31)_____; somewhat dissatisfied (3)_____; dissatisfied (12)_____; very much dissatisfied (30)_____; entirely dissatisfied (21)_____

33. How satisfied, on the whole, is your spouse with your marriage? entirely satisfied (45)_____; very much satisfied (34)_____; satisfied (41)_____; somewhat satisfied (22)_____somewhat dissatisfied (21)_____; dissatisfied (30)_____; very much dissatisfied (12)_____; entirely dissatisfied (3)_____

34. Have you ever been ashamed of your spouse? never (44)_____; once (14)_____; a few times (31)_____; often (40)_____

35. Even if satisfied with your spouse, have you ever felt that you might have been at all happier if married to another type of person? never (26)_____; rarely (41)_____; occasionally (22) _____; frequently (13)_____

36. Do you ever regret your marriage? never (17)_____; rarely (50)_____; occasionally (13)_____; frequently (40)_____

1	2

T

Part Two

In responding to the following items, place a check in the appropriate column to the right of each item below.

Check Column A to indicate the things that have occurred in your marriage but have not interfered with your happiness.

Check Column B to indicate those things that have made your marriage less happy than it should have been.

Check Column C to indicate those things that have done most to make your marriage unhappy.

Check Column D if the item was not present in your marriage.

For the husband or wife to fill out	A 24	B 32	C 13	D 33
Insufficient income				
Poor management of income				
Lack of freedom due to marriage				
Spouse considerably older than I				
Spouse considerably younger than I				
Matters relating to in-laws				
My spouse and I differ in:				
Education				
Intellectual interests				
Religious beliefs				
Choice of friends				
Preferences for amusements and recreation				
Attitude toward drinking				
Tastes in food				
Respect for conventions				
My spouse:				
is argumentative				
For the husband to fill out				
My wife:				
is slovenly in appearance				
has had much poor health				
is interested in other men				
is nervous or emotional				
neglects the children				

For the husband or wife to fill out	A 24	B 32	C 13	D 33
My spouse:				
is not affectionate				
is narrow-minded				
is not faithful to me				
complains too much				
is lazy				
is quick-tempered				
criticizes me				
spoils the children				
is untruthful				
is conceited				
is easily influenced by others				
is jealous				
is selfish and inconsiderate				
is too talkative				
smokes				
drinks				
swears				
For the husband to fill out				
My wife:				
wants to visit or entertain a lot				
does not have meals ready on time				
interferes if I discipline the children				
tries to improve me				

292

For the husband to fill out (cont.)	A 24	B 32	C 13	D 33
My wife:				
is a poor housekeeper				
is not interested in my business				
is extravagant				
lets her feelings be hurt too easily				
is too interested in social affairs				
has annoying habits and mannerisms				
is a poor cook				
interferes with my business				
For the wife to fill out				
My husband:				
pays attention to other women				
is nervous or impatient				
takes no interest in the children				
is untidy				
is always wrapped up in his business				
gambles				
is touchy				
is not interested in the home				
has vulgar habits				
dislikes to go out with me evenings				
is late to meals				
is harsh with the children				
has poor table manners				

For the husband to fill out (cont.)	A 24	B 32	C 13	D 33
My wife:				
is a social climber				
is too interested in clothes				
is insincere				
gossips indiscreetly				
nags me				
interferes with my hobbies				
works outside the home				
is fussy about keeping the house neat				
For the wife to fill out				
My husband:				
is tight with money				
has no backbone				
does not talk things over freely				
is rude				
is bored if I tell him of the things that happen in my everyday life				
is unsuccessful in his business				
does not show his affection for me				
gets angry easily				
drinks too much				
has friends I do not approve of				
is constantly nagging and bickering				
lacks ambition				
T				

Part I____, Part II____, Total____

SECTION I

Personality Measurements

Of the hundreds of personality inventories only two are selected for presentation. These two measures are probably the most widely used personality measures in research today. The *Minnesota Multiphasic Personality Inventory* is described but not reproduced. It is a battery of scales containing 550 statements. It is thorough and so well constructed that it has generally won the confidence of researchers as the best scale to probe the personality. The research applications included in the description of the instrument attest to its use.

The *California F-Scale* to measure the authoritarian personality has been viewed as a measure of important personality pattern. It has also stimulated wide research application.

Of all the personality measures, it was believed the social researcher might find these two scales to be the most useful for his purpose. For a compilation of other measures of personality the following might be consulted:

Edward B. Greene, *Measurements of Human Behavior*, rev. ed., New York: The Odyssey Press, 1952.

Harold H. Anderson and Gladys L. Anderson, *An Introduction to Projective Techniques and Other Devices for Understanding the Dynamics of Human Behavior*, Englewood Cliffs, N.J.: Prentice-Hall, 1951.

F. P. Kilpatrick and Hadley Cantril, "Self Anchoring Scaling, A Measure of Individuals' Unique Reality Worlds," *Journal of Individual Psychology*, November, 1960, 16 (2) 1-8.

The Psychological Corporation has a catalog of personality and other psychological tests. This organization distributes such widely used tests as the *Minnesota Multiphasic Personality Inventory*, Edward's *Personal Preference Schedule, Bernreuter Personality Inventory*, Allport, Vernon, and Lindzey's *Study of Values, Rorschach Technique*, and Murray's *Thematic Apperception Test*. For a catalog of the Test Division, write The Psychological Corporation, 304 East 45 Street, New York, N. Y., 10017.

INDEX: MINNESOTA MULTIPHASIC PERSONALITY
INVENTORY (MMPI)

VARIABLE MEASURED: Measures twenty-six areas of personality traits and attitudes.

DESCRIPTION: The *MMPI* is primarily designed to provide, in a single test, scores on all the more clinically important phases of personality. The instrument itself comprises 550 statements covering a wide range of subject matter, from the physical condition of the individual being tested to his morale and social attitude. For administration of the Inventory the subject is asked to respond to all statements, which are in the first person, as True, False, or Cannot Say. The *MMPI* yields scores on nine scales of personality characteristics indicative of clinical syndromes.

WHERE PUBLISHED: Starke R. Hathaway, *The Minnesota Multiphasic Personality Inventory*, Minneapolis: University of Minnesota Press, 1942.
Starke R. Hathaway and J. Charnley McKinley, *Manual for the Minnesota Multiphasic Personality Inventory*, rev. ed.; New York: The Psychological Corporation, 1951.
W. Grant Dahlstrom and George Schlager Welsh, *An MMPI Handbook: A Guide to Use in Clinical Practice and Research*, Minneapolis: University of Minnesota Press, 1960.

RELIABILITY: $r = .71$ to $.83$. See Starke R. Hathaway and J. Charnley McKinley, *Manual for the Minnesota Multiphasic Personality Inventory*, rev. ed.; New York: The Psychological Corporation, 1951.
See also:
Harrison G. Gough, "Simulated Patterns on the Minnesota Multiphasic Personality Inventory," *The Journal of Abnormal and Social Psychology*, April, 1947, 42: 215-25.
Charles A. Weisgerber, "The Predictive Value of the Minnesota Multiphasic Personality Inventory with Student Nurses," *The Journal of Social Psychology*, February, 1951, 33: 3-11.

VALIDITY: Hathaway and McKinley maintain, "... the chief criterion of excellence has been the valid prediction of clinical cases against the neuro-psychiatric staff diagnosis, rather than statistical measures of reliability and validity." Starke R. Hathaway and J. Charnley McKinley, *Manual for the Minnesota Multiphasic Personality Inventory*, rev. ed.; New York: The Psychological Corporation, 1951.
See also:

A. Ellis, "The Validity of Personality Questionnaires," *The Psychological Bulletin,* September, 1946, 43: 385-440.

Orpha M. Lough and Mary E. Green, "Comparison of the Minnesota Multiphasic Personality Inventory and the Washburne S-A Inventory as Measures of Personality of College Women," *The Journal of Social Psychology,* August, 1950, 32: 23-30.

W. D. Altus and T. T. Tafejian, "MMPI Correlates of the California E-F Scale," *The Journal of Social Psychology,* August, 1953, 38: 145-49.

A. L. Benton and K. A. Probst, "A Comparison of Psychiatric Ratings with Minnesota Multiphasic Personality Inventory Scores," *The Journal of Abnormal and Social Psychology,* January, 1946, 41: 75-78.

Paul E. Meehl and Starke R. Hathaway, "The K Factor as a Suppressor Variable in the Minnesota Multiphasic Personality Inventory," *The Journal of Applied Psychology,* 1946, 30: 525-64.

UTILITY: The Inventory is easily administered. The time required varies from 30 to 90 minutes. No supervision is needed beyond that required for the subject to understand clearly the nature of his task and to assure his optimal cooperation.

RESEARCH APPLICATIONS: Starke R. Hathaway and Elio D. Monachesi, *Analyzing and Predicting Juvenile Delinquency with the MMPI,* Minneapolis: The University of Minnesota Press, 1953.

Elio D. Monachesi, "Some Personality Characteristics of Delinquents and Non-Delinquents," *Journal of Criminal Law and Criminology,* Jan.-Feb., 1948, 37: 487-500.

Starke R. Hathaway and Elio D. Monachesi, "The Minnesota Multiphasic Personality Inventory in the Study of Juvenile Delinquents," *American Sociological Review,* December, 1952, 17: 704-10.

Harrison Gough, "A New Dimension of Status: I. The Development of a Personality Scale," *American Sociological Review,* August, 1948, 13: 401-534.

———, "A New Dimension of Status: II. Relationship of the *St* Scale to other Variables," *American Sociological Review,* October, 1948, 13: 534-37.

———, "A New Dimension of Status: III. Discrepancies Between the *St* Scale and 'Objective' Status," *American Sociological Review,* April, 1949, 14: 275-81.

Lewis E. Drake, "A Social *I.E.* Scale for the Minnesota Multiphasic Personality Inventory," *Journal of Applied Psychology,* 1946, 30: 51-54.

Paul E. Meehl and Starke R. Hathaway, "The *K* Factor as a Suppressor Variable in the Minnesota Multiphasic Personality Inventory," *Journal of Applied Psychology,* 1946, 30: 525-64.

A. H. Maslow *et al.*, "A Clinically Derived Test for Measuring Psychological Security-Insecurity," *Journal of General Psychology*, 1945, 33: 21-41.

Harrison G. Gough, "Simulated Patterns on the Minnesota Multiphasic Personality Inventory," *Journal of Abnormal and Social Psychology*, April, 1947, 42: 215-25.

Abraham Carp, "MMPI Performance and Insulin Shock Therapy," *Journal of Abnormal and Social Psychology*, October, 1950, 45: 721-26.

William Schofield, "A Further Study of the Effects of Therapies on MMPI Responses," *Journal of Abnormal and Social Psychology*, January, 1953, 48: 67-77.

Andrew L. Sopchak, "Parental 'Identification' and 'Tendency toward Disorders' as Measured by the Minnesota Multiphasic Personality Inventory," *Journal of Abnormal and Social Psychology*, April, 1952, 47: 159-65.

Daniel Brower, "The Relations between Minnesota Multiphasic Personality Inventory Scores and Cardio-vascular Measures Before and After Experimentally Induced Visuo-Motor Conflict," *The Journal of Social Psychology*, August, 1947, 26: 55-60.

Peter J. Hampton, "The Minnesota Multiphasic Personality Inventory as a Psychometric Tool for Diagnosing Personality Disorders among College Students," *The Journal of Social Psychology*, August, 1947, 26: 99-108.

Orpha M. Lough and Mary E. Green, "Comparison of the Minnesota Multiphasic Personality Inventory and the Washburne S-A Inventory as Measures of Personality of College Women," *The Journal of Social Psychology*, August, 1950, 32: 23-30.

Charles A. Weisgerber, "The Predictive Value of the Minnesota Multiphasic Personality Inventory with Student Nurses," *The Journal of Social Psychology*, February, 1951, 33: 3-11.

J. H. Clark, "Grade Achievement of Female College Students in Relation to Non-Intellective Factors: MMPI Items," *The Journal of Social Psychology*, May, 1953, 37: 275-81.

Paul Greenberg and A. R. Gilliland, "The Relationship between Basal Metabolism and Personality," *The Journal of Social Psychology*, February, 1952, 35: 3-7.

Don L. Winfield, "The Relationship between IQ Scores and Minnesota Multiphasic Personality Inventory Scores," *The Journal of Social Psychology*, November, 1953, 38: 299-300.

W. D. Altus and T. T. Tafejian, "MMPI Correlates of the California E-F Scale," *The Journal of Social Psychology*, August, 1953, 38: 145-49.

Daniel Brower, "The Relation between Intelligence and Minnesota Multiphasic Personality Inventory Scores," *The Journal of Social Psychology*, May, 1947, 25: 243-45.

Hermann O. Schmidt, "Test Profiles as a Diagnostic Aid: The Minnesota Multiphasic Inventory," *The Journal of Applied Psychology*, April, 1945, 29: 115-31.

Lindsey R. Harmon and Daniel N. Wiener, "Use of the Minnesota Multiphasic Personality Inventory in Vocational Advisement," *The Journal of Applied Psychology*, April, 1945, 29: 132-41.

Willie Maude Verniaud, "Occupational Differences in the Minnesota Multiphasic Personality Inventory," *The Journal of Applied Psychology*, December, 1946, 30: 604-13.

Orpha M. Lough, "Teachers College Students and the Minnesota Multiphasic Personality Inventory," *The Journal of Applied Psychology*, June, 1946, 30: 241-47.

William D. Altus, "A College Achiever and Non-achiever Scale for the Minnesota Multiphasic Personality Inventory," *The Journal of Applied Psychology*, August, 1948, 32: 385-97.

E. E. Daniels and W. A. Hunter, "MMPI Personality Patterns for Various Occupations," *The Journal of Applied Psychology*, December, 1949, 33: 559-65.

Orpha M. Lough, "Women Students in Liberal Arts, Nursing, and Teacher Training Curricula and the Minnesota Multiphasic Personality Inventory," *The Journal of Applied Psychology*, August, 1947, 37: 437-45.

Ralph D. Norman and Miriam Redlo, "MMPI Personality Patterns for Various College Major Groups," *The Journal of Applied Psychology*, December, 1952, 36: 404-9.

Jerry H. Clark, "Application of the *MMPI* in Differentiating A.W.O.L. Recidivist from Non-recidivists," *The Journal of Psychology*, July, 1948, 26: 229-34.

C. N. Cofer, June Chance, and A. J. Judson, "A Study of Malingering on the Minnesota Multiphasic Personality Inventory," *The Journal of Psychology*, April, 1949, 27: 491-99.

Franklin D. Fry, "A Study of the Personality Traits of College Students, and of State Prison Inmates as Measured by the Minnesota Multiphasic Personality Inventory," *The Journal of Psychology*, October, 1949, 28: 439-49.

George M. Guthrie, "Six MMPI Diagnostic Profile Patterns," *The Journal of Psychology*, October, 1950, 30: 317-23.

Arthur Burton, "The Use of the Masculinity-Femininity Scale of the Minnesota Multiphasic Personality Inventory as an Aid in the Diagnosis of Sexual Inversion," *The Journal of Psychology*, July, 1947, 24: 161-64.

Franklin D. Fry, "A Normative Study of the Reactions Manifested by College Students and by State Prison Inmates in Response to the Minnesota Multiphasic Personality Inventory, The Rozenzweig Picture-Frustration Study, and the Thematic Apperception Test," *The Journal of Psychology*, July, 1952, 34: 27-30.

William Schofield, "A Study of Medical Students with the MMPI: I. Scale Norms and Profile Patterns," *The Journal of Psychology*, July, 1953, 36: 59-65.

————, "A Study of Medical Students with the MMPI: II. Group and Individual Changes after Two Years," *The Journal of Psychology*, July, 1953, 36: 137-41.

————, "A Study of Medical Students with the MMPI: III. Personality and Academic Success," *The Journal of Applied Psychology*, February, 1953, 37: 47-52.

Lewis G. Carpenter, Jr., "An Experimental Test of an Hypothesis for Predicting Outcome with Electroshock Therapy," *The Journal of Psychology*, July, 1953, 36: 131-35.

Fred T. Tyler and John U. Michaelis, "Comparison of Manual and College Norms for the MMPI," *Journal of Applied Psychology*, August, 1953, 37: 273-75.

L. E. Drake, "Differential Sex Responses to Items of the MMPI," *Journal of Applied Psychology*, February, 1953, 37: 46.

A. G. Mac Lean *et al.*, "F Minus K Index on the MMPI," *Journal of Applied Psychology*, August, 1953, 37: 315-16.

M. Tydlaska and R. Mengel, "Scale for Measuring Work Attitude for the MMPI," *Journal of Applied Psychology*, December, 1953, 37: 474-77.

William C. Cottle, "Card Versus Booklet Forms of the MMPI," *Journal of Applied Psychology*, August, 1950, 34: 255-59.

John U. Michaelis and Fred T. Tyler, "MMPI and Student Teaching," *Journal of Applied Psychology*, April, 1951, 35: 122-24.

Olga E. de C. Engelhardt and William D. Orbison, "Comparison of the Terman-Miles M-F Test and the Mf Scale of the MMPI," *Journal of Applied Psychology*, October, 1950, 34: 338-42.

Ellsworth B. Cook and Robert J. Wherry, "A Factor Analysis of MMPI and Aptitude Test Data," *Journal of Applied Psychology*, August, 1950, 34: 260-66.

Arthur L. Benton and Kathryn A. Probst, "A Comparison of Psychiatric Ratings with Minnesota Multiphasic Personality Inventory Scores," *The Journal of Abnormal and Social Psychology*, January, 1946, 41: 75-78.

Content of Minnesota Multiphasic Personality Inventory (MMPI) *

1. General health (9 items)
2. General neurologic (19 items)
3. Cranial nerves (11 items)
4. Motility and coordination (6 items)
5. Sensibility (5 items)
6. Vasomotor, trophic, speech, secretory (10 items)
7. Cardio-respiratory system (5 items)
8. Gastro-intestinal system (11 items)
9. Genito-urinary system (5 items)
10. Habits (19 items)
11. Family and marital (26 items)
12. Occupational (18 items)
13. Educational (12 items)
14. Sexual attitudes (16 items)
15. Religious attitudes (19 items)
16. Political attitudes—law and order (46 items)
17. Social attitudes (72 items)
18. Affect, depressive (32 items)
19. Affect, manic (24 items)
20. Obsessive and compulsive states (15 items)
21. Delusions, hallucinations, illusions, ideas of reference (31 items)
22. Phobias (29 items)
23. Sadistic, masochistic trends (7 items)
24. Morale (33 items)
25. Items primarily related to masculinity-femininity (55 items)
26. Items to indicate whether the individual is trying to place himself in an acceptable light (15 items)

* By permission of Hathaway and McKinley and the University of Minnesota Press.

INDEX: AUTHORITARIAN PERSONALITY (F) SCALE, FORMS 45 AND 40

VARIABLE MEASURED: "Authoritarianism" or antidemocratic potential.

DESCRIPTION: The scale consists of thirty items grouped into nine attitudinal categories considered as variables in a personality syndrome. The items are rated on a seven-point scale, from $+3$ to -3, according to the subjects' agreement or disagreement with the statement.

WHERE PUBLISHED: T. W. Adorno, Else Frenkel-Brunswik, D. J. Levinson, and R. N. Sanford, *The Authoritarian Personality,* New York: Harper, 1950.

RELIABILITY:

Authors' report on studies—mean $r = .90$, range $.81$ to $.97$
Correlation with Ethnocentrism Scale—mean $r = .75$ with a range from $r = .59$ to $r = .87$
Using Fisher's Z_r, each item was correlated with every other item—mean $r = .13$ and the range was from $r = -.05$ to $r = .44$
In addition, each item was correlated with the remainder of the scale, the mean r being $.33$, the range $.15$ to $.52$.

See also:
Richard Christie and Marie Jahoda (eds.), *Studies in the Scope and Method of "The Authoritarian Personality,"* Glencoe, Ill.: Free Press, 1954.
Richard Christie, Joan Havel, and Bernard Seidenberg, "Is the *F* Scale Irreversible?" *Journal of Abnormal and Social Psychology,* 1958, 56: 143-59.

VALIDITY: The authors used the case study method to validate the scale. The scale has been correlated with the Campbell Xenophobia: $r = .60$

See also:
Richard Christie and Marie Jahoda (eds.), *Studies in the Scope and Method of "The Authoritarian Personality,"* Glencoe, Ill.: Free Press, 1954.
E. Terry Prothro and Levon Melikian, "The California Public Opinion Scale in an Authoritarian Culture," *The Public Opinion Quarterly,* 1953, 17: 115-35.

Bernard M. Bass, "Authoritarianism or Acquiescence?" *Journal of Abnormal and Social Psychology,* November, 1955, 51: 616-23.

Santo F. Camilleri, "A Factor Analysis of the *F*-Scale," *Social Forces,* May, 1959, 37: 316-23.

Jerome Himelhoch, "Tolerance and Personality Needs: A Study of the Liberalization of Ethnic Attitudes among Minority Group College Students," *American Sociological Review,* February, 1950, 15: 79-88.

UTILITY: The test may be administered either in interviews or by questionnaire.

RESEARCH APPLICATIONS: Richard Christie and Marie Jahoda (eds.), *Studies in the Scope and Method of "The Authoritarian Personality,"* Glencoe, Ill.: Free Press, 1954.

——— and Peggy Cook, "A Guide to Published Literature Relating to the Authoritarian Personality," *Journal of Psychology,* 1958, 45: 171-99 (bibliography).

James G. Martin and Frank R. Westie, "The Tolerant Personality," *American Sociological Review,* August, 1959, 24: 521-28.

Jerome Himelhoch, "Tolerance and Personality Needs: A Study of the Liberalization of Ethnic Attitudes among Minority Group College Students," *American Sociological Review,* February, 1950, 15: 79-88.

Herbert Greenberg and Dolores Hutto, "The Attitudes of West Texas College Students toward School Integration," *Journal of Applied Psychology,* October, 1958, 42: 301-4.

Walter C. Kaufman, "Status, Authoritarianism, and Anti-Semitism," *American Journal of Sociology,* January, 1957, 62: 379-82.

Donald T. Campbell and Thelma H. McCormack, "Military Experience and Attitudes toward Authority," *American Journal of Sociology,* March, 1957, 62: 482-90.

Richard Christie, "Changes in Authoritarianism as Related to Situational Factors," *American Psychologist,* 1952, 8: 307-8.

Alan H. Roberts and Milton Rakeach, "Anomie, Authoritarianism, and Prejudice: A Replication," *American Journal of Sociology,* January, 1956, 61: 355-58.

William J. MacKinnon and Richard Centers, "Authoritarianism and Urban Stratification," *American Journal of Sociology,* May, 1956, 61: 610-20.

Leo Srole, "Social Integration and Certain Corollaries: An Exploratory Study," *American Sociological Review,* December, 1956, 21: 709-16.

William M. O'Neil and Daniel J. Levinson, "A Factorial Exploration of Authoritarianism and Some of Its Ideological Concomitants," *Journal of Personality,* June, 1954, 22: 449-63.

John W. Thibaut and Henry W. Riecken, "Authoritarianism, Status, and the Communication of Aggression," *Human Relations,* May, 1955, 8: 95-120.

William Haythorn, Arthur Couch, Donald Faefner, Peter Langham, and Launor F. Carter, "The Behavior of Authoritarian and Equalitarian Personalities in Groups," *Human Relations,* February, 1956, 9: 57-73.

Solis L. Kates, "First-Impression Formation and Authoritarianism," *Human Relations,* August, 1959, 12: 277-85.

Charles U. Smith and James W. Prothro, "Ethnic Differences in Authoritarian Personality," *Social Forces,* May, 1957, 35: 334-38.

Santo F. Camilleri, "A Factor Analysis of the *F*-Scale," *Social Forces,* May, 1959, 37: 316-23.

E. Terry Prothro and Levon Melikian, "The California Public Opinion Scale in an Authoritarian Culture," *Public Opinion Quarterly,* 1953, 17(3): 353-62.

Elliot G. Mishler, "Personality Characteristics and the Resolution of Role Conflicts," *Public Opinion Quarterly,* 1953, 17(1): 115-35.

Alvin Scodel and Paul Mussen, "Social Perceptions of Authoritarians and Nonauthoritarians," *Journal of Abnormal and Social Psychology,* April, 1953, 48: 181-84.

Roger W. Brown, "A Determinant of the Relationship between Rigidity and Authoritarianism," *Journal of Abnormal and Social Psychology,* October, 1953, 48: 469-76.

Joseph Adelson, "A Study of Minority Group Authoritarianism," *Journal of Abnormal and Social Psychology,* October, 1953, 48: 477-85.

Bernard M. Bass, "Authoritarianism or Acquiescence?" *Journal of Abnormal and Social Psychology,* November, 1955, 51: 616-23.

Anthony Davids, "Some Personality and Intellectual Correlates of Intolerance of Ambiguity," *Journal of Abnormal and Social Psychology,* November, 1955, 51: 415-20.

Samuel J. Meer, "Authoritarianism Attitudes and Dreams," *Journal of Abnormal and Social Psychology,* July, 1955, 51: 74-78.

Solis L. Kates and Lufty N. Diab, "Authoritarian Ideology and Attitudes on Parent-Child Relationships," *Journal of Abnormal and Social Psychology,* July, 1955, 51: 13-16.

Richard Christie, Joan Havel, and Bernard Seidenberg, "Is the *F*-Scale Irreversible?" *Journal of Abnormal and Social Psychology,* 1958, 56: 143-59.

Nevitt Sanford, "Recent Developments in Connection with the Investigation of the Authoritarian Personality," *Sociological Review,* July, 1954, 2: 11-33.

Frederick John Gelbmann, *Authoritarianism and Temperament*, Ph.D. dissertation, Washington, D.C.: The Catholic University of America Press, 1958.

Harrison G. Gough, "Studies of Social Intolerance: I. Some Psychological and Sociological Correlates of Anti-Semitism," *Journal of Social Psychology*, May, 1951, 33: 237-46.

——, "Studies of Social Intolerance: II. A Personality Scale for Anti-Semitism," *Journal of Social Psychology*, May, 1951, 33: 247-55.

——, "Studies of Social Intolerance: III. Relationship of the *Pr* Scale to Other Variables," *Journal of Social Psychology*, May, 1951, 33: 257-62.

Richard Christie and John Garcia, "Subcultural Variation in Authoritarian Personality," *Journal of Abnormal and Social Psychology*, October, 1951, 46: 457-69.

Edward E. Jones, "Authoritarianism as a Determinant of First-Impression Formation," *Journal of Personality*, September, 1954, 23: 107-27.

F-SCALE CLUSTERS: FORMS 45 AND 40 *

A. Conventionalism: Rigid adherence to conventional, middle-class values.
  1. Obedience and respect for authority are the most important virtues children should learn.
  12. A person who has bad manners, habits, and breeding can hardly expect to get along with decent people.
  37. If people would talk less and work more, everybody would be better off.
  41. The businessman and the manufacturer are much more important to society than the artist and the professor.

B. Authoritarian Submission: Submissive, uncritical attitude toward idealized moral authorities of the ingroup.
  1. Obedience and respect for authority are the most important virtues children should learn.
  4. Science has its place, but there are many important things that can never possibly be understood by the human mind.
  8. Every person should have complete faith in some supernatural power whose decisions he obeys without question.
  21. Young people sometimes get rebellious ideas, but as they grow up they ought to get over them and settle down.
  23. What this country needs most, more than laws and political programs, is a few courageous, tireless, devoted leaders in whom the people can put their faith.
  42. No sane, normal, decent person could ever think of hurting a close friend or relative.
  44. Nobody ever learned anything really important except through suffering.

C. Authoritarian Aggression: Tendency to be on the lookout for, and to condemn, reject, and punish, people who violate conventional values.
  12. A person who has bad manners, habits, and breeding can hardly expect to get along with decent people.
  13. What youth needs most is strict discipline, rugged determination, and the will to work and fight for family and country.

* "F-Scale Clusters: Forms 45 and 40," from T. W. Adorno *et. al., The Authoritarian Personality,* New York: Harper & Row, Publishers, 1950.

19. An insult to our honor should always be punished.
25. Sex crimes, such as rape and attacks on children, deserve more than mere imprisonment; such criminals ought to be publicly whipped, or worse.
27. There is hardly anything lower than a person who does not feel a great love, gratitude, and respect for his parents.
34. Most of our social problems would be solved if we could somehow get rid of the immoral, crooked, and feebleminded people.
37. If people would talk less and work more, everybody would be better off.
39. Homosexuals are hardly better than criminals and ought to be severely punished.

D. Anti-intraception: Opposition to the subjective, the imaginative, the tender-minded.
9. When a person has a problem or worry, it is best for him not to think about it, but to keep busy with more cheerful things.
31. Nowadays more and more people are prying into matters that should remain personal and private.
37. If people would talk less and work more, everybody would be better off.
41. The businessman and the manufacturer are much more important to society than the artist and the professor.

E. Superstition and Stereotypy: The belief in mystical determinants of the individual's fate; the disposition to think in rigid categories.
4. Science has its place, but there are many important things that can never possibly be understood by the human mind.
8. Every person should have complete faith in some supernatural power whose decisions he obeys without question.
16. Some people are born with an urge to jump from high places.
26. People can be divided into two distinct classes: the weak and the strong.
29. Some day it will probably be shown that astrology can explain a lot of things.
33. Wars and social troubles may someday be ended by an earthquake or flood that will destroy the whole world.

F. Power and "Toughness": Preoccupation with the dominance-submission, strong-weak, leader-follower dimension; identification with power figures; overemphasis upon the conventionalized attributes of the ego; exaggerated assertion of strength and toughness.
2. No weakness or difficulty can hold us back if we have enough willpower.

13. What youth needs most is strict discipline, rugged determination, and the will to work and fight for family and country.
19. An insult to our honor should always be punished.
22. It is best to use some prewar authorities in Germany to keep order and prevent chaos.
23. What this country needs most, more than laws and political programs, is a few courageous, tireless, devoted leaders in whom the people can put their faith.
26. People can be divided into two distinct classes: the weak and the strong.
38. Most people don't realize how much our lives are controlled by plots hatched in secret places.

G. Destructiveness and Cynicism: Generalized hostility, vilification of the human.
    6. Human nature being what it is, there will always be war and conflict.
    43. Familiarity breeds contempt.

H. Projectivity: The disposition to believe that wild and dangerous things go on in the world; the projection outwards of unconscious emotional impulses.
    18. Nowadays when so many different kinds of people move around and mix together so much, a person has to protect himself especially carefully against catching an infection or disease from them.
    31. Nowadays more and more people are prying into matters that should remain personal and private.
    33. Wars and social troubles may someday be ended by an earthquake or flood that will destroy the whole world.
    35. The wild sex life of the old Greeks and Romans was tame compared to some of the goings-on in this country, even in places where people might least expect it.
    38. Most people don't realize how much our lives are controlled by plots hatched in secret places.

I. Sex: Exaggerated concern with sexual "goings-on."
    25. Sex crimes, such as rape and attacks on children, deserve more than mere imprisonment; such criminals ought to be publicly whipped, or worse.
    35. The wild sex life of the old Greeks and Romans was tame compared to some of the goings-on in this country, even in places where people might least expect it.
    39. Homosexuals are hardly better than criminals and ought to be severely punished.

SECTION J

An Inventory of Measures Utilized in the American Sociological Review during 1951-60

Instructions for use of Inventory:

A researcher who has not found scales in the handbook to fit his particular problem may be aided by examining the following inventory. Skim the right-hand column and identify similar areas of research interest. The left-hand column contains the scale or indexes used by the researcher. Go to the *American Sociological Review* for the published source of the instrument.

SCALE INVENTORY OF THE *AMERICAN SOCIOLOGICAL REVIEW*, 1951-60 *

Scales for Measuring Social Status

Edwards' Scale of Occupational Categories

Richard M. Stephenson, "Mobility Orientation and Stratification of 1,000 Ninth Graders," April, 1957, 22: 204-12.

Edwards' Index of Socioeconomic Status

Raymond A. Mulligan, "Social Characteristics of College Students," June, 1953, 18: 305-10.

Hollingshead's Index of Social Position

Melvin L. Kohn, "Social Class and the Exercise of Parental Authority," June, 1959, 24: 352-66.
Fred L. Strodtbeck, Margaret R. McDonald, and Bernard C. Rosen, "Evaluation of Occupations: A Reflection of Jewish and Italian Mo-

* Assembled by Frank Castro.

308

bility Differences," October, 1957, 22: 546-53.

Robert A. Ellis, "Social Stratification and Social Relations: An Empirical Test of the Disjunctiveness of Social Class," October, 1957, 22: 570-78.

George Psathas, "Ethnicity, Social Class, and Adolescent Independence from Parental Control," August, 1957, 22: 415-23.

(modified)	Bernard C. Rosen, "Race, Ethnicity, and Achievement," February, 1959, 24: 47-60.
Hollingshead's Two Factor Index of Social Position	Raymond G. Hurst, Orville Gureslin, and Jack L. Roach, "Social Status and Psychiatric Services in a Child Guidance Clinic," February, 1958, 23: 81-83.
	Ephraim H. Mizruchi, "Social Structure and Anomia in a Small City," October, 1960, 25: 645-54.
Hollingshead's Two and Three Factor Indexes of Social Position	Bulkeley Smith, Jr., "The Differential Residential Segregation of Working Class Negroes in New Haven," August, 1959, 24: 529-33.
North-Hatt Occupational Prestige Scale	Peter M. Blau, "Occupational Bias and Mobility," August, 1957, 22: 392-99.
	William H. Sewell, Archie O. Haller, and Murray A. Straus, "Social Status and Educational and Occupational Aspiration," February, 1957, 22: 67-73.
	Alfred C. Clarke, "The Use of Leisure and Its Relation to Levels of Occupational Prestige," June, 1956.
	Ward S. Mason and Neal Gross, "Intra-Occupational Prestige Differentiation: The School Superintendency," June, 1955, 20: 326-31.

	Leonard Reissman, "Levels of Aspiration and Social Class," June, 1953, 18: 233-42.
	Evelyn Ellis, "Social Psychological Correlates of Upward Social Mobility among Unmarried Career Women," October, 1952, 17: 558-63.
(adapted for Negro respondents)	Morgan C. Brown, "The Status of Jobs and Occupations as Evaluated by an Urban Negro Sample," October, 1955, 20: 561-66.
North-Hatt Occupational Prestige Scale and Smith Occupational Prestige Scale	LaMar T. Empey, "Social Class and Occupational Aspirations: A Comparison of Absolute and Relative Measurement," December, 1956, 21: 703-9.
Warner's Index of Status Characteristics	Howard E. Freeman and Ozzie G. Simmons, "Social Class and Post-Hospital Performance," June, 1959, 24: 345-51.
	Martha Sturm White, "Social Class, Child Rearing Practices, and Child Behavior," December, 1957, 22: 704-12.
	A. Alexander Fanelli, "Extensiveness of Communication Contacts and Perceptions of the Community," August, 1956, 21: 439-45.
	Joseph A. Kahl and James A. Davis, "A Comparison of Indexes of Socio-Economic Status," June, 1955, 20: 317-25.
(McGuire-Loeb Modification)	Jules Roth and Robert F. Peck, "Social Class and Social Mobility Factors Related to Marital Adjustment," August, 1951, 16: 478-87.
Warner's Index of Status Characteristics and Centers' Class Self-identification	Howard E. Freeman, Edwin Novak, and Leo Reeder, "Correlates of Membership in Voluntary Associations," October, 1957, 22: 528-33.

J. R. Haer, "Predictive Utility of Five Indices of Social Stratification," October, 1957, 22: 541-46.

John L. Haer, "The Classification Techniques of Warner and Centers," December, 1955, 20: 689-92.

Warner's Index of Status Characteristics and Warner's Index of Social Position

Gregory P. Stone and William H. Form, "Instabilities in Status: The Problem of Hierarchy in the Community Study of Status Arrangements," April, 1953, 18: 149-62.

Warner's Scale of Occupations

Irwin Goffman, "Status Consistency and Preference for Changes in Power Distribution," June, 1957, 22: 275-81.

Robert J. Havighurst and Allison Davis, "A Comparison of the Chicago and Harvard Studies of Social Class Differences in Child Rearing," August, 1955, 20: 438-42.

Centers' Self-Identification Index of Class

Jackson Toby, "Universalistic and Particularistic Factors in Role Assignment," April, 1953, 18: 134-41.

Chapin's Social Status Scale

Walter T. Martin, "A Consideration of Differences in the Extent and Location of the Formal Associational Activities of Rural-Urban Fringe Residents," December, 1952, 17: 685-94.

Chapman and Sims Index of Socio-Economic Status

Charles F. Westoff, Philip C. Sagi, and E. Lowell Kelly, "Fertility through Twenty Years of Marriage: A Study in Predictive Possibilities," October, 1958, 23: 549-56.

Counts's Indices of Socio-Economic Status (adapted)

Erwin O. Smigel, "Public Attitudes toward 'Chiseling' with Reference to Unemployment Compensation," February, 1953, 18: 59-67.

Generational Occupational Mobility Measurement	Melvin M. Tumin and Arnold S. Feldman, "Theory and Measurement of Occupational Mobility," June, 1957, 22: 281-88.
Guttman Scale (Farber-Osinach Index)	Bernard Farber and John C. Osinach, "An Index of Socio-Economic Rank of Census Tracts in Urban Area," October, 1959, 24: 630-40.
Guttman Scales for Social Status and Distance	Frank R. Westie, "Negro-White Status Differentials and Social Distance," October, 1952, 17: 550-58.
Likert-Type Scale	Solomon Rettig, Frank N. Jacobson, and Benjamin Pasamanick, "Status Overestimation, Objective Status, and Job Satisfaction among Professions," February, 1958, 23: 75-81.
	Martin Gold and Carol Slater, "Office, Factory, Store—and Family: A Study of Integration Setting," February, 1958, 23: 64-74.
The Magnetic Board Rating Technique	Solomon Rettig, Frank N. Jacobson, and Benjamin Pasamanick, "Status Overestimation, Objective Status, and Job Satisfaction among Professions," February, 1958, 23: 75-81.
Measures of Mobility	Charles A. Westoff, Marvin Bressler, and Philip C. Sagi, "The Concept of Social Mobility; An Empirical Inquiry," June, 1960, 25: 375-85.
Measure of Status Integration	Jack P. Gibbs and Walter T. Martin, "A Theory of Status Integration and Relationship to Suicide," April, 1958, 23: 140-47.
Measurement of Social Class and Social Position	Stanley Hetzler, "An Investigation of the Distinctiveness of Social Classes," October, 1953, 18: 493-97.
Mobility Achievement Scale (Likert-Type)	Melvin Seeman, "Social Mobility and Administrative Behavior," December, 1958, 23: 633-42.

Social Class Boundary Index	Werner S. Landecker, "Class Boundaries," December, 1960, 25: 868-77.
Socio-Economic Status Composite Index	Charles V. Willie, "Age, Status, and Residential Stratification," April, 1960, 25: 260-64.
Technique for systematic analysis of horizontal differentiation of occupational structure	Richard T. Morris and Raymond J. Murphy, "The Situs Dimension in Occupational Structure," April, 1959, 24: 231-39.
Vaughan Socio-Economic Status Scale	Russell Middleton, "Ethnic Prejudice and Susceptibility to Persuasion," October, 1960, 25: 679-86.

Scales for Measuring Group Structure and Dynamics

Bales's Interaction Process Analysis	Henry Landsberger, "Interaction Process Analysis of Professional Behavior: A Study of Labor Mediators in Twelve Labor-Management Disputes," October, 1955, 20: 566-75.
	Phillip E. Slater, "Role Differentiation in Small Groups," June, 1955, 20: 300-310.
	Fred L. Strodtbeck, "The Family as a Three-Person Group," February, 1954, 19: 23-29.
	Theodore M. Mills, "Power Relations in Three-Person Groups," August, 1958, 18: 351-59.
	R. F. Bales, F. L. Strodtbeck, T. M. Mills, and M. E. Roseborough, "Channels of Communication in Small Groups," August, 1951, 16: 461-68.
Bogardus Social Distance Scale	Russell L. Langworthy, "Community Status and Influence in a High School," August, 1959, 24:537-39.
	Emory S. Bogardus, "Measuring Changes in Ethnic Relations," February, 1951, 16: 48-51.

Sociometric Procedures

Peter M. Blau, "Structural Effects," April, 1960, 25: 178-93.

James A. Jones, "An Index of Consensus on Rankings in Small Groups," August, 1959, 24: 533-37.

Delbert C. Miller, "Industry and Community Power Structure: A Comparative Study of an American and an English City," February, 1958, 23: 9-15.

Robert A. Ellis, "Social Stratification and Social Relations: An Empirical Test of the Disjunctiveness of Social Class," October, 1957, 22: 570-78.

Clarence Schrag, "Leadership among Prison Inmates," February, 1954, 19: 37-42.

O. J. Harvey, "An Experimental Approach to the Study of Status Relations in Informal Groups," August, 1953, 18: 357-67.

Jackson Toby, "Universalistic and Particularistic Factors in Role Assignment," April, 1953, 18: 134-41.

James C. Brown, "An Experiment in Role Taking," October, 1952, 17: 587-95.

Sociometric Test (Criswell's Self-Preference Index)

George A. Lundberg and Lenore Dickson, "Selective Association Among Ethnic Groups in a High School Population," February, 1952, 17: 23-35.

Sociometric Analysis and Personal Contact Checklist Form

Robert S. Weiss and Eugene Jacobson, "A Method for the Analysis of the Structure of Complex Organizations," December, 1955, 20: 661-68.

Dymond's Scale for the Measurement of Empathic Ability (Likert method of scoring used)

Glenn M. Vernon and Robert L. Stewart, "Empathy as a Process in the Dating Situation," February, 1957, 22: 48-52.

Gross's Index of Integration	Edward Gross, "Symbiosis and Consensus as Integrative Factors in Small Groups," April, 1956, 21: 174-79.
Interactional Telemeter	Delbert C. Miller and Warren W. Philbric, "The Measurement of Group Learning Process by Use of the Interactional Telemeter," April, 1953, 18: 184-89.
Measures of Valuation of Membership	Harold H. Kelley and Edmund H. Volkart, "Resistance to Change of Group-Anchored Attitudes," August, 1952, 17: 453-65.
Westie's Social Distance Scale	Frank R. Westie and David H. Howard, "Social Status Differentials and the Race Attitudes of Negroes," October, 1954, 19: 584-91.

Scales for Measuring Job Satisfaction and Morale

Job Satisfaction Measure (Guttman scale analysis)	Judson B. Pearson, Gordon H. Barker, and Rodney D. Elliott, "Sales Success and Job Satisfaction," August, 1957, 22: 424-33.

Scales for Measuring Community Factors

Shevky-Bell Social Area Analysis	Dorothy L. Meier and Wendell Bell, "Anomia and Differential Access to the Achievement of Life Goals," April, 1959, 24: 189-202.
	Wendell Bell and Maryanne T. Force, "Urban Neighborhood Types and Participation in Formal Associations," February, 1956, 21: 25-34.
	Scott Greer, "Urbanism Reconsidered: A Comparative Study of Local Areas in a Metropolis," February, 1956, 21: 19-25.
Shevky and Williams Urban Typology	Wendell Bell, "The Social Areas of the San Francisco Bay Region," February, 1953, 18:39-47.

Shevky's Social Area Analysis

Maurice D. Van Arsdol, Jr., Santo F. Camilleri, and Calvin F. Schmid, "The Generality of Urban Social Area Indexes," June, 1958, 23:277-84.

Guttman Scale Analysis

Joel Smith, "A Method for the Classification of Areas on the Basis of Demographically Homogeneous Populations," April, 1954, 19: 201-7.

Index of Community Identification

A. Alexander Fanelli, "Extensiveness of Communication Contacts and Perceptions of the Community," August, 1956, 21: 439-45.

Adapted Socio-Physical System Analysis

Norman E. Green, "Scale Analysis of Urban Structures: A Study of Birmingham, Alabama," February, 1956, 21: 8-13.

Scales for Measuring Social Participation

Chapin's Social Participation Scale

Ephraim H. Mizruchi, "Social Structure and Anomia in a Small City," October, 1960, 25: 645-54.

Donald W. Olmstead, "Organizational Leadership and Social Structure in a Small City," June, 1954, 19: 273-81.

Walter T. Martin, "A Consideration of the Differences in the Extent and Location of the Formal Associational Activities of Rural-Urban Fringe Residents," December, 1952, 17: 685-94.

Srole's Scale of Anomia

Ephraim H. Mizruchi, "Social Structure and Anomia in a Small City," October, 1960, 25: 645-54.

Dorothy L. Meier and Wendell Bell, "Anomia and Differential Access to the Achievement of Life Goals," April, 1959, 24: 189-202.

	Leo Srole, "Social Integration and Certain Corollaries: An Exploratory Study," December, 1956, 21: 704-16.
Wallin's Neighborliness Scale	Sylvia Fleis Flava, "Suburbanism as a Way of Life," February, 1956, 21: 34-37.
	Scott Greer, "Urbanism Reconsidered: A Comparative Study of Local Areas in a Metropolis," February, 1956, 21: 19-25.
Anderson's Rural Living Opinion Scale	Sylvia Fleis Flava, "Suburbanism as a Way of Life," February, 1956, 21: 34-37.
Foskett and Hohle Technique for measurement of influence in community affairs	Robert E. Agger and Daniel Goldrich, "Community Power Structures and Partisanship," August, 1958, 23: 383-92.
Committee Participation Scale	Delbert C. Miller, "Industry and Community Power Structure: A Comparative Study of an American and an English City," February, 1958, 23: 9-15.
General Community Participation Scale	John M. Foskett, "Social Structure and Social Participation," August, 1955, 20: 431-38.
Guttman Scaling Procedure	Harry R. Dick, "A Method for Ranking Community Influentials," June, 1960, 25: 395-99.
Beer-Bell Anomia Scale	Russell Middleton, "Ethnic Prejudice and Susceptibility to Persuasion," October, 1960, 25: 679-86.
Reputational and Issue Techniques for measurement of influence in community affairs	Delbert C. Miller, "Industry and Community Power Structure: A Comparative Study of an American and an English City," February, 1958, 23: 9-15.
Warner's Index of Social Participation	Melvin L. Kohn and John A. Clausen, "Social Isolation and Schizophrenia," June, 1955, 20: 265-73.

Scales to Measure Leadership

Halpin Leadership Behavior Description Questionnaire (modified)	Melvin Seeman, "Social Mobility and Administrative Behavior," December, 1958, 23: 633-42.
Likert-Type Scale	Stanley A. Hetzler, "Variation in Role-Playing Patterns among Different Leaders," December, 1955, 20: 700-706.

Scales to Measure Attitudes and Values

Guttman Scales	Melvin Tumin, Paul Burton, and Bernie Burrus, "Education, Prejudice, and Discrimination: A Study in Readiness for Desegregation," February, 1958, 23: 41-49.
	Andrew F. Henry and Edgar F. Borgatta, "A Comparison of Attitudes of Enlisted and Commissioned Air Force Personnel," December, 1953, 18: 669-71.
	Edward A. Suchman, Robin M. Williams, Jr., and Rose K. Goldsen, "Student Reaction to Impending Military Service," June, 1953, 18: 293-304.
Likert-Type Scale	Erwin O. Smigel, "Public Attitudes toward Stealing as Related to the Size of the Victim Organization," June, 1956, 21: 320-27.
	Erwin O. Smigel, "Public Attitudes toward 'Chiseling' with Reference to Unemployment Compensation," February, 1953, 18: 59-67.
	Clifford Kirkpatrick, Sheldon Stryker, and Philip Buell. "Attitudes toward Male Sex Behavior with Reference to Kinsey Findings," October, 1952, 17: 580-87.

Raymond L. Garden, "Interaction between Attitude and the Definition of the Situation in the Expression of Opinion," February, 1952, 17: 50-58.

Westie Summated Differences Scales	James G. Martin and Frank R. Westie, "The Tolerant Personality," August, 1959, 24: 521-28.

Melvin L. DeFleur and Frank R. Westie, "Verbal Attitudes and Overt Acts: An Experiment on the Salience of Attitudes," December, 1958, 23: 667-73.

Frank R. Westie, "A Technique for the Measurement of Race Attitudes," February, 1953, 18: 73-78.

Anti-Negro Likert Scale
Berkeley *AS* Scale (Anti-Semitic)

Russell Middleton, "Ethnic Prejudice and Susceptibility to Persuasion," October, 1960, 25: 679-86.

Attitude Scale (Stice and Knoll Method)

Robert L. Hall, "Social Influence on the Aircraft Commander's Role," June, 1955, 20: 292-99.

Burgess, Cavan, and Havighurst Attitude Inventory

David O. Moberg, "The Christian Religion and Personal Adjustment in Old Age," February, 1953, 18: 87-90.

Centers' Conservatism-Radicalism Battery

Herman M. Case, "An Independent Test of the Interest Group Theory of Social Class," December, 1952, 17: 751-55.

Church and Sect Scale (Likert Type)

Russell R. Dynes, "Church-Sect Typology and Socio-Economic Status," October, 1955, 20: 555-60.

Crissman's Changes in Moral Judgments

Solomon Rettig and Benjamin Pasamanick, "Changes in Moral Values among College Students: A Factorial Study," December, 1959, 24: 856-63.

Kaufman Status Concern Scale
McClosky Conservatism Scale
Putney-Middleton Religious Orthodoxy

Russell Middleton, "Ethnic Prejudice and Susceptibility to Persuasion," October, 1960, 25: 679-86.

McGranahan's Social Attitudes (adapted)	Bartlett H. Stoodley, "Normative Attitudes of Filipino Youth Compared with German and American Youth," October, 1957, 22: 553-56.
Measurement of Moral Values	Solomon Rettig and Benjamin Pasamanick, "Differences in Structure of Moral Values of Students and Alumni," August, 1960, 25: 550-55.
Measures of Attitudes toward Camping and Forest Activities (Guttman Scale)	Harold H. Kelley and Edmund H. Volkart, "Resistance to Change of Group-Anchored Attitudes," August, 1952, 17: 453-65.
Measures of Change	Harold H. Kelley and Edmund H. Volkart, "Resistance to Change of Group-Anchored Attitudes," August, 1952, 17: 453-65.
Open-Ended Questionnaire Measuring Moral Ideals	William A. Scott, "Empirical Assessment of Values and Ideologies," June, 1959, 24: 299-310.
Reissman's Aspiration Scale	Russell R. Dynes, Alfred C. Clarke, and Simon Dinitz, "Levels of Occupational Aspiration: Some Aspects of Family Experience as a Variable," April, 1956, 21: 212-15.
Scale Measuring Attitude Content and Intensity	Orville G. Brim, Jr., "Attitude Content-Intensity and Probability Expectations," February, 1955, 20: 68-76.
Self-Attitude Schedule (Guttman Scale)	Manford H. Kuhn and Thomas S. McPartland, "An Empirical Investigation of Self-Attitudes," February, 1954, 19: 68-76.
Thurstone-Chave Scale	Allan W. Eister, "Some Aspects of Institutional Behavior with Reference to Churches," February, 1952, 17: 64-69.
Thurstone's Method of Paired Comparisons	William R. Catton, Jr., "Exploring Techniques for Measuring Human Values," February, 1954, 19: 49-55.

Value Scale (Achievement, Motive, and Value Orientation)

Bernard C. Rosen, "The Achievement Syndrome: A Psychocultural Dimension of Social Stratification," April, 1956, 21: 203-11.

Scales Measuring Family and Marriage Factors

Adjustment Scale of Married Offspring to their Parents

Sheldon Stryker, "The Adjustment of Married Offspring to Their Parents," April, 1955, 20: 149-54.

Adolescent-Parent Adjustment Scale (Likert Type)

Ivan Nye, "Adolescent-Parent Adjustment: Socio-Economic Level as a Variable," June, 1951, 16: 341-49.

Family Opinion Survey (Likert Type Scale)

Clifford Kirkpatrick and Charles Hobart, "Disagreement, Disagreement Estimate, and Non-Empathic Imputations for Intimacy Groups Varying from Favorite Date to Married," February, 1954, 19: 10-19.

Family Solidarity

Luther T. Jansen, "Measuring Family Solidarity," December, 1952, 17: 727-33.

Index of Parent-Child Interaction

Russell R. Dynes, Alfred C. Clarke, and Simon Dinitz, "Levels of Occupational Aspiration: Some Aspects of Family Experience as a Variable," April, 1956, 21: 212-15.

Jansen Measurement of Family Solidarity

Eugene A. Wilkening, "Change in Farm Technology as Related to Familism, Family Decision Making, and Family Integration," February, 1954, 19: 29-37.

Measures of Inter-Family Dependence on Familism

Eugene A. Wilkening, "Change in Farm Technology as Related to Familism, Family Decision Making, and Family Integration," February, 1954, 19: 29-37.

Minnesota Scale for the Survey of Opinions (Family Adjustment)

Charles E. Ramsey and Lowry Nelson, "Changes in Values, and Attitudes toward the Family," October, 1956, 21: 605-9.

Burgess-Cottrell Marriage-Prediction Scale
Burgess-Cottrell Marital-Adjustment Scale

Atlee L. Stroup, "Predicting Marital Success or Failure in Urban Population," October, 1953, 18: 558-62.

Burgess-Cottrell and Locke Marital-Adjustment Scale

Robert C. Williamson, "Socio-Economic Factors and Marital Adjustment in an Urban Setting," April, 1954, 19: 213-16.

Burgess-Cottrell-Wallin Marriage-Adjustment Form

Harold T. Christensen and Robert E. Philbrick, "Family Size as a Factor in the Marital Adjustment of College Couples," June, 1952, 17: 306-12.

Burgess and Wallin Index of Marital Role Tension (adapted)

Bernard Forbes and Leonard S. Blackman, "Marital Role Tensions and Number and Sex of Children," October, 1956, 21: 596-601.

Favorableness of Attitude to Marriage (Guttman Type Scale)

Paul Wallin, "Marital Happiness of Parents and Their Children's Attitude to Marriage," February, 1954, 19: 20-23.

Likert-Type Scale

Alver Hilding Jacobson, "Conflict of Attitudes toward the Roles of the Husband and Wife in Marriage," April, 1952, 17: 146-50.

Locke Marital Adjustment Test

Harvey J. Locke and Georg Karlsson, "Marital Adjustment and Prediction in Sweden and the United States," February, 1952, 17: 10-17.

Marriage Prediction of Success or Failure

Jules Roth and Robert F. Peck, "Social Class and Social Mobility Factors Related to Marital Adjustment," August, 1951, 16: 478-87.

Peterson and Williamson Measure of Marital Adjustment (taken from Locke's Test)

Harvey J. Locke and Robert C. Williamson, "Marital Adjustment: A Factor Analysis Study," October, 1958, 23: 562-69.

Measures of Personality Factors

Bell Adjustment Inventory (Student Form)	Carol L. Stone, "Sorority, Status, and Personality Adjustment," August, 1951, 16: 538-41.
Bell Adjustment Inventory Bernreuter Personality Inventory	Charles F. Westoff, Philip C. Sagi, and E. Lowell Kelly, "Fertility through Twenty Years of Marriage: A Study in Predictive Possibilities," October, 1958, 23: 549-56.
Bell Adjustment Inventory California Test of Personality	Floyd M. Martinson, "Ego Deficiency as a Factor in Marriage," April, 1955, 20: 161-64.
California Test of Personality	William H. Sewell and A. O. Haller, "Factors in the Relationship between Social Status and the Personality Adjustment of the Child," August, 1959, 24: 511-20.
California Personality Inventory	Frank R. Scarpetti, Ellen Murray, Simon Dinitz, and Walter C. Reckless, "The 'Good' Boy in a High Delinquency Area: Four Years Later," August, 1960, 25: 555-58.
	Walter C. Reckless, Simon Dinitz, and Barbara Kay, "The Self Component in Potential Delinquency and Potential Non-Delinquency," October, 1957, 22: 566-70.
Edwards' Personal Preference Schedule	Charles E. Bowerman and Barbara R. Day, "A Test of the Theory of Complimentary Needs as Applied to Couples during Courtship," October, 1956, 21: 602-5.
F-Scale	Russell Middleton, "Ethnic Prejudice and Susceptibility to Persuasion," October, 1960, 25: 679-86.
	James G. Martin and Frank R. Westie, "The Tolerant Personality," August, 1959, 24: 521-28.

F-Scale Anti-Femininity Scale in Men	Dean A. Allen, "Anti-Femininity in Men," October, 1954, 19: 591-93.
MMPI	Starke R. Hathaway and Elio D. Monachesi, "The Minnesota Multiphasic Personality Inventory in the Study of Juvenile Delinquents," December, 1952, 17: 704-10.
Measurement of Alienation	John P. Clark, "Measuring Alienation within a Social Structure," December, 1959, 24: 849-52.
Nettler Alienation Scale	Gwynn Nettler, "Antisocial Sentiment and Criminality," April, 1959, 24: 202-8.
	Gwynn Nettler, "A Measure of Alienation," December, 1957, 22: 670-77.
Terman-Miles Masculinity-Femininity Test	Frederick B. Parker, "Sex Temperament and Alcohol," June, 1959, 24: 366-74.
Nye and Short Delinquency Scale	Frank R. Scarpetti, Ellen Murray, Simon Dinitz, and Walter C. Reckless, "The 'Good' Boy in a High Delinquency Area: Four Years Later," August, 1960, 25: 555-58.
Traditional-Companionship Role Conception Inventory	Annabelle Bender Motz, "The Role Conception Inventory: A Tool for Research in Social Psychology," August, 1952, 17: 465-71.
Measurement of Altruism (Likert-type scale)	Robert W. Fredericks, "Alter Versus Ego: An Exploratory Assessment of Altruism," August, 1960, 25: 496-508.

Measures of Intelligence and Achievement

California Test of Mental Maturity (Advanced, Short Form)	Murray A. Strauss, "Mental Ability and Cultural Needs: A Psychocultural Interpretation of the Intelligence Test Performance of Ceylon University Entrants," June, 1951, 16: 371-75.

Concept Development Scale

Anselm Strauss and Karl Schuessler, "Socialization, Logical Reasoning, and Concept Development in the Child," August, 1951, 16: 514-23.

Otis Mental Ability Test

Charles T. Westoff, Philip C. Sagi, and E. Lowell Kelly, "Fertility through Twenty Years of Marriage: A Study in Predictive Possibilities," October, 1958, 23: 549-56.

Measure of Level of Achievement

Leonard Reissman, "Levels of Aspiration and Social Class," June, 1953, 18: 233-42.

Measures of Interest

Kuder Preference Record

Floyd M. Martinson, "Ego Deficiency as a Factor in Marriage," April, 1955, 20: 161-64.

Jackson Toby, "Universalistic and Particularistic Factors in Role Assignment," April, 1953, 18: 134-41.

Occupational Preference Scale

Walter C. Reckless, Simon Dinitz, and Barbara Kay, "The Self Component in Potential Delinquency and Potential Non-Delinquency," October, 1957, 22: 566-70.

Miscellaneous Scales

Guttman Scale

Harold Mulfor and Donald Miller, "Drinking Behavior Related to Definitions of Alcohol: A Report of Research in Progress," June, 1959, 24: 385-89.

(Determinism of Behavior)

Gwynn Nettler, "Cruelty, Dignity, and Determinism," June, 1959, 24: 375-84.

John Finley Scott, "Two Dimensions of Delinquent Behavior," April, 1959, 24: 240-43.

(Measurement of Delinquent Behavior)

F. Ivan Nye and James F. Short, Jr., "Scaling Delinquent Behavior," June, 1957, 22: 392-99.

(Faith in People Index) — Morris Rosenberg, "Misanthropy and Political Ideology," December, 1956, 21: 690-95.

(Interviewer Effect on Scale Reproducibility) — Kurt W. Black, Reuben Hill, and J. M. Stycos, "Interviewer Effect on Scale Reproducibility," August, 1955, 20: 443-46.

Anselm L. Strauss, "The Development of Transformation of Monetary Meanings in the Child," June, 1952, 17: 275-86.

Discussion on Subjective and Objective Scales Using Guttman Scale as an Example — Matilda W. Riley and Jackson Toby, "Subject and Object Scales: A Sociological Application," June, 1952, 17: 287-96.

Guttman Scaling Procedure — J. A. Jahn, "Some Further Contributions to Guttman's Theory of Scale Analysis," April, 1951, 16: 233-39.

Cooperator-Subject Reporting Method — Clifford Kirkpatrick and John Cotton, "Physical Attractiveness, Age, and Marital Adjustment," February, 1951, 16: 81-86.

Cornell-Type Scale — Walter T. Martin, "Some Socio-Psychological Aspects of Adjustment to Residence Location in the Rural-Urban Fringe," June, 1953, 18: 248-53.

Criminal Indices — Gwynn Nettler, "Antisocial Sentiment and Criminality," April, 1959, 24: 202-8.

Definitions of Alcohol — Harold Mulfor and Donald Miller, "Drinking Behavior Related to Definitions of Alcohol: A Report of Research in Progress," June, 1959, 24: 385-89.

Discussion on Scaling Open-Ended Questionnaire Responses — Robert McGinnis, "Scaling Interview Data," October, 1953, 18:514-21.

Magnetic Board Rating Technique	Mark Lefton, Simon Dinitz, and Benjamin Pasamanick, "Decision-Making in a Mental Hospital: Real, Perceived, and Ideal," December, 1959, 24: 822-29.
Meer-Bell Index of Life Chances	Dorothy L. Meier and Wendell Bell, "Anomia and Differential Access to the Achievement of Life Goals," April, 1959, 24: 189-202.
NORC Prestige Scales	Charles F. Westoff, Philip C. Sagi, and E. Lowell Kelly, "Fertility through Twenty Years of Marriage: A Study in Predictive Possibilities," October, 1958, 23: 549-56.
Personal Television Index Program Television Index	Emory S. Bogardus, "A Television Scale and Television Index," April, 1952, 17: 220-23.
Questionnaire to Determine Patterns of Race Relations Using John's List of Stereotypes of American Negro	Roger Bastide and Pierre Van Den Berghe, "Stereotypes, Norms and Interracial Behavior in São Paulo, Brazil," December, 1957, 22: 689-94.
Thurstone's Method of Paired Comparisons	J. P. Sutcliffe and M. Haverman, "Factors Influencing Choice in Role Conflict Situations," December, 1956, 21: 695-703.
Thurstone's Technique of "Equal-Appearing Intervals"	Frances G. Scott, "Factors in the Personal Adjustment of Institutionalized and Non-Institutionalized Aged," October, 1955, 20: 538-46.

PART IV

Research Costing and Reporting

The good research design plans each step of the research process in advance. Research costing is a task that requires knowledge and experience. Most researchers drastically underestimate the time and effort that will be required to complete a research task. There are many unforeseen handicaps and delays.

In this part a *Guide to Research Costing* IV.1 is included. Before it can be used, the researcher must secure the going wage rate for interviewers, the cost of transportation, the rate for machine calculation, etc. These can not be provided here since they vary by time and place. However, the guide will alert the social scientist to the factors he must take into account in planning the cost of the research.

Finally, plans for the report must be made. *The Specifications for Sociological Report Rating* IV.2 indicate the criteria that judges will commonly use in appraising the publishing possibilities of the report. The *Form for Sociological Report Rating* IV.3 will provide a final check on the research design at the point where it counts—transmission to the profession.

IV.1. GUIDE TO RESEARCH COSTING

GUIDE TO RESEARCH COSTING * †

Activity	Total	Week Ending	Week Ending	Week Ending	_____

1. Total
   a) Man-hours
   b) Cost ($)
   c) % of total completed					

2. Planning
   a) Man-hours
   b) Cost
   c) % completed					

3. Pilot Study and Pretests
   a) Man-hours
   b) Cost
   c) % completed					

4. Drawing Sample
   a) Man-hours
   b) Cost
   c) % completed					

5. Preparing Observational Materials
   a) Man-hours
   b) Cost
   c) % completed					

6. Selection and Training
   a) Man-hours
   b) Cost
   c) % completed					

7. Trial Run
   a) Man-hours
   b) Cost
   c) % completed					

8. Revising Plans
   a) Man-hours
   b) Cost
   c) % completed					

9. Collecting Data
   a) Man-hours
   b) Cost
   c) % completed					

10. Processing Data
   a) Man-hours
   b) Cost
   c) % completed					

11. Preparing Final Report
   a) Man-hours
   b) Cost
   c) % completed					

* Source: Russell K. Ackoff, *Design for Social Research*, Chicago: University of Chicago Press, 1953. Copyright 1953 by the University of Chicago.

† Suggested form for budget-time schedule summary. (There is nothing necessary or sufficient about this listing of activities, nor is the order absolute in any sense.)

IV.2. SPECIFICATIONS FOR SOCIOLOGICAL REPORT RATING

SPECIFICATIONS FOR SOCIOLOGICAL REPORT RATING *

	Defective	Substandard	Standard	Superior
Statement of Problem:				
1. Clarity of Statement	Statement is ambiguous, unclear, biased, inconsistent, or irrelevant to the research.	Problem must be inferred from incomplete or unclear statement.	Statement is unambiguous and includes precise description of research objectives.	Statement is unambiguous and includes formal propositions, and specifications for testing them.
2. Significance of Problem	No problem stated, or problem is meaningless, unsolvable, or trivial.	Solution of the problem would be of interest to a few specialists.	Solution of the problem would be of interest to many sociologists.	Solution of the problem would be of interest to most sociologists.
3. Documentation	No documentation to earlier work, or documentation is incorrect.	Documentation to earlier work is incomplete or contains errors of citation or interpretation	Documentation to earlier work is reasonably complete.	Documentation shows in detail the evolution of the research problem from previous research findings.
Description of Method:				
4. Appropriateness of Method	Problem cannot be solved by this method.	Only a partial or tentative solution can be obtained by this methd.	Solution of the problem by this method is possible, but uncertain.	Problem is definitely solvable by this method.
5. Adequacy of Sample or Field	Sample is too small, or not suitable, or biased, or of unknown sampling characteristics.	The cases studied are meaningful, but findings can not be projected.	Findings are projectable, but with errors of considerable, or of unknown, magnitude.	Results are projectable with known small errors, or the entire universe has been enumerated.
6. Replicability	Not replicable.	Replicable in substance, but not in detail.	Replicable in detail with additional information from the author(s).	Replicable in detail from the information given.

330

Presentation of Results:

	7. Completeness / 8. Comprehensibility	9. Yield	Interpretation: 10. Accuracy	11. Bias	12. Usefulness
	Relevant details are presented in detail.	Definitive solution of problem.	Positive checks of accuracy included in the procedures.	Positive precautions against bias included in procedures.	Probable influence on all future work in this area.
	Relevant results are presented, partly in detail, partly in summary form.	Tentative solution of problem.	Errors unlikely with the procedures used. No errors detected.	No evidence of bias.	Possible influence on some future work in this area.
	Comprehension of results requires special knowledge or skills.	Useful hints or suggestions toward solution of problem.	Errors likely with the procedures used. No major errors detected.	Some bias in interpretation, but not in presentation of results.	Possible influence on some future work in this area.
	Results are incomprehensible, or enigmatic.	No contribution to solution of problem.	Errors of calculation, transcription, dictation, logic, or fact detected.	Evident bias in presentation of results and in interpretation.	Not useful.

331

* Source: Theodore Caplow designed this form. It was tested by the Committee on Research, American Sociological Society. See "Official Reports and Proceedings," *American Sociological Review*, December, 1958, pp. 704-11. Cf. Stuart C. Dodd and Louis N. Gray, "Scientific Scales for Measuring Methodology," Seattle, Wash.: Institute for Sociological Research, University of Washington, 1962 (Mimeograph copies available on request).

IV.3. FORM FOR SOCIOLOGICAL REPORT RATING *

Author _____

Title _____

Publication Reference _____

Rater _____

Date _____

Check (√) Appropriate Columns	Defective 0	Substandard 1	Standard 2	Superior 3
STATEMENT OF PROBLEM:				
1. Clarity of Statement				
2. Significance of Problem				
3. Documentation				
DESCRIPTION OF METHOD:				
4. Appropriateness of Method				
5. Adequacy of Sample or Field				
6. Replicability				
PRESENTATION OF RESULTS:				
7. Completeness				
8. Comprehensibility				
9. Yield				
INTERPRETATION:				
10. Accuracy				
11. Bias				
12. Usefulness				

Enter number of checks in   _ × 0 = 0   _ × 1 = _   _ × 2 = _   _ × 3 = _
each column in appropriate
blanks; weight as indicated,   [*Total Rating*   ]
and add for Total Rating   [   ]

* Theodore Caplow designed this rating form. Test Reliabilities appear in "Official Reports and Proceedings," *American Sociological Review,* December, 1958, 23: 704-11. See also the reports of the Educational Testing Service, Princeton, New Jersey, for ingenious rating scales on a large variety of subjects.

332